Picked-By-You Guides®
Top Rated Outdoor Series

Top Rated™ Fly Fishing
Salt and Freshwaters
of North America

by Maurizio Valerio

799.124
VAL

PICKED-BY-YOU GUIDES®

Top Rated Outdoor Series

Copies of this book can be ordered from:

Picked-By-You

PO Box 718

Baker City, OR 97814

Phone: (800) 279-0479 • Fax: (541) 523-5028

www.topguides.com • e-mail: maurice@topguides.com

Artwork by Steamroller Studios, Cover Art by Fifth Street Design
Maps by Map Art, Cartesia Software
Printed in Korea

Publisher's Cataloging-in-Publication
(Provided by Quality Books, Inc.)

Valerio, Maurice.
   Top rated fly fishing : salt and freshwaters of North
America / by Maurizio Valerio. -- 1st ed.
      p. cm. -- (Top rated outdoor series)
   Includes indexes.
   Preassigned LCCN: 98-67993
   ISBN: 1-889807-01-X

   1. Fly fishing--North America--Directories. 2. Fishing
lodges--North America--Directories. 3. Fishing guides--North
America--Directories. 4. Fishing equipment industry--North
America--Directories   I. Title.

SH462. V35 1999   799.1'24'0257
                                   QBI98-1375

To Allison, Marco and Nini

About the Author

Maurizio (Maurice) Valerio received a Doctoral degree Summa cum Laude in Natural Science, majoring in Animal Behaviour, from the University of Parma (Italy) in 1981, and a Master of Arts degree in Zoology from the University of California, Berkeley in 1984.

He is a rancher, a writer and a devoted outdoorsman who decided to live with the wild animals that he cherishes so much in the Wallowa Mountains of Northeast Oregon. He has traveled extensively in the Old and New World, for more than 25 years. He is dedicated to preserving everyone's individual right of a respectful, knowledgeable and diversified use of our Outdoor Resources.

Table of Contents

Acknowledgments

It is customary in this section to give credit to those who have contributed to the realization of the end product. The Picked-By-You Guides® started three years ago as a little personal crusade and has evolved into a totally challenging, stimulating and rewarding full time commitment.

My deep thanks must go first to all the Captains, Ranchers, Guides, Lodges and Outfitters who decided to trust our honesty and integrity. They have taken a leap of faith in sharing their lists of clients with us and for this we are truly honored and thankful.

They have constantly encouraged our idea. Captains have taught us the difference between skinny fishing and skinny dipping, while River Guides have patiently help us to identify rafters , purlins , catarafts and J-rig rafts. They were also ready to give us a badly needed push forward every time this very time-consuming idea came to a stall. We have come to know many of them through pleasant phone chats, e-mails, faxes and letters. They now sound like old friends on the phone and we are certain we all share a deep respect for the mountains, the deserts and the waters of this great country of ours.

The Picked-By-You Team (both in the office and abroad), with months of hard work, skills, ingenuity, good sense of humor and pride, have then transformed a simple good idea into something a bit more tangible and much more exciting. They all have put their hearts in the concept and their hands and feet in the dirt. Some with a full-time schedule, some with a part-time collaboration, all of them bring their unique and invaluable style and contribution.

My true thanks to Brent Beck, Lindsay Benson, Bob Erdmann, Robert Evans, Cheryl Fisher, Brian Florence, Sally Georgeson, Grace Martin, Kevin McNamara, Jerry Meek, Allison C. Mickens, Tom Novak, Shelby Sherrod, Dyanne Van Swoll, Giuseppe Verdi and Mr. Peet's Coffee and Tea.

Last, but not least, my sincere, profound, and loving gratitude to my wife Allison. Her patient support, her understanding, her help and her skills have been the fuel which started and stoked this fire. Her laughter has been the wind to fan it.

To you Allie, with a toast to the next project...just kidding!

Maurizio (Maurice) Valerio

Preface

The value of information depends on its usefulness. Simply put, whatever allows you to make informed choices will be to your advantage. To that end, Picked-By-You Guides® aims to take the guesswork out of selecting services for outdoor activities. Did you get what you paid for? From Picked-By-You Guides®' point of view, the most reliable indicator is customer satisfaction.

The information in this book is as reliable as those who chose to participate. In the process of selecting the top professionals, Picked-By-You Guides® contacted all licensed guides, outfitters and businesses which provide services for outdoor activities. They sought to include everyone but not all who were contacted agreed to participate according to the rules. Thus, the omission of a guide, outfitter or service does not automatically mean they didn't qualify based on customer dissatisfaction.

The market abounds with guidebooks by 'experts' who rate a wide range of services based on their personal preferences. The value of the Picked-By-You concept is that businesses earn a place in these books only when they receive favorable ratings from a majority of clients. If ninety percent of the customers agree that their purchase of services met or exceeded their expectations, then it's realistic to assume that you will also be satisfied when you purchase services from the outdoor professionals and businesses included in this book.

It's a fact of life; not everyone is satisfied all of the time or by the same thing. Individual experiences are highly subjective and are quite often based on expectations. One person's favorable response to a situation might provoke the opposite reaction in another. A novice might be open to any experience without any preconceived notions while a veteran will be disappointed when anything less than great expectations aren't met.

If you select any of the businesses in this book, chances are excellent that you will know what you are buying. A diversity of clients endorsed them because they believed the services they received met or exceeded their expectations. Picked-By-You Guides® regards that information more valuable than a single observer or expert's point of view.

The intent behind Picked-By-You Guides® is to protect the consumer from being misled or deceived. It is obvious that these clients were given accurate information which resulted in a positive experience and a top rating.

The number of questionnaire responses which included detailed and sometimes lengthy comments impressed upon us the degree to which people value their experiences. Many regard them as "once-in-a-lifetime" and "priceless," and they heaped generous praise on those whose services made it possible.

Picked-By-You Guides® has quantified the value of customer satisfaction and created a greater awareness of top-rated outdoor professionals. It remains up to you to choose and be the judge of your own experience. With the help of this book, you will have the advantage of being better informed when making that pick.

Robert Evans, *information specialist*

The Picked-By-You Guides® Idea

Mission Statement

The intent of this publication is to provide the outdoor enthusiast and his/her family with an objective and easy-to-read reference source that would list only those businesses and outdoor professionals who have **agreed to be rated** and have been overwhelmingly endorsed by their past clients.

There are many great outdoor professionals (Guides, Captains, Ranches, Lodges, Outfitters) who deserve full recognition for putting their experience, knowledge, long hours, and big heart, into this difficult job. With this book we want to reward those deserving professionals while providing an invaluable tool to the general public.

Picked-By-You Guides® are the only consumer guides to outdoor activities.

In this respect it would be useful to share the philosophy of our Company succinctly illustrated by our Mission Statement:

"To encourage and promote the highest professional and ethical standards among those individuals, Companies, Groups or Organizations who provide services to the Outdoor Community.

To communicate and share the findings and values of our research and surveys to the public and other key groups.

To preserve everyone's individual right of a respectful, knowledgeable and diversified use of our Outdoor Resources".

Our business niche is well defined and our job is simply to listen carefully.

THEY 'the experts' Vs. WE 'the People'

Picked-By-You books were researched and compiled by **asking people such as yourself**, who rafted, fished, hunted or rode a horse on a pack trip with a particular outdoor professional or business, to rate their services, knowledge, skills and performance.

Only the ones who received A- to A+ scores from their clients are found listed in these pages.

The market is flooded with various publications written by 'experts' claiming to be the ultimate source of information for your vacation. We read books with titles such as " The Greatest River Guides", "The Complete Guide to the Greatest Fishing Lodges" etc.

We do not claim to be experts in any given field, but we rather pass to history as good....listeners. In the preparation of the Questionnaires we listened first to the outdoor professionals' point of view and then to the comments and opinions of thousands of outdoor enthusiasts. We then organized the findings of our research and surveys in this and other publications of this series.

Thus we will not attempt to tell how to fish, how to paddle or what to bring on your trip. We are leaving this to the outdoor professionals featured in this book, for they have proven to be outstanding in providing much valuable information before, during and after your trip.

True [paid] advertising: an oxymoron

Chili with beans is considered a redundant statement for the overwhelming majority of cooks but it is an insulting oxymoron for any native Texan.

In the same way while 'true paid advertising' is a correct statement for some, it is a clear contradiction in terms for us and certainly many of you. A classic oxymoron.

This is why we do not accept commissions, donations, invitations, or, as many publishers cleverly express it, "...extra fees to help defray the cost of publication". Many articles are written every month in numerous specialized magazines in which the authors tour the country from lodge to lodge and camp to camp sponsored, invited, or otherwise compensated in many different shapes or forms.

It is indeed a form of direct advertising and, although this type of writing usually conveys a good amount of general information, in most cases it lacks the impartiality so valuable when it comes time to make the final selection for your vacation or outdoor adventure.

Without belittling the invaluable job of the professional writers and their integrity, we decided to approach the task of **researching information and sharing it with the public** with a different angle and from an opposite direction.

Money? .. No thanks!

We are firmly **committed to preserve the impartiality** and the novelty of the Picked-By-You idea.

For this reason we want to reassure the reader that the outdoor professionals and businesses featured in this book have not paid (nor will they pay), any remuneration to Picked-by-You Guides ® or the author in the form of money, invitations or any other considerations.

They have earned a valued page in this book solely as the result of *their hard work and dedication to their clients.*

"A spot in this book cannot be purchased: it must be earned"

Size of a business in not a function of its performance

Since the embryonic stage of the Picked-By-You idea, during the compilation of the first Picked-By-You book, we faced a puzzling dilemma.

Should we establish a minimum number of clients under which a business or outdoor professional will not be allowed to participate in our evaluating process?

This would be a 'safe' decision when it comes the time to elaborate the responses of the questionnaires. But we quickly learned that many outdoor professionals limit, by choice, the total number of clients and, by philosophy of life, contain and control the size of their business. They do not want to grow too big and sacrifice the personal touches or the freshness of their services. In their words "we don't want to take the chance to get burned out by people." They do not consider their activity just a job, but rather a way of living.

"WHY, NO MAM, WE NEVER HAVE HAD ANY OF THOSE SASQUATCH SIGHTINGS IN THESE PARTS."

But if this approach greatly limits the number of clients accepted every year we must say that these outdoor professionals are the ones who often receive outstanding ratings and truly touching comments from their past clients.

Some businesses have provided us with a list of clients of 40,000, some with 25 . In this book **you will find both the large and the small**.

From a statistical point, it is obvious that a fly fishing guide who submitted a list of 32 clients, by virtue of the sample size of the individuals surveyed, will implicitly have a lower level of accuracy if compared to a business for which we surveyed 300 guests. (Please refer to the Rating and Data

Elaboration Sections for details on how we established the rules for qualification and thus operated our selection).

We do not believe that the size of business is a function of its good performance and we feel strongly that those dedicated professionals who choose to remain small deserve an equal chance to be included.

We tip our hats

We want to recognize all the Guides, Captains, Ranches, Lodges and Outfitters who have participated in our endeavor, whether they qualified or not. The fact alone that they accepted to be rated by their past clients is a clear indication of how much they care, and how willing they are to make changes.

We also want to credit all those outdoor enthusiasts who have taken the time to complete the questionnaires and share their memories and impressions with us and thus with you. Some of the comments sent to us were hilarious, some were truly touching.

We were immensely pleased by the reaction of the outdoor community at large. The idea of "Picked-by-You Guides®" was supported from the beginning by serious professionals and outdoor enthusiasts alike. We listened to their suggestions, their comments, their criticisms and we are now happy to share this information with you.

Questionnaires

"Our books will be only as good as the questions we ask."

We posted this phrase in the office as a reminder of the importance of the 'tool' of this trade. The questions.

Specific Questionnaires were tailored to each one of the different activities surveyed for this series of books. While a few of the general questions remained the same throughout, many were specific to particular activities. The final objective of the questionnaire was to probe the many different facets of that diversified field known as the outdoors.

The first important factor we had to consider in the preparation of the Questionnaires was the total number of questions to be asked. Research shows an *inversely proportionate relation* between the total number of questions and the percentage of the response: the higher the number of questions, the lower the level of response. Thus we had to balance an acceptable return rate with a meaningful significance. We settled for a compromise and we decided to keep 20 as the maximum number.

The first and the final versions of the Questionnaires on which we based our surveys turned out to be very different. We asked all the businesses and outdoor professionals we contacted for suggestions and criticisms. They helped us a great deal: we weighed their different points of view and we incorporated all their suggestions into the final versions.

We initially considered using a phone survey, but we quickly agreed with the businesses and outdoor professional that we all are already bothered by too many solicitation calls when we are trying to have a quiet dinner at home. We do not want you to add Picked-By-You to the list of companies that you do not want to talk to, nor we want you to add our 800 number to your caller ID black list.

In using the mail we knew that we were going to have a slightly lower percentage of questionnaires answered, but this method is, in our opinion, a more respectful one.

We also encouraged the public to participate in the designing of the questionnaire by posting on our Web at www.topguides.com the opportunity to submit a question and ...."Win a book". Many sent their suggestions and , if they were chosen to be used in one of our questionnaires, they were given the book of their choice.

Please send us your question and/or your suggestions for our future surveys at:

PICKED-BY-YOU Guides®, P.O. Box 718, Baker City, OR 97814

Rating (there is more than one way to skin the cat)

We considered many different ways to score the questionnaires, keeping in mind at all times our task:

translate an opinion into a numerical value

Some of the approaches considered were simple *averages* [arithmetical means], others were sophisticated statistical tests. In the end we opted for simplicity, sacrificing to the God of statistical significance. WARNING: if $p \leq 0.001$ has any meaning in your life stop reading right here: you will be disappointed with the rest.

For the rest of us, we also made extensive use in our computation of the *median*, a statistic of location, which divides the frequency distribution of a set of data into two halves. A quick example, with our imaginary Happy Goose Outfitter, will illustrate how in many instances the *median* value, being the center observation, helps describing the distribution, which is the truly weak point of the *average*:

Average salary at Happy Goose Outfitters $ 21,571

Median salary at Happy Goose Outfitters $ 11,000

5,000	10,000	10,000	11,000	12,000	15,000	98,000
Wrangler	Guide	Guide	Senior Guide	Asst.Cook	Cook	Boss

Do not ask the boss : "What's the average salary?"

These are the values assigned to **Questions 1-15**:

5.00 points	OUTSTANDING
4.75 points	EXCELLENT
4.25 points	GOOD
3.50 points	ACCEPTABLE
3.00 points	POOR
0.00 points	UNACCEPTABLE

Question 16, relating to the weather conditions, was treated as bonus points to be added to the final score.

Good=0   Fair=1   Poor=2

The intention here was to reward the outdoor professional who had to work in adverse weather conditions.

Questions 17 - 18 = 5 points

Questions 19 - 20 = 10 points

The individual scores of each Questionnaire were expressed as a percentage to avoid the total score from being drastically affected by one question left unanswered or marked "not applicable." All the scores received for each individual outdoor professional and business were thus added and computed.

The 90 points were considered our cutoff point. Note how the outfitters must receive a combination of Excellent with only a few Good marks (or better) in order to qualify.

Only the Outfitters, Captains, Lodges, Guides who received an A- to A+ score did qualify and they are featured in this book.

We also decided not to report in the book pages the final scores with which the businesses and the outdoor professionals ultimately qualified. In a way we thought that this could be distractive.

In the end, we must admit, it was tough to leave out some outfitters who scored very close to the cutoff mark.

It would be presumptuous to think that our scoring system will please everybody, but we want to assure the reader that we tested different computations of the data. We feel the system that we have chosen respects the overall opinion of the guest/client and maintains a more than acceptable level of accuracy.

We know that …. "You can change without improving, but you cannot improve without changing."

The Power of Graphs (how to lie by telling the scientific truth)

The following examples illustrate the sensational (and unethical) way with which the 'scientific' computation of data can be distorted to suit one's needs or goals.

The *Herald* presents a feature article on the drastic increase of total tonnage of honey stolen by bears (mostly Poohs) in a given area during 1997.

Total tonnage of honey stolen by bears (Poohs)

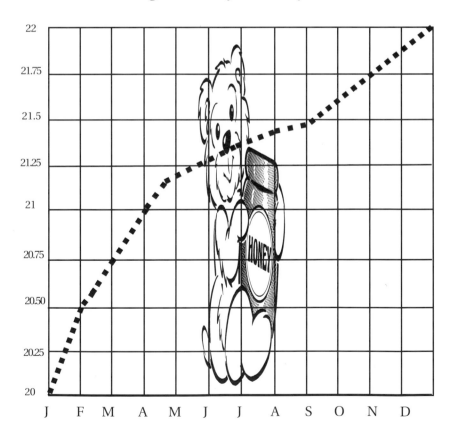

Total tonnage of honey stolen by bears (Poohs)

It is clear how a journalist, researcher or author must ultimately choose one type of graph. But the question here is whether or not he/she is trying to make "his/her point" by choosing one type versus the other, rather than simply communicate some findings.

Please note that the bears, in our example, are shameless, and remain such in both instances, for they truly love honey!

Graphs were not used in this book. We were just too worried we wouldn't use the correct ones.

The Book Making Process

Research

We **researched** the name and address of every business and outdoor professional **in the United States and** in all the **provinces of Canada** (see list in the Appendix). Some states do not require guides and outfitters or businesses providing outdoor services to be registered, and in these instances the information must be obtained from many different sources [Outfitter's Associations, Marine Fisheries, Dept. of Tourism, Dept. Environmental Conservation, Dept. of Natural Resources, Dept. of Fish and Game, US Coast Guard, Chamber of Commerce, etc.].

In the end the database on which we based this series of Picked-By-You Guides® amounted to more than 23,000 names of Outfitters, Guides, Ranches, Captains etc. Our research continues and this number is increasing every day. The Appendix in the back of this book is only a partial list and refers specifically to Top Rated Fly Fishing.

Participation

We **invited** businesses and outdoor professionals, with a letter and a brochure explaining the Picked-By-You concept, to join our endeavor by simply sending us a **complete** **list of their clients** of the past two years. With the "Confidentiality Statement" we reassured them that the list was going to be kept **absolutely confidential** and to be *used one time only* for the specific purpose of evaluating their operation. Then it would be destroyed.

We truly oppose this "black market" of names so abused by the mail marketing business. If you are ever contacted by Picked-By-You you may rest assured that your name, referred to us by your outdoor professional, will never be sold, traded or otherwise used a second time by us for marketing purposes.

Questionnaires

We then **sent a questionnaire** to **every single client on each list** (to a maximum of 300 randomly picked for those who submitted large lists with priority given to overnight or multiple day trips), asking them to rate the

services, the **knowledge** and **performance** of the business or outdoor professional by completing our comprehensive questionnaire (see pages 168-169). The businesses and outdoor professionals found in these pages may or may not be the ones who invest large sums of money to advertise in magazines, or to participate at the annual conventions of different clubs and foundations. However, they are clearly the ones, according to our survey, that put customer satisfaction and true dedication to their clients first and foremost.

Data Elaboration

A **numerical value was assigned to each question**. All the **scores were computed**. Both the **average** and the **median** were calculated and considered for eligibility. Please note that the total score was computed as a percentile value.

This allows some flexibility where one question was left unanswered or was answered with a N/A. Furthermore, we decided not to consider the high and the low score to ensure a more evenly distributed representation and to reduce the influence which an extreme judgement could have either way (especially with the small sample sizes).

We also set a **minimum number of questionnaires** which needed to be answered to allow a business or an outdoor professional to qualify. Such number was set as a function of the total number of clients in the list: the smaller the list of clients, the higher was the percentage of responses needed for qualification.

In some cases the outfitter's average score came within 1 points of the A-cutoff mark. In these instances, we considered both the median and the average were considered as well as the guests' comments and the total number of times that this particular business was recommended by the clients by answering with a 'yes' question 19 and 20.

Sharing the results

Picked-By-You will share the results of this survey with the businesses and the outdoor professionals. This will be done at no cost to them whether or not they qualified for publication. All questionnaires received will, in fact, be returned along with a summary result to the business, keeping the confidentiality of the client's name when this was requested. This will prove an invaluable tool to help improving those areas that have received some criticisms.

The intention of this series of books is to research the opinions and the comments of outdoor enthusiasts, and to share the results of our research with the public and other key groups.

One outfitter wrote us about our Picked-by-You Guides® series, "I feel your idea is an exciting and unique concept. Hopefully our past clientele will rate us with enough points to 'earn' a spot in your publication. If not, could we please get a copy of our points/questionnaires to see where we need to improve. Sincerely..."

This outfitter failed to qualify by just a few points, but such willingness to improve leaves us no doubt that his/her name will be one of those featured in our second edition. In the end it was not easy to exclude some of them from publication, but we are certain that, with the feedback provided by this survey, they will be able to improve those areas that need extra attention.

We made a real effort to keep a position of absolute impartiality in this process and, in this respect, we would like to repeat that the outfitters have not paid, nor they will pay, one single penny to Picked-By-You Guides® or the Author to be included in this book.

The research continues.

Icon Legend
General Services and Accommodations

Family

Kids

Senior Citizen

Handicap

Women Only Camps/Dates

Drop Camp

Spike Tent Camp

Hot Springs/Spas

Swimming Pool

Archeological Sites

Tennis

Lodge

Cabin

Wall Tent Camp

Trailer

Sleep Aboard

Full Board

Natural/Gourmet
Meals

Hotel/Motel

Icon Legend

General Services

Unguided Activities

Guided Activities

Overnight Trips

Fish Cleaning
Service

Day Trips

Season(s) of Operation

Fall

Year-round

Summer

Winter

Spring

Icon Legend
Locations

Blue Ribbon Stream

Blue Ribbon Waterway

River Delta

Salt Water

Estuary

Lake

Open Ocean

Pond

Large River

Stream

Marsh/Wetlands

Icon Legend
Activities/Fishing Techniques

Catch and Release

Wade Fly Fishing

Skinny Fishing (flats, bays)

River Fishing with Dory

Whitewater Trips

River Fishing with Raft

Spin Casting

Trophy Fishing

Deep Water Fishing

Fly Tying School

Fly Fishing School

Crabbing / Shrimping

Icon Legend
Activities

Sporting Clay,
Trap, Skeet

Big Game Hunting

Bird Hunting

Whale Watching

Wildlife Viewing

Trekking / Backpacking

Cross Country Skiing

Snow Shoeing

Horseback Riding

Horse Pack Trips

Llama Pack Trips

Mountain Biking

Icon Legend
Fish

Largemouth Bass

Crappie(s)

Smallmouth Bass

Muskellunge

Striped Bass

Northern Pike

Bluegill

Perch(es)

Arctic Grayling

Snook

Icon Legend
Fish

Chinook (King) Salmon

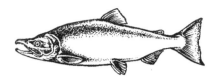

Sockeye (Red) Salmon

Coho (Silver) Salmon

Atlantic Salmon

Pink (Humpback) Salmon

Chum (Dog) Salmon

Brown Trout

Rainbow Trout

Arctic Char

Brook Trout

Icon Legend
Fish

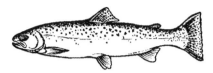

Steelhead Trout

Lake Trout

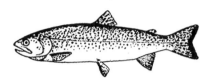

Cutthroat trout

Dolly Varden

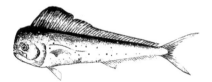

Dolphin Fish

Spotted Sea Trout

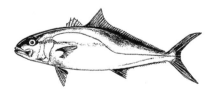

Amberjack(s)

Swordfish

Mackerel(s)

Icon Legend
Fish

Redfish(es)

Permit

Barracuda(s)

Tarpon(s)

Sea Bass

Shark(s)

Bonefish

Marlin(s)

Tuna(s)

Sailfish

Icon Legend

Boat Types and Transportation

Airplane on Floaters

Skinny Fishing Boat

Cataraft

Inflatable Kayak

Canoe

Raft

Sea Kayaking

Motor Boat

Hovercraft

Jon Boat

Icon Legend
Boat Types and Transportation

Dory / McKenzie River
Boat

Fly Bridge

Bass Boat

Zodiac

Jet Boat

Open Console Boat

Cabin Cruiser

Mako

Fly Fishing
Outfitters, Guides, and Lodges

Picked-By-You Professionals in
Alaska

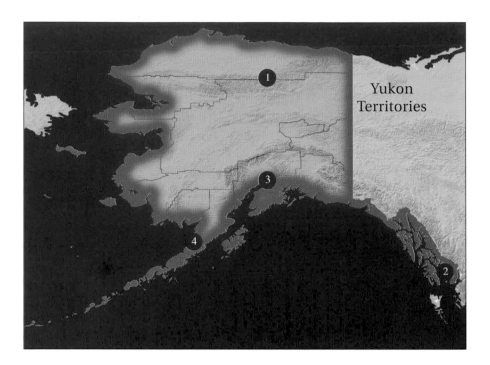

Outdoor Professionals

1. Alaska Fish & Trails Unlimited
2. Classic Alaska Charters
3. George Ortman Adventure Guiding
4. Tracy Vrem's Blue Mountain Lodge

License and Report Requirements

• State requires licensing of Outdoor Professionals.

• State requires a "Hunt Record" for big game.

• State to implement a "logbook" program for charter vessel/guided catches of King Salmon in Southeast Alaska by the 1998 season.

Useful information for the state of
Alaska

State and Federal Agencies

Alaska Dept. of Fish & Game
PO Box 25556
Juneau, AK 99802-5526
phone: (907) 465-4100

Alaska Region Forest Service
709 West 9th Street
Box 21628
Juneau, AK 99802-1628
phone: (907) 586-8863
TTY: (907) 586-7816

Chugach National Forest
3301 C Street, Ste. 300
Anchorage, AK 99503-3998
phone: (907) 271-2500
TTY: (907) 271-2332

Tongass National Forest:
Chatham Area
204 Siginaka Way
Sitka, AK 99835
phone: (907) 747-6671
TTY: (907) 747-8840

Bureau of Land Management
Alaska State Office
222 W. 7th Avenue, #13
Anchorage, AK 99513-7599
phone: (907) 271-5960
or (907)271-plus extension
fax: (907) 271-4596

Office Hours: 7:30 a.m. - 4:15 p.m.

National Parks

Denali National Park
phone: (907) 683-2294

Gates of the Arctic National Park
phone: (907) 456-0281

Glacier Bay National Park
phone: (907) 697-2230

Katmai National Park
phone: (907) 246-3305

Kenai Fjords National Park
phone: (907) 224-3175

Kobuk Valley National Park
phone: (907) 442-3890

Lake Clark National Park
phone: (907) 271-3751

Wrangell-St. Elias National Park
phone: (909) 822-5235

Associations, Publications, etc.

American Fisheries Society
2720 Set Net Ct.
Kenai, AK 99611
phone: (907) 260-2909
fax: (907) 262-7646

Trout Unlimited Alaska Council
PO Box 3055
Soldotna, AK 99669
phone: (907) 262-9494

Federation of Fly Fishers
http://www.fedflyfishers.org

Alaska Fish and Trails Unlimited

Jerald D. Stansel

1177 Shypoke Dr. • Fairbanks, AK 99709
PO Box 26045, Bettles Field, AK 99726
phone: (907) 479-7630 • www2.polarnet.com/-aktrails

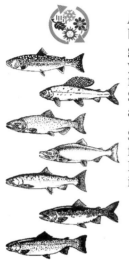

Alaska Fish and Trails Unlimited is owned by guide and bush pilot Jerry Stansel, who has been operating and guiding in the Brooks Range Gates of the Arctic for 25 years. His tours specialize in guided and unguided fly-in fishing, rafting, backpacking and photography trips. Species of fish include arctic char, sheefish, lake trout, arctic grayling, whitefish, northern pike and salmon.

So come, breathe Alaska's crisp, clean air. Drink its pure, fresh water. Fly across the Arctic Circle and Arctic Divide. Fish for a variety of species, either around Fairbanks or in the Arctic.

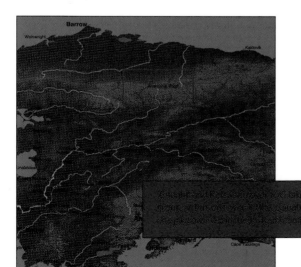

Classic Alaska Charters

Capt. Robert Scherer

P.O. Box 6117 • Ketchikan, AK 99901
phone: (907) 225-0608

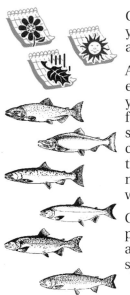

Classic Alaska Charters is unique. We consult directly with you as to your particular interests and design a vacation around you.

Alaskan fishing is among the best in the world. You'll experience unspoiled fishing grounds all to yourself at your pace. Whether an expert or novice, you'll catch the fever when you hook into a monster halibut or stand in a salmon-swollen river. Or fish all day in the safety and comfort of our motor yacht. You can also take walks along the tideflats to photograph black and brown bear, marine mammals, bald eagles, harbor seals, waterfalls and wildflowers.

Captain Rob is U.S.C.G. certified and has been professionally guiding in Alaska since 1984. He is a wildlife and nature photographer and can guide you into spectacular wilderness photo opportunities.

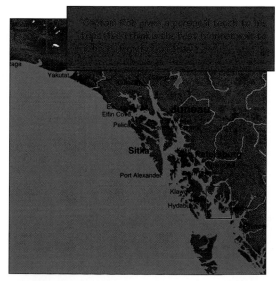

George Ortman Adventure Guiding

George Ortman
Box 261 • Willow, AK 99688
phone/fax: (907) 495-6515

I offer the finest in wilderness fishing and travel. My expertise and knowledge will provide you with a fantastic wilderness experience. Your complete comfort, safety, and satisfaction are my priority and goal.

During the summer, we have many fishing options, such as the Kokwok, Kenektok and Izavieknik rivers. Each has its own characteristics and attractions with varying degrees of difficulty. I will organize your trip around your personal goals and fishing style. I offer substantial discounts with two destinations and many guests choose to do two rivers for a broader experience, both with fishing and seeing the country. Lake trout can be sought on Upnuk Lake where lakers over 30 pounds are regularly taken.

I provide a complete guiding service, including all gear, food, and flights from your arrival in Dillingham through departure.

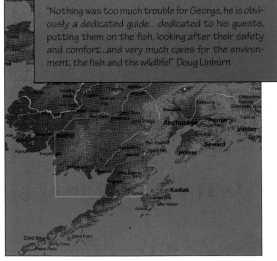

"Nothing was too much trouble for George, he is obviously a dedicated guide... dedicated to his guests, putting them on the fish, looking after their safety and comfort...and very much cares for the environment, the fish and the wildlife!" Doug Linburn

Tracy Vrem's Blue Mountain Lodge

Tracy Vrem

P.O. Box 670130 • Chugiak, AK 99567
phone: (907) 688-2419 • fax: (907) 688-0491

We're in the heart of the best fishing in the Alaska Peninsula. Blue Mountain Lodge is located in the Becherof Ugashik lakes region. These lakes are spawning grounds for millions of salmon. It's not uncommon to catch and release more than 30 fish a day, from trophy-sized grayling, to acrobatic rainbow trout, lunker arctic char, lake trout, northern pike, or all five species of salmon.

We rarely lose a day of fishing due to the weather. And, with the excellent fishing, you'll have an opportunity to sight bear, caribou and moose. A short flight to Katmai National Monument is part of our agenda.

The wood frame and aluminum-sided lodge is a far cry from being plush, but it's comfortable and unique. There is a shower and washroom; the toilet facility is an outhouse.

"...the fishing can not be described, one must experience it to believe it. On the trip home one of our group told me 'Ben, we can't tell anyone about this, they will think we are lying.'" Ben Miller

Arkansas

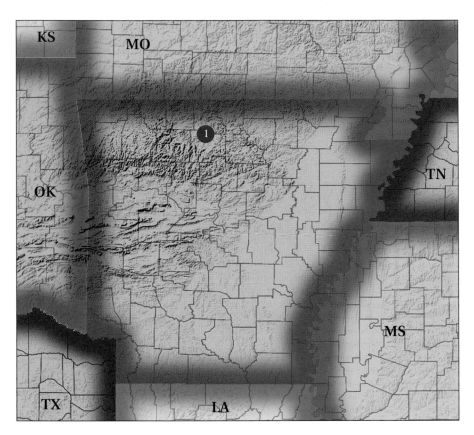

Outdoor Professionals

1 The John B. Gully Flyfishing Guide Service

License and Report Requirements

• State does not license or register Outfitters, Guides or Lodges.

• State has no report require

Useful information for the state of
Arkansas

State and Federal Agencies

Arkansas Game & Fish Commission
#2 Natural Resources Dr.
Little Rock, AR 72205
(501) 23-6300

Bureau of Land Management
Eastern States
7450 Boston Boulevard
Springfield, Virginia 22153
phone: (703) 440-1660
or (703) 440-plus extension
fax: (703) 440-1599

Office Hours: 8:00 a.m. - 4:30 p.m.

Eastern States
Jackson Field Office
411 Briarwood Drive, Suite 404
Jackson, Mississippi 39206
phone: (601) 977-5400

Forest Service
Southern Region
1720 Peachtree Road NW
Atlanta, GA 30367
phone: (404) 347-4177
TTY: (404) 347-4278

Ouachita National Forest
Federal Building
PO Box 1270
Hot Springs, AR 71902
phone: (501) 321-5202
TTY: (501) 321-5307

Ozark-St. Francis National Forests
605 West Main Street
PO Box 1008
Russellville, AR 72811
phone: (501) 968-2354
TTY: (501) 964-7201

National Parks

Hot Springs National Park
PO Box 1860
Hot Springs, AR 71902
phone: (501) 624-3383

Associations, Publications, etc.

American Fisheries Society
Arkansas Chapter
401 Harden Road
Little Rock, AR 72211
phone: (501) 228-3620
fax: (501) 228-3601

Trout Unlimited Arkansas Council
70 N. College Ave., Ste. 11
Fayetteville, AR 72701
phone: (501) 521-7011
fax: (501) 443-4333

Federation of Fly Fishers
http://www.fedflyfishers.org

Arkansas Bass Chapter Federation
119 Lilly Street
Searcy, AR 72143
phone: (501) 268-6659

The Ozark Society
PO Box 2914
Little Rock, AR 72203

The John B. Gulley Fly Fishing Guide Service

John B. Gulley II

1703 River Ridge Rd. • Norfork, AR 72658-9005
phone: (870) 499-7517 • fax: (870) 499-5132
email: John_Gulley@juno.com

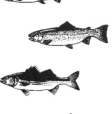

John Gulley's Orvis-endorsed Fly Fishing Service is designed for the rivers and lakes of Arkansas. Arkansas trout waters are 99% tailwater fisheries, therefore, guides need to be extremely versatile in order to fish all the conditions necessary to catch trout. It is also a year-round fishery and is considered world-class because of the many world record trout caught in Arkansas. As a guide, I have developed methods to deal with all conditions.

Our operation includes walk-in wade fishing at private and public access points and highwater float trips. Our service also includes the opportunity for the flyfisherman to catch some of the best freshwater striper action in America.

An Arkansas native, my experience in guiding flyfishermen and casting instruction totals more than 24 years. My flies include many innovative patterns that I have developed for trout, bass and stripers.

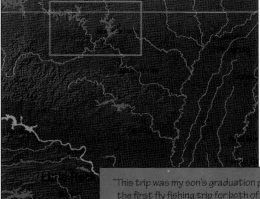

"This trip was my son's graduation present, also the first fly fishing trip for both of us. We have planned a trip next year to the same place using John Gully. Excellent trip and guide." Pat Gavin

46

Picked-By-You Professionals in
California

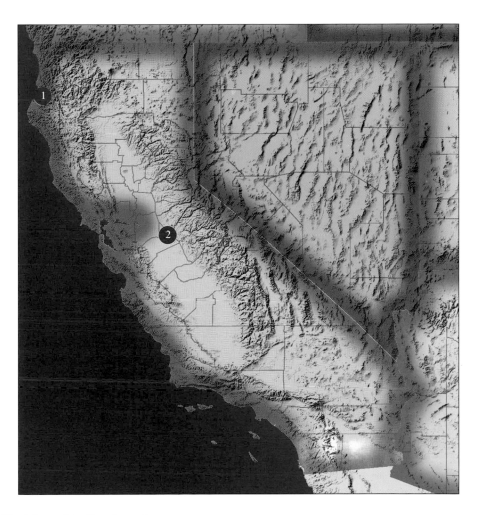

Outdoor Professionals

1 Bruce Slightom
2 Tim Bermingham's Drift Boat Guide Service

Useful information for the state of
California

State and Federal Agencies

California Fish & Game Commission
License & Revenue Branch
1416 9th Street
Sacramento, CA 95814
phone: (916) 27-2244

Pacific Southwest
Forest Service Region
630 Sansome St.
San Francisco, CA 94111
phone: (415) 705-2874
TTY: (415) 705-1098

Bureau of Land Management
California State Office
2135 Butano Drive
Sacramento, CA 95825
phone: (916) 978-4400
or (916) 978-plus extension
fax: (916) 978-4620

Office Hours: 7:30 - 4:00 pm (PST)

National Parks

Lassen Volcanic National Park
phone: (916) 595-4444

Redwood National Park
phone: (707) 464-6101

Sequoia & Kings Canyon Natl. Parks
phone: (209) 565-3341

Yosemite National Park
phone: (209) 372-0200

Channel Islands National Park
phone: (805) 658-5700

Associations, Publications, etc.

California Trout, Inc.
870 Market St. #859
San Francisco, CA 94102
phone: (415) 392-8887

Trout Unlimited
5200 Huntington Ave. Ste. 300
Richmond, CA 94804
phone: (510) 528-5390
fax: (510) 525-3664

Federation of Fly Fishers
http://www.fedflyfishers.org

Bass Chapter Federation
751 Melva Ave.
Oakdale, CA 95361
phone: (209) 541-3673
or (209) 847-3272

California Outdoors
PO Box 401
Coloma, CA 95613
phone: (800) 552-3625

License and Report Requirements
• State requires licensing of Outdoor Professionals.

• State requires the filing of a "Monthly Guide Log" for fishing and hunting.

• River Outfitters need a "Use Permit", required for BLM, National Forest, Indian reservations, and National Parks.

Bruce Slightom

Bruce Slightom
4841 Cummings Rd. • Eureka, CA 95503
phone: (707) 443-8746 • email: Cheryls@Humboldt1.com

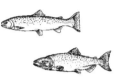

Bruce Slightom has been guiding fall flyfishers on the Klamath and Trinity rivers for more than 20 years. He has been an instructor in the local university's beginning and advanced fly casting classes for 15 years. With this experience, Bruce can get you into fish as well as help anglers of all levels hone their skills.

In winter, conventional gear is used to pursue steelhead on the coastal rivers of Northern California. Based in Eureka, the Eel, Mattole, Smith and other rivers are all close by, offering a choice of rivers to fish as conditions change.

Jet boat, drift boat, raft or walk-in trips — we can go where the fish are. Not only will you catch fish but you can also take advantage of Bruce's skill in teaching how to fish.

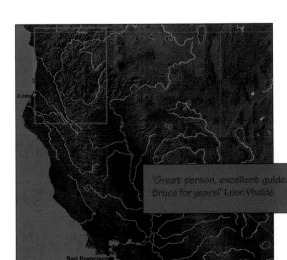

"Great person, excellent guide...have fished with Bruce for years!" Leon Vhalds

Tim Bermingham's Drift Boat Guide Service

Tim Bermingham

840070 Melones Dam Rd. • Jamestown, CA 95327
phone/fax: (209) 984-4007
email: info@driftfish.com • http://www.driftfish.com/index.html

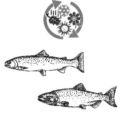

Tim Bermingham has fished California inland waters for more than 30 years. Raised in Merced, he knows the Merced River better than anybody. Fishing mainly on the Merced River during spring, summer and fall, we also have jet or driftboat trips on the Tuolumne, Stanislaus and Mokelumne rivers, and the Smith and Mattole rivers in northwest California during the winter.

We boast a 100% success rate; not one of my client's has ever failed to land fish. Rainbow, brook or brown trout, salmon, steelhead, largemouth, smallmouth and striped bass success is a sure bet.

Fly, spin or baitfishing, all tackle provided. All you need is a California fishing license.

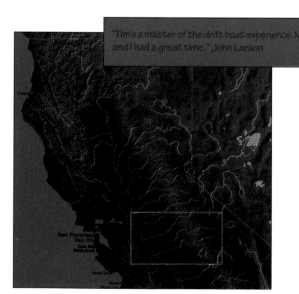

"Tim's a master of the drift boat experience. My son and I had a great time." John Larson

Picked-By-You Professionals in
Colorado

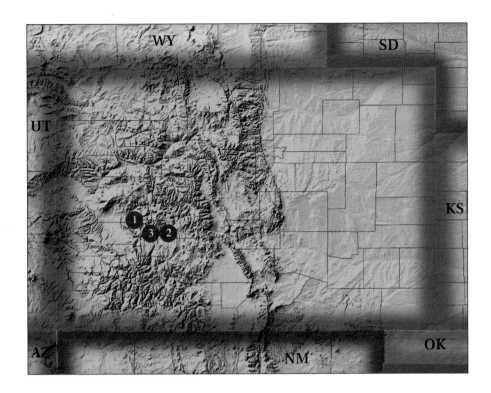

Outdoor Professionals

1. Dragonfly Anglers
2. Mike Wilson's High Mountain Drifters
3. The Troutfitter

• State requires licensing of Outdoor Professionals.

• State requires an "Inter-Office Copy of Contract with Client" be submitted each time a client goes with an Outfitter. Colorado Agencies of Outfitters Registry sends this copy to client to fill out and return to their agency.

Useful information for the state of
Colorado

State and Federal Agencies

Colorado Agencies of Outfitters Registry
1560 Broadway, Suite 1340
Denver, CO 80202
phone: (303) 894-7778

Colorado Dept. of Natural Resources
1313 Sherman, Room 718
Denver, CO 80203
phone: (303) 866-3311

Forest Service
Rocky Mountain Region
740 Simms Street
PO Box 25127
Lakewood, CO 80225
phone: (303) 275-5350
TTY: (303) 275-5367

Arapaho-Roosevelt National Forests
Pawnee National Grassland
phone: (970) 498-2770

Grand Mesa-Umcompahgre
Gunnison National Forests
phone: (970) 874-7641

Pike-San Isabel National Forests
Commanche & Cimarron National
Grasslands
phone: (719) 545-8737

San Juan-Rio Grande National Forest
phone: (719) 852-5941

White River National Forest
phone: (970) 945-2521

Bureau of Land Management
Colorado State Office
2850 Youngfield St.
Lakewood, Co. 80215-7093
phone: (303) 239-3600
fax: (303) 239-3933
Tdd: (303) 239-3635
Email: msowa@co.blm.gov
Office Hours: 7:45 a.m. - 4:15 p.m.

National Parks

Mesa Verde National Park, CO 81330
phone: (303) 529-4465

Rocky Mountain National Park
phone: (303) 586-2371

Associations, Publications, etc.

American Fisheries Society
Colorado & Wyoming Chapter
PO Box 6249
Sheridan, WY 82801
phone: (307) 672-7418
fax: (307) 672-0594

Trout Unlimited CO Council
2001 E. Easter, #100
Littleton, CO 80122
phone: (303) 795-3302

Federation of Fly Fishers
http://www.fedflyfishers.org

CO Bass Chapter Federation
2713 Garden Drive
Ft. Collins, CO 80526
phone: (303) 221-3608

Dragonfly Anglers

Rod and Roger Cesario

307 Elk Ave., P.O. Box 1116 • Crested Butte, CO 81224
phone: (800) 491-3079 • (970) 349-1228 • (970) 349-9836 • Lic. #711

Dragonfly Anglers offers guided fly fishing trips for the beginner to the experienced fisherman in Gunnison County and Western Colorado. We fish large rivers, small streams, private water and everything in between.

Also available are guided overnight or day trips to the gold medal Black Canyon of the Gunnison River. Custom overnight trips to our remote lodge in northwestern Gunnison County offer an unforgettable fly fishing experience and provides a different river or stream each day.

Dragonfly Anglers is licensed, bonded and insured and operates under special-use permits from USDA Forest Service, Gunnison National Forest and BLM.

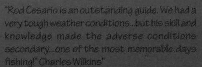

"Rod Cesario is an outstanding guide. We had a very tough weather conditions...but his skill and knowledge made the adverse conditions secondary...one of the most memorable days fishing!" Charles Wilkins"

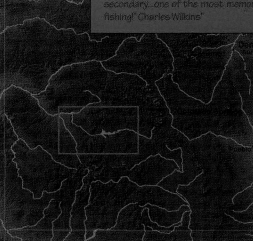

Mike Wilson's High Mountain Drifters

Mike Wilson

115 South Wisconsin St. • Gunnison, CO 81230
phone: (800) 793-4243 • (970) 641-4243

High Mountain Drifters is the Gunnison Basin's leading fly shop and guide service. We fish the most diverse and exclusive waters in the area and pride ourselves in making every trip fun. We have male and female guides available, and they are young, experienced and enthusiastic. We offer the highest quality and most miles of private water in the valley. Trips are available for all ages and abilities. Our trips start at 9 a.m. and full day trips get back when you want them to, not at 5 p.m.

We offer free casting clinics every Saturday morning taught by the valley's only two certified casting instructors. We are a full-service, year-round shop and a dealer for Winston, Scott, Redington, Sage, Hexagraph and Cortland rods. We also carry Simms, Fly-Tech, Patagonia and Filson clothing and waders. Our catalog is available upon request.

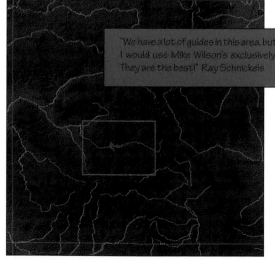

The Troutfitter

Dominque Eymere and Bradley Sorock

313 Elk Ave., PO Box 2779 • Crested Butte, CO 81224
phone: (970) 349-1323 • fax: (970) 349-5066 • Lic. #1655

The Troutfitter is located in the beautiful historic town of Crested Butte, Colorado. We offer walk/wade trips on a variety of exclusive private stretches of water.

We take that extra step to make your trip a pleasurable experience, including a catered lunch from a fine local dining establishment, two-to-one client/guide ratio, and pristine fishing water which we limit to four fisherman per day.

Our guides meet rigorous requirements of experience and are friendly, outgoing and personable.

All trips include any rental needs, including waders, boots, fly vests, and quality flyrods from G-Loomis and St. Croix. Come fish with us.

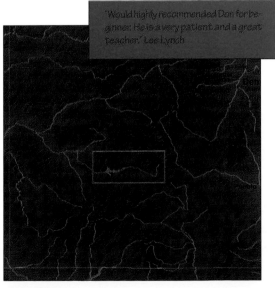

"Would highly recommended Don for beginner. He is a very patient and a great teacher." Lee Lynch

Florida

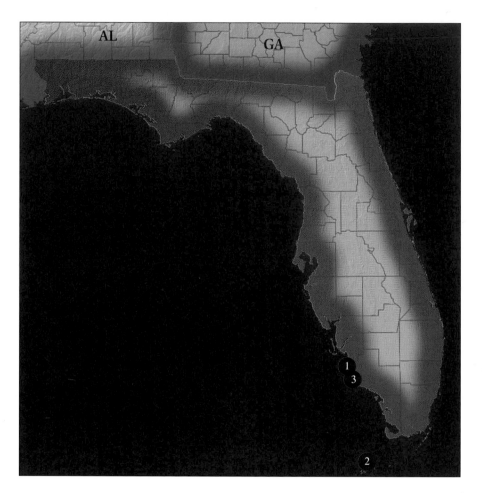

Outdoor Professionals

1 Capt. Doug Hanks
2 Fly Fishing Paradise
3 Look-N-Hook Charters

License and Report Requirements

• State requires licensing of Saltwater Outdoor Professionals

• Game & Fresh Water Fish Dept. requires a "trip ticket" from Captain whose clients leave fish on board and Captain sells to the public. "Trip ticket" includes length of stay out, county and area, but no client names. "Trip tickets" must be turned in after each trip.

Florida

State and Federal Agencies

Game & Fresh Water Fish Dept.
620 S. Meridian St.
Tallahassee, FL 32399-1600
phone: (904) 488-4676
or (904) 488-1960

Forest Service
Southern Region
1720 Peachtree Road NW
Atlanta, GA 30367
phone: (404) 347-4177
TTY: (404) 347-4278

Apalachicola, Ocala, Osceola National
Forests
325 John Knox Rd., Ste. F100
Tallahassee, FL 32303
phone: (904) 942-9300

TTY: (904) 42-9351

Bureau of Land Management
Eastern States
7450 Boston Boulevard
Springfield, Virginia 22153
phone: (703) 440-1660
or (703) 440-plus extension
fax: (703) 440-1599
Office Hours: 8:00 a.m. - 4:30 p.m.

Eastern States
Jackson Field Office
411 Briarwood Drive, Suite 404
Jackson, Mississippi 39206
phone: (601) 977-5400
fax: (601) 977-5440

National Parks

Biscayne National Park
phone: (305) 247-2044

Everglades National Park
phone: (305) 242-7700

Associations, Publications, etc.

American Fisheries Society
Florida Chapter
100 8th Avenue, SE
St. Petersburg, FL 33701

Trout Unlimited Florida Council
4006 S. Florida Avenue
Lakeland, FL 33813
phone: (813) 646-1476

Federation of Fly Fishers
http://www.fedflyfishers.org

International Game Fish Association
1301 E. Atlantic Blvd.
Pompano Beach, FL 33060
phone: (305) 954-3474
fax: (305) 954-5868
email: 16FA@netcom.com

Florida Bass Chapter Federation
44 Muskogee Road
San Mateo, FL 32187
phone: (904) 328-6035

Florida Sportsmen's Conservation
Association
PO Box 20051
West Palm Beach, FL 33416-0051
phone: (561) 478-5965
fax: (561) 688-2553

Marine Industries Association of South
Florida
phone: (954) 524-0633

Capt. Doug Hanks

Capt. Doug Hanks

3600 Cottage Club Lane • Naples, FL 34105
phone: (941) 263-7478 • fax: (941) 263-4621

Capt. Doug Hanks operates his backcountry guide service in the Everglades National Park. Anglers travel from all locales to experience fishing in this unique environment. Alligators, manatees and abundant bird life inhabit the remote Mangrove Swamp.

The diverse wildlife only adds to the real attraction — the spectacular fishing. Fishermen can expect to catch snook, redfish and tarpon using traditional or flyfishing tackle.

Capt. Doug Hanks supplies all tackle and licenses. All equipment is top-quality, including his specialized Silverking flats skiff.

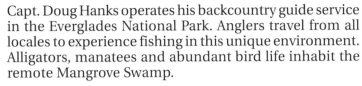

"Capt. Doug is a very capable guide who provided me with an outstanding fishing trip and new insights to the Florida Everglades / 10,000 Islands."
George Atkinson

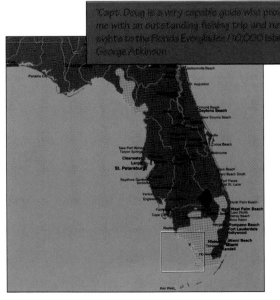

Fly Fishing Paradise

Capt. Dexter Simmons

P.O. Box 145 • Sugarloaf, FL 33044
reservations and information: (305) 745-3304
email: LCZZ92a@prodigy.com • http://www.pages.prodigy.com/captdexter

Fly fish or use light tackle to fish the saltwater flats of Key West, the Marquesas, the Florida Keys, the Bahamas, the Caribbean or Central America. Catch and release tarpon, bonefish, permit, barracuda, shark, cobia and mutton snapper aboard "FlatsMaster" (an 18-foot Action Craft flats skiff) with Capt. Dexter Simmons.

Full day, half day and week-long charters available. Overnight excursions to the Marquesas, Bahamas, Belize, Yucatan or Central America offer an angling adventure. Deluxe accommodations available.

Top-notch fly fishing and light tackle gear, and friendly, helpful instruction included.

"A true well-educated fisherman and conservationist. I highly recommend him" Jack Copass

Look-N-Hook Charters

Capt. Jim and Shari Nickerson

3100 4th St. N.E. • Naples, FL 34120-1339
phone: (941) 353-5448 • fax: (941) 353-5879
email: tarpon500@aol.com

Capt. Jim is an experienced backcountry guide who specializes in sight fishing for snook, redfish, and tarpon on a fly or spin rod in Everglades National Park and Ten Thousand Islands. Established in 1989, Look-N-Hook is endorsed by Orvis and is a member of Yamaha's elite guide program.

Look-N-Hook, Capt. Jim's 17-foot Action Craft flats skiff, roams the nation's ninth largest national park in search of prized game fish. Enjoy the calm waters and the tranquil beauty shared by nature's creatures such as manatee, dolphin, alligator and a variety of birds. It is truly a fisherman's dream and a nature lover's paradise.

The boat is limited to two anglers, but Capt. Jim will accommodate larger groups by booking additional boats. Half-day and full-day trips available.

"Wonderful trip, great guide, great fishing...couldn't have asked for a better time!" Phillip Schwartz

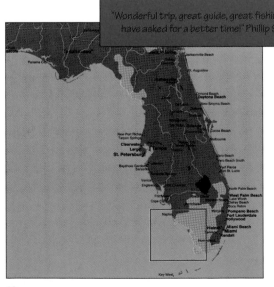

Picked-By-You Professionals in
Idaho

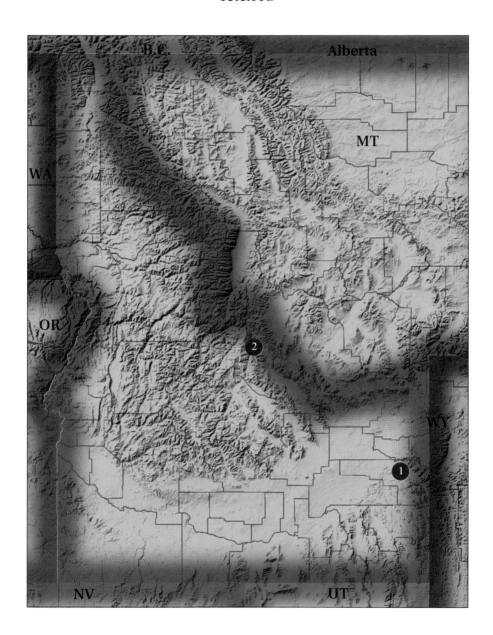

Outdoor Professionals

1. Heise Expeditions
2. Solitude River Trips

Useful information for the state of
Idaho

State and Federal Agencies

Idaho Fish & Game Dept.
600 South Walnut
Boise, ID 83707
phone: (208) 334-3700

Outfitter & Guides Licensing Board
1365 N. Orchard, Room 172
Boise, ID 83706
phone: (208) 327-7380
fax: (208) 327-7382

Forest Service
Northern Region
Federal Bldg.
PO Box 7669
Missoula, MT 59807-7669
phone: (406) 329-3616
TTY: (406) 329-3510

Clearwater National Forest
phone: (208) 476-4541

Idaho Panhandle, Coeur d'Alene,
Kaniksu, St. Joe National Forests
phone / TTY: (208) 765-7223

Nez Perce National Forest
phone: (208) 983-1950

Bureau of Land Management
Idaho State Office
1387 S. Vinnell Way
Boise, ID 83709-1657
phone: (208) 373-3896
or (208) 373-plus extension
fax: (208) 373-3899

Office Hours 7:45 a.m. - 4:15 p.m.

Associations, Publications, etc.

Trout Unlimited Idaho Council
3845 Whiskey Jack Road
Sandpoint, ID 83864-9466
phone: (208) 263-6937
fax: (208) 265-2996

American Fisheries Society
1525 Kathleen
Coeur d'Alene, ID 83814
phone: (208) 769-1414

Federation of Fly Fishers
http://www.fedflyfishers.org

Idaho Bass Chapter Federation
8012 W. Arapaho Ct.
Boise, ID 83703
phone: (208) 853-9039

Idaho Outfitters & Guides Association
PO Box 95
Boise, ID 83701
phone: (208) 342-1438

License and Report Requirements

• State requires licensing of Outdoor Professionals.

• State requires that every Outfitter be it bird, fish, big game, river rafting, trail riding or packing file a "Use Report" annually.

• Currently, no requirements for Guest/Dude Ranches.

Heise Expeditions

Mike Quinn

5116 E. Heise Rd. • Ririe, ID 83443

phone: (800) 828-3984 • (208) 538-7453 • fax: (208) 538-6039

Heise Resort is nestled in the heart of the world's finest cutthroat trout fishing, just 20 miles east of Idaho Falls. Airport transportation can be arranged; car rentals are available.

Our professional guides are customer-oriented to provide everything necessary for an exciting and enjoyable trip. Experience the beauty, serenity and uniqueness of Idaho's "blueribbon" cutthroat fishing on the South Fork of the Snake River. With hot springs, lodging, golf course and beautiful scenery, you'll get hooked on what we have to offer.

For over 100 years, the family-owned Heise Resort has set traditions of excellence which have kept customers coming back. Blending history with modern recreation, Heise Expeditions continues to provide that unique experience with nature that will keep you coming back.

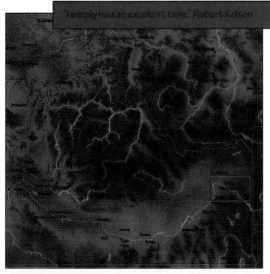

"I simply had an excellent time." Robert Kelson

Solitude River Trips

Al and Jeana Bukowsky

main office: P.O. Box 907 • Merlin, OR 97532
summer (June-August): P.O. Box 702 • Salmon, ID 83467
phone: (800) 396-1776 • www.rivertrips.com

Although just floating the river is an exhilarating and enlightening experience, flyfishermen will find the Middle Fork of the Salmon River a heaven on Earth.

Since 1973, a catch-and-release, single, barbless hook-only policy has been in effect. The native cutthroat trout, the predominant species, has thrived and, along with a few native rainbow and Dolly Varden trout, provides some of the finest fishing in the country. The trout average 12 to 15 inches in length, with some up to 19 inches. You don't even have to be an expert to catch these beautiful fish. Our guides offer patient fly-casting instruction for the novice, while also providing helpful tips for the most experienced angler.

The plentiful trout make the Middle Fork a great place to learn, or to simply improve one's fishing skills.

"Top river float in the West for dry fly action on native Cutthroat...great staff and food." Gene and Debbi Hering

Maine

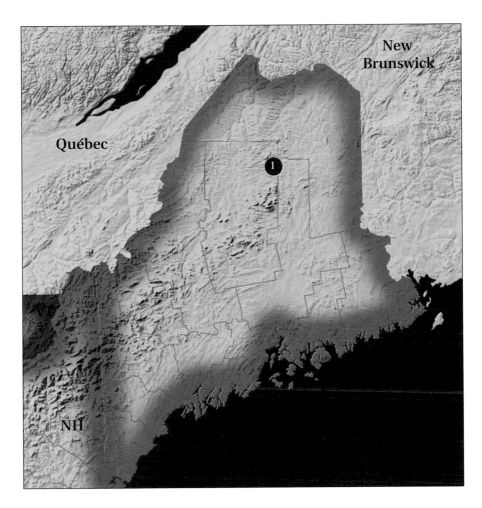

Outdoor Professionals

1 ## Libby Sporting Camps

License and Report Requirements

• State requires licensing of Outdoor Professionals.

• Monthly Head Fee Guides Report required for Whitewater River Companies.

• No report required for Hunting and Fishing Professionals.

Useful information for the state of
Maine

State and Federal Agencies

Maine Dept. of Fish & Wildlife
284 State St. Station #41
Augusta, ME 04333
phone: (207) 287-8000

Forest Service
Eastern Region
310 West Wisconsin Ave. Rm 500
Milwaukee, WI 53203
phone: (414) 297-3646
TTY: (414) 297-3507

White Mountain National Forest
Federal Building
719 North Main Street
Laconia, NH 03246
phone: (603) 528-8721

Bureau of Land Management
Eastern States
7450 Boston Boulevard
Springfield, Virginia 22153
phone: (703) 440-1660
or (703) 440- Plus Extension
fax: (703) 440-1599

Office Hours: 8:00 a.m. - 4:30 p.m.

Eastern States
Milwaukee District Office
310 W. Wisconsin Ave., Suite 450
(P.O. Box 631 53201-0631)
Milwaukee, Wisconsin 53203
phone: (414) 297-4450
fax: (414) 297-4409

National Parks

Acadia National Park
phone: (207) 288-3338

Associations, Publications, etc.

Trout Unlimited Maine Council
PO Box 53
Hallowell, ME 04347-0053
phone: (207) 724-3576
fax: (207) 724-3576

Federation of Fly Fishers
http://www.fedflyfishers.org

Maine Atlantic Salmon Authority
650 State St.
Bangor, ME 04401-5654
phone: (207) 941-4449
fax: (207) 941-4443

American Bass Assoc. of Maine
20 Marshwood Estates
Eliot, ME 03903
phone: (207) 748-1744

Sportsman's Alliance of Maine
RR 1, Box 1174
Church Hill Road
Augusta, ME 04330-9749
phone: (207) 622-5503

Maine Bass Chapter Federation
RR 1. Box 332
Hollis Center, ME 04042
phone: (207) 929-8553

Sportsman's Alliance of Maine
RR 1, Box 1174
Church Hill Road
Augusta, ME 04330-9749
phone: (207) 622-5503

Maine Professional Guide Association
phone: (207) 785-2061

The Maine Sportsman
phone: (207) 287-3995

Libby Sporting Camps

Matthew and Ellen Libby

P.O. Box V, Dept. 0 • Ashland, ME 04732
radio phone: (207) 435-8274 • fax: (207) 435-3230
email: libbycam@libbycam.sdi.agate.net

The Libby family has operated a lodge and guide service in the Aroostook and Allagash River headwaters of Maine since 1890. The camp is located 150 miles north of Bangor in the heart of a 4-million acre wilderness near the Canadian border. Hunting for trophy deer, bear and moose is second to none in the state. An abundance of grouse rounds out the hunter's dream.

The six guest cabins are comfortable, clean, spacious and private. The food is home-cooked and served family-style in the dining room overlooking the lake. The cabins are handcrafted — from the peeled log timbers and immense fieldstone fireplace in the lodge to the handmade quilts on the beds.

Perfect accommodations for families, business groups and honeymooners.

"If you fish you have to fish at Libby's at least once in your life. It is an outstanding experience in every way." Tom Baynes

Montana

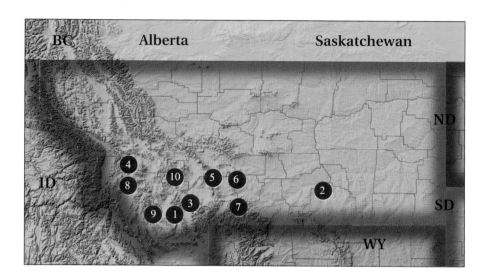

Outdoor Professionals

1 Broken Arrow Lodge
2 Eagle Nest Lodge
3 East Slope Anglers
4 Esper's Under Wild Skies Lodge & Outfitters
5 Grossenbacher Guides
6 Hatch Finders
7 Rocky Fork Guide Service
8 The Complete Fly Fisher
9 The Reflective Angler
10 Tite Line Fishing

License and Report Requirements
• State requires licensing of Outdoor Professionals.
• State requires an "Annual Client Report Log" for all Hunting and Fishing Outfitters.
• State does not regulate River Guides.
• Guest/Dude Ranches need to get an Outfitter license only if they take guest to fish or hunt on land that they do not own.

Useful information for the state of
Montana

State and Federal Agencies

Montana Board of Outfitters
Dept. of Commerce
Arcade Building - 111 North Jackson
Helena, MT 59620-0407
phone: (406) 444-3738

Montana Dept. of Fish, Wildlife & Parks
1420 East 6th
Helena, MT 59620
phone: (406) 444-2535

Forest Service
Northern Region
Federal Building
PO Box 7669
Missoula, MT 59807-7669
phone: (406) 329-3616
TTY: (406) 329-3510

Bitterroot National Forest
phone: (406) 363-7117

Custer National Forest
phone / TTY: (406) 657-6361

Flathead National Forest
phone: (406) 755-5401

Gallatin National Forest
phone / TTY: (406) 587-6920

Helena National Forest
phone: (406) 449-5201

Kootenai National Forest
phone: (406) 293-6211

Lewis & Clark National Forest
phone: (406) 791-7700

Lolo National Forest
phone: (406) 329-3750

Bureau of Land Management

Montana State Office
Granite Tower
222 North 32nd Street
P.O. Box 36800
Billings, Montana 59107-6800
phone: (406) 255-2885
fax: (406) 255-2762
Email - mtinfo@mt.blm.gov
Office Hours: 8:00 a.m. - 4:30 p.m.

National Parks

Glacier National Park
phone: (406) 888-5441

Associations, Publications, etc.

Fishing Outfitters Assoc. of Montana
Box 311
Gallatin Gateway, MT 59730
phone: (406) 763-5436

Federation of Fly Fishers
PO Box 1595
502 South 19th, Ste. #1
Bozeman, MT 59771
phone: (406) 585-7592
fax: (406) 585-7596
http://www.fedflyfishers.org

Trout Unlimited Montana Council
PO Box 1638
Polson, MT 59860
phone: (406) 887-2495

Montana Bass Chapter Federation
12345 O'Keefe Road
Missoula, MT 59812
phone: (406) 728-8842

Broken Arrow Lodge

Erwin and Sherry Clark

2200 Upper Ruby Rd., P.O. Box 177 • Alder, MT 59710
phone: (800) 775-2928 • phone/fax: (406) 842-5437
www.recworld.com/state/mt/hunt/broken/broken.html

With private access and minimal fishing pressure, the Ruby offers some of the finest fishing in Montana and tends to be the most popular with our guests.

The Ruby is a friendly stream, easily waded. The small streams in the backcountry are easily accessible and offer great fishing for cutthroats along with breathtaking scenery and abundant wildlife. Lake fishing on Clark Canyon provides an opportunity to catch the "big fish," rainbows and browns average 4-1/2 pounds. A short distance from the lodge, float trips on the Big Hole, Madison, Yellowstone, Beaverhead and Jefferson rivers are available on request and provide exhilarating experiences with beautiful scenery, quality fishing and the thrill of floating the river. We recommend mid-June until late September for the most rewarding fishing trip.

We offer the option to fish on your own or with a guide.

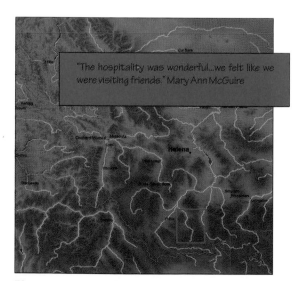

"The hospitality was wonderful...we felt like we were visiting friends." Mary Ann McGuire

Eagle Nest Lodge

Keith Kelly

P.O. Box 509 • Hardin, MT 59034
phone: (406) 665-3711 • fax: (406) 665-3712

Eagle Nest Lodge is one of the world's premier fly-fishing destinations and has the distinction of being one of the first Orvis-endorsed operations. A family business since its conception in 1982, Eagle Nest is owned and managed by the Kellys. The services, lodging and dining of this Montana sporting lodge have satisfied the most discerning anglers for more than a decade.

Eagle Nest is secluded on the banks of the Bighorn River, a fishery heralded as one of the world's finest for the remarkable number of trophy browns and rainbows it holds. Out of the Big Horn Mountains flows the Tongue River, a stream that boasts fantastic scenery in addition to solitude and an abundance of cutthroat, rainbow and brown trout.

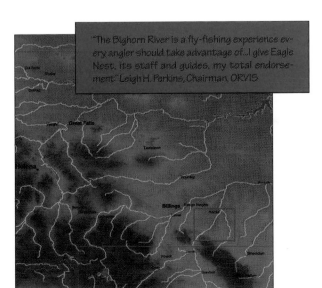

"The Bighorn River is a fly-fishing experience every angler should take advantage of...I give Eagle Nest, its staff and guides, my total endorsement." Leigh H. Perkins, Chairman, ORVIS

East Slope Anglers

Brad Parsch and Wayne Rooney
P.O. Box 160249 • Big Sky, MT 59716
phone: (888) Fly Fysh (359-3974) • (406) 995-4369

Our fishing guides are among the best available. They have the knowledge to be successful and the ability to impart their knowledge in a helpful and friendly manner. From beginner to expert, we can make your fishing experience a rewarding one. Youngsters are welcome.

Float trips are day-long on one of the float-fishing rivers in the area. Wade trips can be arranged for a half or full day with a maximum of three fishermen per guide. Full-day trips include lunch and can involve any number of waters in the area. We also provide instruction by the hour.

One-day and overnight horseback trips to less accessible waters around Big Sky are also available through East Slope Anglers. These trips can be enjoyed with non-fishing members. Most trips involve rides to alpine lakes and the use of float-tubes.

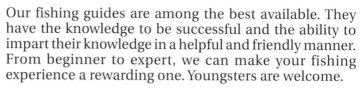

"I couldn't believe the number of fish we caught and released. Would give my unqualified recommendation to anyone to use these services!" Don Tillery

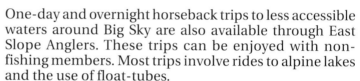

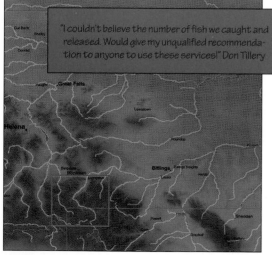

Esper's Under Wild Skies Lodge & Outfitters

Vaughn and Judy Esper

P.O. Box 849 • Philipsburg, MT 59858
phone: (406) 859-3000 • fax: (406) 859-3161

Under Wild Skies Lodge and Outfitters is located in the Deerlodge National Forest at the boundary of the Anaconda Pintler Wilderness.

Our guest ranch offers something for everyone. For the fisherman we have two lakes on the ranch. The Middle Fork of Rock Creek, which traverses the property, offers four species of trout. Take a scenic wilderness horseback ride for a day or overnight pack trip into the majestic Pintler mountains, or just relax in the casual elegance of the lodge.

At Under Wild Skies we take pride in our facilities, services and the meticulous attention we pay to every detail of your stay. You come as a guest and leave as a friend.

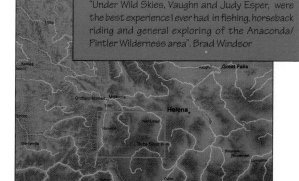

"Under Wild Skies, Vaughn and Judy Esper, were the best experience I ever had in fishing, horseback riding and general exploring of the Anaconda/Pintler Wilderness area". Brad Windsor

Grossenbacher Guides

Brian and Jenny Grossenbacher

P.O. Box 6704 • Bozeman, MT 59771
phone: (406) 582-1760 • fax: (406) 582-0589

At Grossenbacher Guides, we guarantee customer service and satisfaction. We not only work hard to get you into fish, but also to fill your expectations of a paramount flyfishing adventure.

Our philosophy, *The Total Flyfishing Experience*, follows the belief that a great day of fishing not only includes plenty of fish, but also an appreciation for the surrounding ecosystems, regional history and geology.

We place a premium on education; whether it's an improvement on your cast, a faster way to tie knots, or a brief lesson in ornithology, you will take home more than just memories of a great trip.

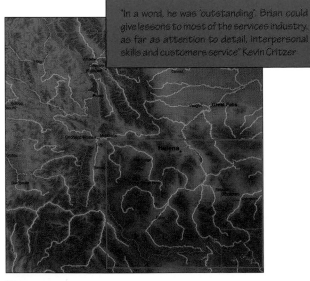

"In a word, he was 'outstanding'. Brian could give lessons to most of the services industry, as far as attention to detail, interpersonal skills and customers service" Kevin Critzer

Hatch Finders

Dean A. Reiner

120 South M St. • Livingston, MT 59047
phone: (406) 222-0989
email: hatchfinders@mcn.net • www. mcn.net/~hatchfinders

Spring and summer fishing on the Yellowstone River can be the challenge of a lifetime. Prolific caddis hatches in May produce the first major dry fly fishing of the year. The river comes alive with aggressive fish beginning with the salmon fly hatch in early July followed by hoppers in August and September.

DePuy's and Armstrong's Spring creeks are the mecca of fly fishing summer or winter. Hatches occur daily along 2.5 miles of the creek. Nymphing and dry fly fishing are not for the faint of heart.

Float trips by drift boats seat two fishermen at a time. Large parties can easily be accommodated. Enjoy the beautiful Paradise Valley where wildlife abounds and the scenery is breathtaking.

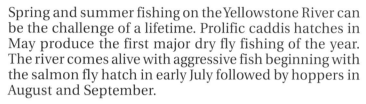

"Dean did an outstanding job overall to make my trip a lasting great memory." Capt. Rodney Smith

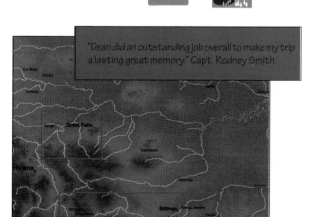

Rocky Fork Guide Service

Ernie Strum

HC 50, Box 4849 • Red Lodge, MT 59068
phone: (406) 446-2514

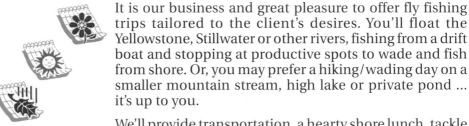

It is our business and great pleasure to offer fly fishing trips tailored to the client's desires. You'll float the Yellowstone, Stillwater or other rivers, fishing from a drift boat and stopping at productive spots to wade and fish from shore. Or, you may prefer a hiking/wading day on a smaller mountain stream, high lake or private pond ... it's up to you.

We'll provide transportation, a hearty shore lunch, tackle and flies if desired, and as much instruction and advice as you wish. Our guides are experienced, licensed and insured.

Outfitter Ernie Strum is a Federation of Fly Fishers-certified casting instructor.

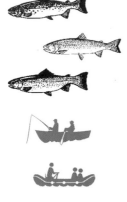

"...great people who are extremely knowledgable and proficient in the art and skill of fly fishing. I would certainly recommend Rocky Guide Service most highly." L. Rex Smith

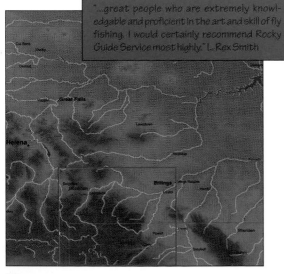

The Complete Fly Fisher

David W. and Stuart Decker

Box 127 • Wise River, MT 59762
phone: (406) 832-3175 • fax: (406) 832-3169

There are few places on this earth where legendary water, wild trout and five-star hospitality come together to provide the perfect balance. Where solitude, relaxation, challenge and excitement coexist. This is where life and angling combine to create the Complete Fly Fisher.

What makes one fly fishing experience different from another? Well, there's the river and we've got some of the world's best. There's the level of experience of the angler, or the guide, and we've definitely got the best.

But what really sets your time at The Complete Fly Fisher apart is the hospitality. Our staff and our guides are totally committed to anticipating your needs.

We've fine-tuned the perfect fly fishing experience.

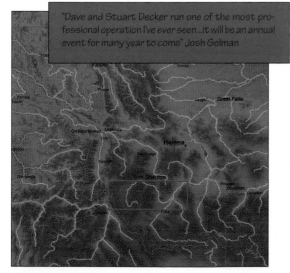

"Dave and Stuart Decker run one of the most professional operation I've ever seen...it will be an annual event for many year to come" Josh Gelman

The Reflective Angler

Eric and Al Troth

P.O. Box 6401 • Bozeman, MT 59771 (winter)
P.O. Box 1307 • Dillon, MT 59725 (summer)
phone: (406) 582-7600 (Bozeman) • (406) 683-2752 (Dillon)

We stalked to within two rod lengths of a large brown trout feeding on mayflies beneath a bank of willows. A perfect cast and the water exploded with a splash as the 20-incher seized the fly. It was the beginning of an unforgettable memory.

I seek to provide the extra dimension and personal attention that makes your trip truly satisfying. I share waters that I know intimately from more than 20 years' experience, and I specialize in instructing the fine points of dry fly and nymphing techniques.

Our daily float/wade excursions to southwestern Montana's blue-ribbon Beaverhead and Big Hole rivers begin in Dillon (a range of accommodations are available). I cater to individuals, pairs and small parties and personally guide all trips.

"A first class guide who's main year round profession is guiding fly fishermen. An excellent teacher! He ties and provides all flies for various waters and situation. The BEST!"

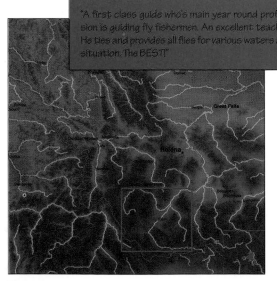

Tite Line Fishing

John Seidel

1520 Pancheri Dr. • Idaho Falls, ID 83402

toll free: (877) LV2-FISH • phone: (208) 529-4343 • fax: (208) 529-4397

email: jseidel@hydeboats.com

Tite Line Fishing offers the absolute best in fly fishing on the Missouri River, and some of the best fishing in all of Montana and the western United States. Our professional resident guides will put you where the fish are. Their enthusiasm helps make them experts on the river's hatches and effective fly patterns. We practice catch and release.

From the beginning angler to the seasoned, Tite Line Fishing will ensure your trip is a lifetime experience. The Missouri River is populated by 5,500 trout per mile with the average length 16 to 17 inches.

In addition to the trout, you will find a variety of Montana wildlife and breathtaking scenery.

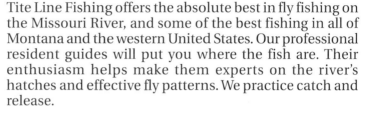

"One of the very best guided floats I've been on ... very enjoyable, what more could one want!" Robert S. Pulcipher

New Mexico

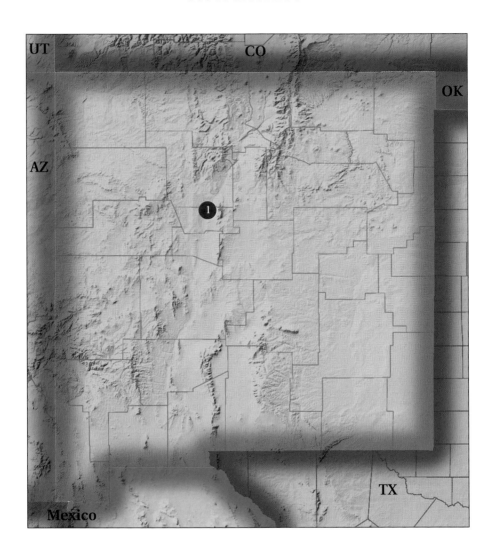

Outdoor Professionals

1 The Reel Life

Useful information for the state of

New Mexico

State and Federal Agencies

New Mexico Game & Fish Dept.
Villagra Building
Santa Fe, NM 87503
phone: (505) 27-7975

Forest Service
Southwestern Region
Federal Building
517 Gold Avenue SW
Albuquerque, NM 87102
phone: (505) 842-3300
TTY: (505) 842-3898

Carson National Forest
phone: (505) 758-6200

Cibola National Forest
phone / TTY: (505) 761-4650

Gila National Forest
phone: (505) 388-8201

Lincoln National Forest
phone: (505) 434-7200

Santa Fe National Forest
phone: (505) 438-7840

Bureau of Land Management
New Mexico State Office
1474 Rodeo Road
Santa Fe, NM 87505

Mailing Address:
P.O. Box 27115
Santa Fe, NM 87502-0115

Information Number: (505) 438-7400
fax: (505) 438-7435
Office Hours: 7:45 a.m. - 4:30 p.m.

National Parks

Carlsbad Caverns National Park
3225 National Parks Hwy.
Carlsbad, NM 88220
phone: (505) 785-2232

Associations, Publications, etc.

American Fisheries Society
PO Box 30003, Dept. 4901
Las Cruces, NM 88003
phone: (505) 521-7279

Federation of Fly Fishers
http://www.fedflyfishers.org

Trout Unlimited Rio Grande Chapter
9307 Galaxia Way, NE,
Albequerque, NM 87111
phone: (505) 243-1336

New Mexico Bass Chapter Federation
PO Box 717
Socorro, NM 87801
phone: (505) 835-1200

New Mexico Council of Outfitters &
Guides, Inc.
160 Washington SE #75
Albuquerque, NM 87108
phone: (505) 764-2670

License and Report Requirements
• State requires that Hunting Outfitters be licensed.
• State requires the filing of an "Annual Report of Outfitters' Clients" for hunting only.
• "Use Permit" required for Fish and River Outfitters using BLM and Forest Service
 lands. They are not required to file any reports.

PBY - New Mexico   81

The Reel Life

Manuel J. Monasterio

1100 San Mateo Blvd. NE, Ste. 10 • Albuquerque, NM 87110
510 Montezuma • Santa Fe, NM 87501
phone: (888) 268-3474 • (505) 268-1693

New Mexico is one of fly fishing's best-kept secrets. Excellent weather, beautiful scenery and plentiful trout waters provide truly memorable, year-round fly fishing. Whether you are conducting business in Albuquerque, sight-seeing in Santa Fe or skiing in Taos, our experienced guides can meet you at or drive you to the most productive stretch of water. Choose from world-class, private spring creeks on the Rio Penasco; private stretches on medium-sized tailwaters such as the Cimarron, Costilla or Culebra; and scenic western freestone rivers like the Pecos or Rio Grande; or phenomenal high lakes.

Anglers seeking solitude will enjoy our overnight llama pack trips. Our Albuquerque shop is located 10 minutes from the airport, and our new Santa Fe location is a short walk from the historic plaza district. Both shops offer an extensive selection of Orvis tackle, clothing and gifts.

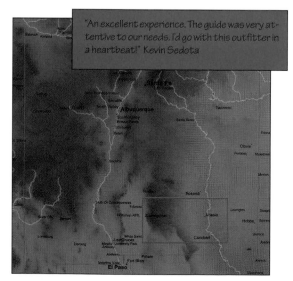

"An excellent experience. The guide was very attentive to our needs. I'd go with this outfitter in a heartbeat!" Kevin Sedota

New York

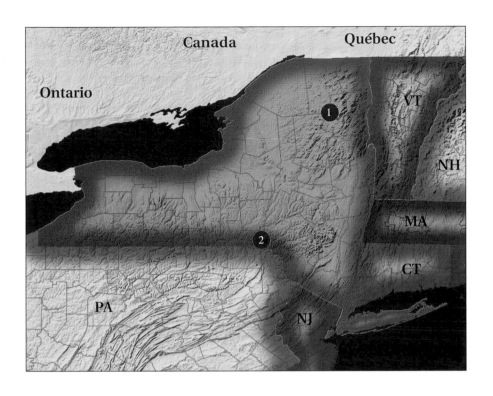

Outdoor Professionals

1. The Hungry Trout Motor Inn
2. West Branch Angler and Sportsman's Resort

Useful information for the state of

New York

State and Federal Agencies

Dept. of Environmental Conservation
50 Wolf Rd.
Albany, NY 12233
phone: (518) 457-3400

Bureau of Land Management
Eastern States
7450 Boston Boulevard
Springfield, Virginia 22153
phone: (703) 440-1660
or (703) 440- Plus Extension
fax: (703) 440-1599

Office Hours: 8:00 a.m. - 4:30 p.m.

Eastern States
Milwaukee District Office
310 W. Wisconsin Ave., Suite 450
(P.O. Box 631 53201-0631)
Milwaukee, Wisconsin 53203
phone: (414) 297-4450
fax: (414) 297-4409

Fire Island National Seashore
120 Laurel Street
Patchogue, NY 11772

Associations, Publications, etc.

Trout Unlimited New York Council
2711 Girdle Road
Elma, NY 14059
phone: (716) 655-1331

American Fisheries Society
Cornell Biological Field Station
R.D. 1
Bridgeport, NY 13030
phone: (315) 633-9243

Federation of Fly Fishers
http://www.fedflyfishers.org

Great Lakes Sport Fishing Council
PO Box 297
Elmhurst, IL 60126
phone: (630) 941-1351
fax: (630) 941-1196
email: glsfc@netwave.net
http://www.execpc.com/glsfc

New York Bass Chapter Federation
274 N. Goodman Street
Rochester, NY
phone: (716) 271-7000

New York State Outdoor Guides Assoc.
(NYSOGA)
PO Box 4704
Queensbury, NY 12804
phone/fax: (518) 798-1253

License and Report Requirements

• State requires licensing of Guides.

• State requires that Guides be re-certified each year.

• State has no report requirements.

The Hungry Trout Motor Inn

Jerry and Linda Bottcher

Rt. 86 • Whiteface Mountain, NY 12997
phone: (800)-766-9137 • (518) 946-2217 • fax: (518) 946-7418
email: hungrytrout@whiteface.net • www.hungrytrout.com

The Hungry Trout Motor Inn rests on the banks of the legendary West Branch of the Ausable River in New York's Adirondack Mountains. Fifteen minutes from Lake Placid, The Hungry Trout has been headquarters for anglers and bird hunters wishing upscale lodging, gourmet dining and access to private water and superb grouse hunting. The Hungry Trout Fly Shop is a leading outfitter in the area and offers professional fishing and grouse hunting guide service throughout the season.

Starting in late fall, you can combine trout fishing and grouse hunting on the same day as the Adirondacks harbor some of the best grouse cover in New York State. The Inn has first-class packages that combine lodging, dining and guide service.

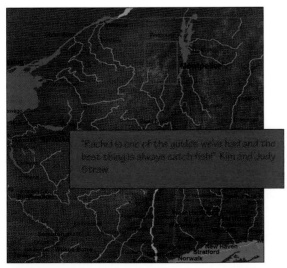

West Branch Angler and Sportsman's Resort

Harry Batschehet and Ray Finney
150 Faulkner Rd., PO Box 102 • Deposit, NY 13754
phone: (607) 467-5525 • fax: (607) 467-2215
email: wbangler@spectra.net • www.westbranchangler.com

The West Branch Angler and Sportsman's Resort is nestled in the beautiful Catskill Mountains on the famous West Branch of the Delaware River.

Our resort offers the fly angler cozy, upscale accommodations with 17 fully self-contained cabins, set on the banks of this magnificent tailwater fishery. We have a world-class fly shop on premises. We can provide experienced fishing guides and canoe and boat rentals. Additionally, we have a spectacular restaurant and bar services, and we provide family activities with our swimming pool, trout pond, sporting clays, hiking and mountain biking. Our winter activities include snowshoeing and cross country skiing.

"West Branch was an excellent , clean place. Food was good and the price reasonable." Ed Foss

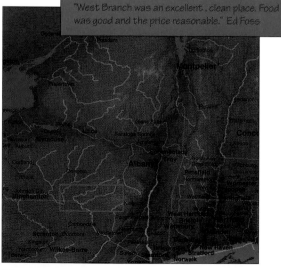

Oregon

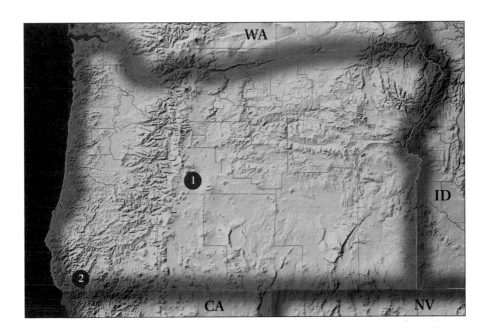

Outdoor Professionals

1 Fishing on the Fly
2 Sweet Old Boys Guide Service

License and Report Requirements

• State requires licensing of Outdoor Professionals.

• State requires a "Year-End Report" for Outfitters hunting and/or fishing on BLM land.

• U.S. Coast Guard licensing required for guides and captains that fish in "Near Coastal Waters".

Useful information for the state of
Oregon

State and Federal Agencies

Oregon Dept. of Fish & Wildlife
PO Box 59
Portland, OR 97207
phone: (503) 872-5268

Oregon Marine Board
435 Commercial St. NE
Salem, OR 97310
phone: (503) 373-1405
or (503) 378-8587

Columbia River Gorge Ntl. Scenic Area
902 Wasco Avenue, Ste 200
Hood River, OR 97031
phone: (541) 386-2333

Forest Service
Pacific Northwest Region
333 SW 1st Avenue
PO Box 3623
Portland, OR 97208
phone: (503) 326-2971
TTY: (503) 326-6448

Rogue River National Forest
phone:(541) 858-2200

Siskiyou National Forest
phone: (541) 471-6500

Siuslaw National Forest
phone: (541) 750-7000

Umpqua National Forest
phone: (541) 672-6601

Winema National Forest
phone: (541) 883-6714

Bureau of Land Management
Oregon State Office
1515 SW 5th Ave.
P.O. Box 2965
Portland, OR 97208-2965

phone: (503) 952-6001
or (503) 952-Plus Extension
fax: (503) 952-6308
Tdd: (503) 952-6372

Electronic mail
General Information:
or912mb@or.blm.gov
Webmaster: orwww@or.blm.gov

National Parks

Crater Lake National Park
phone: (541) 594-2211

Associations, Publications, etc.

American Fisheries Society
19948 S. Leland Road
Oregon City, OR 97045
phone: (503) 731-1267
fax: (503) 235-4228

Oregon Trout, Inc.
117 SW Front Ave.
Portland, OR 97204
phone: (503) 222-9091

Trout Unlimited Oregon Council
22875 NW Chestnut Street
Hillsboro, OR 97124-6545
phone: (541) 640-2123
fax: (503) 844-9929

Federation of Fly Fishers
http://www.fedflyfishers.org

Oregon Bass Chapter Federation
2475 N. Baker Drive
Canby, OR 97013
phone: (503) 266-7729

Oregon Outdoor Association
PO Box 9486
Bend, OR 97708-9486
phone: (541) 382-9758

Fishing on the Fly

Tim Dority
P.O. Box 242 • Bend, OR 97709
phone: (541) 389-3252 • fax: (541) 317-1483

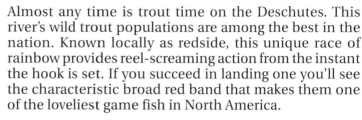

Almost any time is trout time on the Deschutes. This river's wild trout populations are among the best in the nation. Known locally as redside, this unique race of rainbow provides reel-screaming action from the instant the hook is set. If you succeed in landing one you'll see the characteristic broad red band that makes them one of the loveliest game fish in North America.

Nothing quite matches the thrill of hooking a steelhead on a fly. Steelhead begin arriving in the Deschutes in midsummer. These tenacious fish provide fly anglers with unparalleled excitement through December. Jet boat excursions near the mouth of the river are offered beginning in August, and drift boat trips are available later in the year.

Fishing on the Fly specializes in teaching the art of flyfishing, be it nymph or dry fly techniques, entomology or stream reading and tactics.

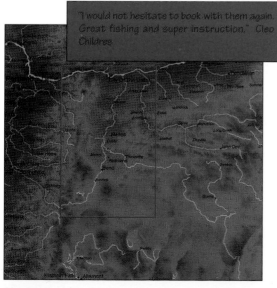

"I would not hesitate to book with them again. Great fishing and super instruction." Cleo Childres

Sweet Old Boys Guide Service

Marsden P. (Tiny) Case

1790 Laurel Rd. • Cave Junction, OR 97523
phone: (541) 592-4552

We fish the Rogue River from Cole Rivers Hatchery above Shady Cove to Graves Creek Landing, depending on the season and water conditions.

Using a drift boat and up-to-date fishing equipment, we provide you with the opportunity to catch steelhead, salmon and trout. Flyfishing available by request for all three.

You need to bring an Oregon fishing license and tags (day license with tag is available), camera (chance for wildlife pictures), lunch, drink, a hat and sunscreen. You should dress in layers, as some mornings are cool.

Fish fall salmon August through October; spring salmon mid-May through July; winter steelhead November through April; summer steelhead July through October, and trout year-round.

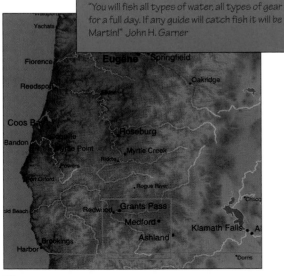

"You will fish all types of water, all types of gear for a full day. If any guide will catch fish it will be Martin!" John H. Garner

Pennsylvania

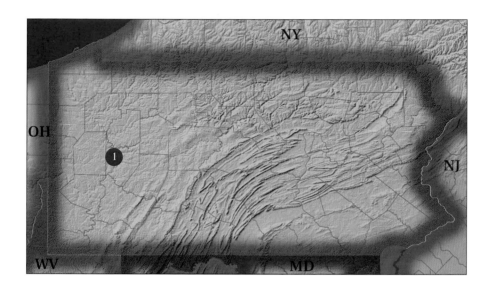

Outdoor Professionals

1 Serene Fly-Fishing Adventures

Useful information for the state of
Pennsylvania

State and Federal Agencies

Pennsylvania Game Commission
2001 Elmerton Ave.
Harrisburg, PA 17110
hunting: (717) 787-4250
fishing: (717) 657-4518

Division of Tourism
Commonwealth of Pennsylvania
phone: (800) 847-4872

Forest Service
Eastern Region
310 West Wisconsin Avenue, Room 500
Milwaukee, WI 53203
phone: (414) 297-3646
TTY: (414) 297-3507

Allegheny National Forest
222 Liberty Street
PO Box 847
Warren, PA 16365
phone: (814) 723-5150
TTY: (814) 726-2710

Bureau of Land Management
Eastern States
7450 Boston Boulevard
Springfield, Virginia 22153
phone: (703) 440-1660
or (703) 440- Plus Extension
fax: (703) 440-1599

Office Hours: 8:00 a.m. - 4:30 p.m.

Eastern States
Milwaukee District Office
310 W. Wisconsin Ave., Suite 450
(P.O. Box 631 53201-0631)
Milwaukee, Wisconsin 53203
phone: (414) 297-4450
fax: (414) 297-4409

Associations, Publications, etc.

Trout Unlimited Pennsylvania Council
PO Box 1126
Federal Square Station
Harrisburg, PA 17108

Federation of Fly Fishers
http://www.fedflyfishers.org

Pennsylvania Bass Chapter Fed., Inc.
769 N. Cottage Road
Mercer, PA 16137
phone: (412) 475-2422

Great Lakes Sport Fishing Council
PO Box 297
Elmhurst, IL 60126
phone: (630) 941-1351
fax: (630) 941-1196
email: glsfc@netwave.net
http://www.execpc.com/glsfc

North American Native Fisheries Assoc.
123 W. Mt. Airy Ave.
Philadelphia, PA 19119

License and Report Requirements
• State requires licensing of Outdoor Professionals.

• State requires the filing of the "Charter Boat/Fishing Guide Report".

Serene Fly-Fishing Adventures

Pete Serene

RD 2, Box 139 G • Kittanning, PA 16201
phone: (412) 783-6346 • (412) 783-6678
email: mmsl@alltel.net

We offer guided flyfishing on all of Pennsylvania's top streams, from Erie tributaries for steelhead to the W.B. Delaware for wild trout and everything in between. I have 25 years' flyfishing experience and specialize in central Pennsylvania's limestone streams. We also have special package trips to Michigan's famous Pere Marquette River for salmon in the fall and steelhead in the spring.

Float in a Hyde driftboat when possible or wade. One- to seven-day packages includes use of a 24-foot motorhome, which provides all the comforts of home. Lunches are provided. With friendly instruction and tips, we work hard to provide a pleasant and relaxing atmosphere in order for you to get the maximum satisfaction out of your flyfishing experience.

Let me take you on a trip that you will always remember.

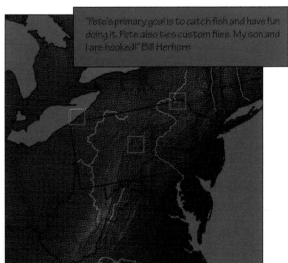

"Pete's primary goal is to catch fish and have fun doing it. Pete also ties custom flies. My son and I are hooked." Bill Herhorn

Texas

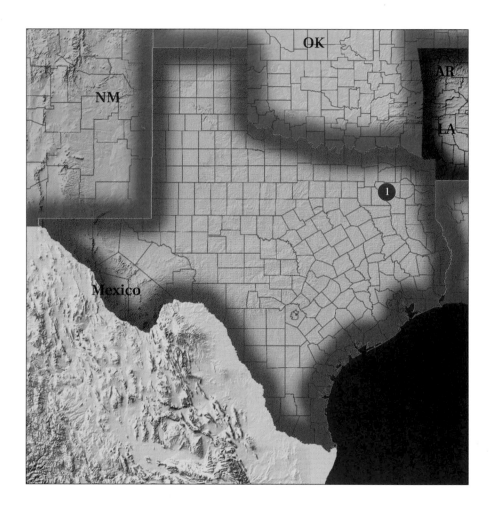

Outdoor Professionals

1 G & W Guide Service

License and Report Requirements
• State does not license or register Outfitters, Guides, or Lodges.

• State has no report requirements.

Texas

State and Federal Agencies

Texas Parks & Wildlife Dept.
4200 Smith School Rd.
Austin, TX 78744
phone: (512) 389-4800

Forest Service
Southern Region
1720 Peachtree Road NW
Atlanta, GA 30367
phone: (404) 47-4177
TTY: (404) 347-4278

Angelina, Davy Crockett, Sabine, Sam
Houston National Forests
Homer Garrison Federal Bldg.
701 North First Street
Lufkin, TX 75901
phone/TTY: (409) 639-8501

Padre Island National Seashore
9405 S. Padre Island Drive
Corpus Christi, TX 78418
phone: (512) 937-2621

Bureau of Land Management
New Mexico State Office
(serves Kansas, Oklahoma & Texas)
Street Address:
1474 Rodeo Road
Santa Fe, NM 87505

Mailing Address:
P.O. Box 27115
Santa Fe, NM 87502-0115

Information Number: 505-438-7400
fax: (505) 438-7435
Public Lands Information Center (PLIC):
(505) 438-7542

Office Hours: 7:45 a.m. - 4:30 p.m.

National Parks

Big Bend National Park
Big Bend National Park, TX 79834
phone: (915) 477-2251

Guadalupe Mountains National Park
HC 60, Box 400
Salt Flat, TX 79847-9400
phone: (915) 828-3351

Associations, Publications, etc.

American Fisheries Society, Texas
Chapter
11045 Spur 164
Tyler, TX 75709
phone: (903) 592-7570
fax: (903) 592-6769

Trout Unlimited Guadelupe River Chapter
113 S. Cuerna Vaca Drive
Austin, TX 78733
phone: (512) 263-9619

Federation of Fly Fishers
http://www.fedflyfishers.org

Texas Bass Chapter Federation
1529 Sunview Drive
Dallas, TX 75253
phone: (214) 352-7531

G & W Guide Service

Brian Gambill

1100 N. Shore • Little Elm, TX 75068
phone: (972) 294-3202

Flyfisher Brian Gambill, who has more than 15 years of guiding experience, was one of the first flyfishing guides on Lake Fork, a premier trophy bass lake located east of Dallas near Quitman.

With a maximum depth of 70 feet and an average depth of 25 feet, the 27,690 acre lake has regularly produces fish in the 5- to 10-pound range.

Specialty flies, lunch and drinks are provided. Equipment rental is available at a nominal rate.

"Brian ties all his own flies and he develops patterns to help his business. He has developed techniques to fish 12 ft., 20 ft., whatever it takes to be effective on a flyrod." Paul Koenig

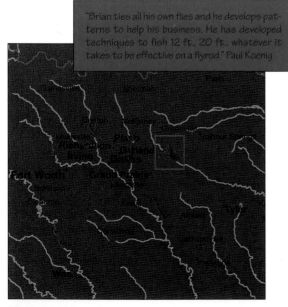

Utah

Outdoor Professionals

1 Alpine Anglers Fly Shop & Boulder Mountain
Adventures

Useful information for the state of
Utah

State and Federal Agencies

Utah Dept. of Natural Resources
1636 W. North Temple
Salt Lake City, UT 84116
phone: (801) 538-4700

Forest Service
Intermountain Region
324 25th Street
Ogden, UT 84401-2310
phone: (801) 625-5306
TTY: (801) 625-5307

Ashley National Forest
phone: (801) 789-1181

Dixie National Forest
phone: (801) 865-3700

Fishlake National Forest
phone: (801) 896-9233

Manti-LaSal National Forest
phone / TTY: (801) 637-2817

Uinta National Forest
phone: (801) 342-5100

Wasatch-Cache National Forests
phone: (801) 524-5030

Bureau of Land Management
Utah State Office
324 South State Street, Suite 301
P.O. Box 45155
Salt Lake City, Utah 84145-0155

Information Number: (801) 539-4001
fax: (801) 539-4013
Office Hours: 8:00 a.m. - 4:00 p.m.

National Parks

Arches National Park
Moab, UT 84532
phone: (801) 259-8161

Bryce Canyon National Park
Bryce Canyon, UT 84717
phone: (801) 834-5322

Canyonlands National Park
Moab, UT 84532
phone: (801) 259-3911

Capitol Reef National Park
Torrey, UT 84775
phone: (801) 425-3791

Zion National Park
Springdale, UT 84767
phone: (801) 772-3256

Associations, Publications, etc.

Trout Unlimited Rio Grande Chapter
9307 Galaxia Way, NE,
Albequerque, NM 87111
phone: (505) 243-1336

Federation of Fly Fishers
http://www.fedflyfishers.org

New Mexico Bass Chapter Federation
PO Box 717
Socorro, NM 87801
phone: (505) 835-1200

License and Report Requirements
• State does not license or register Outfitters, Guides, Captains or Lodges.
• State Parks & Recreation Division requires that River Rafting Guides and Outfitters register and file a "River Outfitting Company Registration".
• BLM, Forest Service and National Park Service require a "Use Permit" and "User Fee" for Boating, Fish and River Outfitters using their lands. Guides and Outfitters required to file a "Year End Report of Activities".

Alpine Anglers Flyshop and Boulder Mountain Adventures

Rich and Lori Cropper

310 W. Main, P.O. Box 750308 • Torrey, UT 84775
phone: (435) 425-3660 • (888) 484-3331
email: brookies@color-country.net • www.color-country.net/~brookies

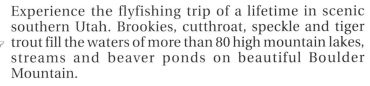

Experience the flyfishing trip of a lifetime in scenic southern Utah. Brookies, cutthroat, speckle and tiger trout fill the waters of more than 80 high mountain lakes, streams and beaver ponds on beautiful Boulder Mountain.

We offer day trips and overnight flyfishing pack trips. Our flyshop will outfit you with top-of-the-line flyfishing equipment.

Friendly, knowledgeable guides provide a rewarding experience for the novice as well as the seasoned angler.

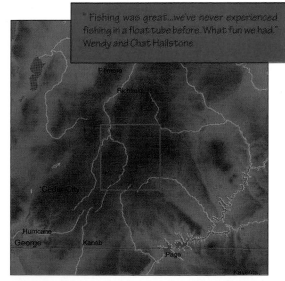

" Fishing was great...we've never experienced fishing in a float tube before. What fun we had."
Wendy and Chat Hailstone

Vermont

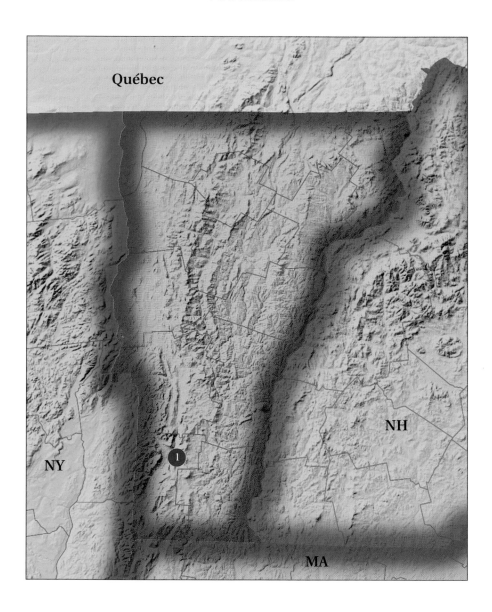

Outdoor Professionals

1 The Battenkill Anglers

Useful information for the state of

Vermont

State and Federal Agencies

Vermont Fish & Wildlife Dept.
103 South Main St.
Waterbury, VT 05671-0501
phone: (802) 241-3700

Eastern Region National Forest
310 West Wisconsin Ave., Room 500
Milwaukee, WI 53203
phone: (414) 297-3646
TTY: (414) 297-3507

Green Mountain, Finger Lakes National
Forests
231 North Main Street
Rutland, VT 05701
phone: (802) 747-6765

Bureau of Land Management
Eastern States
7450 Boston Boulevard
Springfield, Virginia 22153
phone: (703) 440-1660
or (703) 440-plus extension
fax: (703) 440-1599

Office Hours: 8:00 a.m. - 4:30 p.m.

Eastern States
Milwaukee District Office
310 W. Wisconsin Ave., Suite 450
(P.O. Box 631 53201-0631)
Milwaukee, Wisconsin 53203
phone: (414) 297-4450
fax: (414) 297-4409

Associations, Publications, etc.

Trout Unlimited Vermont Council
Toad Pond Rd.
RR 1, Box 35A
Morgan, VT
phone: (802) 895-4220

Federation of Fly Fishers
http://www.fedflyfishers.org

Vermont Bass Chapter Federation
19 Pinewood Rd.
Montpelier, VT 05602
phone: (802) 223-7793

Vermont Federation of Sportsmen

License and Report Requirements

• State does not license or register Outfitters, Guides, or Lodges.

• State has no report requirements.

The Battenkill Anglers

Tom Goodman

RR #1, Box 2303 • Manchester Center, VT 05255
phone: (802) 362-3184

The Battenkill Anglers focus on learning techniques, strategies and tactics for taking trout, as well as the secrets of some of New England's finest trout rivers. We adhere to no schedule and our guides are not salespeople. All of our instructor/guides are full-time professional fly fishers who have been hand-picked for their devotion to the study of taking trout on artificial flies. Our guides have academic backgrounds in stream ecology and entomology, which qualifies them to give you an experience with depth in the science of angling for trout, and really put you in touch with the pulse of our rivers.

Fly fishing for trout is an ancient craft, a blend of art and science that offers many options to the student.

The Battenkill Anglers can help you achieve your angling goals in the classroom or on one of our rivers.

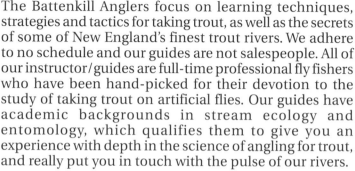

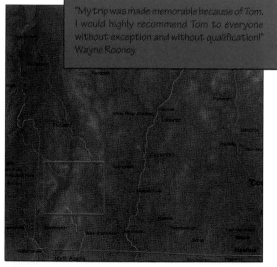

"My trip was made memorable because of Tom. I would highly recommend Tom to everyone without exception and without qualification!"
Wayne Rooney

Virginia

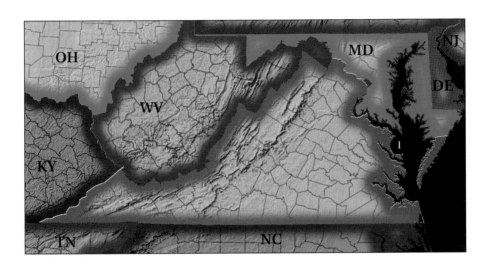

Outdoor Professionals

❶   Chesapeake Bay Charters

License and Report Requirements

• State does not license or register Outfitters, Guides, Captains or Lodges.

• State has no report requirements.

Virginia

State and Federal Agencies

Dept. of Game & Inland Fisheries
4010 W. Brood St.
Richmond, VA 23230
phone: (804) 367-1000

Forest Service
Southern Region
1720 Peachtree Road NW
Atlanta, GA 30367
phone: (404) 347-4177
TTY: (404) 347-4278

George Washington & Jefferson National
Forests
5162 Valley Pointe Parkway
Roanoke, VA 24091
phone: (540) 265-5100
TTY: (540) 265-6089

Bureau of Land Management
Eastern States
7450 Boston Boulevard
Springfield, Virginia 22153
phone: (703) 440-1660
or (703) 440-plus extension
fax: (703) 440-1599

Office Hours: 8:00 a.m. - 4:30 p.m.

Eastern States
Jackson Field Office
411 Briarwood Drive, Suite 404
Jackson, Mississippi 39206
phone: (601) 977-5400
fax: (601) 977-5440

National Parks

Shenandoah National Park
Rt. 4, Box 348
Luray, VA 22835
phone: (703) 999-2243

Associations, Publications, etc.

Trout Unlimited Virginia Council
302 Danray Drive
Richmond, VA 23227
phone: (804) 264-6941

Federation of Fly Fishers
http://www.fedflyfishers.org

American Fisheries Society
Virginia Chapter
Dept. of Biol. Science
Mary Washington College
Fredricksburg, VA 22401
phone: (540) 654-1426

Virginia Bass Chapter Federation
113 Lavergne Lane
Virginia Beach, VA 23454
phone: (804) 428-4280

American Bass Assoc., Inc.
PO Box 896
Gate City, VA 24251
phone: (540) 386-2109

Future Fisherman Foundation
1033 N. Fairfax St., Ste. 200
Alexandria, VA 22314
phone: (703) 519-9691

Chesapeake Bay Charters

Capt. Leroy G. Carr

Rt. 3, Box 217F, 205 Riverview Rd. • Heathville, VA 22473
phone: (home) (804) 453-4050 • (boat) (804) 450-4050

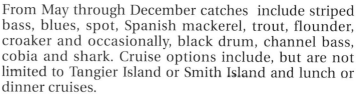

The Blue Streak provides fishing charters and cruises in Chesapeake Bay, Virginia and Maryland. Our objective is to offer personal and courteous service for cruising and/or fishing.

From May through December catches include striped bass, blues, spot, Spanish mackerel, trout, flounder, croaker and occasionally, black drum, channel bass, cobia and shark. Cruise options include, but are not limited to Tangier Island or Smith Island and lunch or dinner cruises.

The Blue Streak is a 36-foot flybridged sport fishing boat, Coast Guard licensed, fully fitted with electronics, twin engines and all safety equipment. We belong to the National Charter Boat Association and serve on the board of directors for Virginia Charter Boat Association.

"The only one I will go fishing with on the Chesapeake Bay." James F. Bailey, Jr.

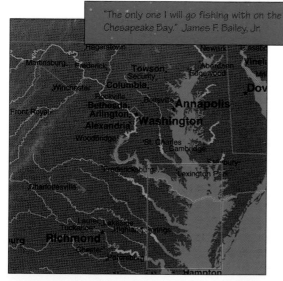

West Virginia

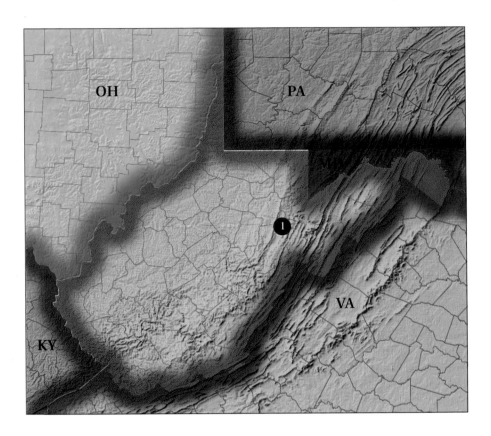

Outdoor Professionals

① Kelly Creek Flyfishers

License and Report Requirements

• State requires licensing of Outdoor Professionals.

• State requires that Commercial Whitewater Guides file a "Monthly Report of Customers".

Useful information for the state of
West Virginia

State and Federal Agencies

Dept. of Natural Resources
1900 Kanawha Blvd. East
State Building 3
Charleston, WV 25305
Fisheries: (304) 558-2771
Law Enforcement: (304) 558-2771

Forest Service
Eastern Region
310 West Wisconsin Avenue, Room 500
Milwaukee, WI 53203
phone: (414) 297-3646
TTY: (414) 297-3507

Monongahela National Forest
USDA Building
200 Sycamore Street
Elkins, WV 26241-3962
phone/TTY: (304) 636-1800

Bureau of Land Management
Eastern States
7450 Boston Boulevard
Springfield, Virginia 22153
phone: (703) 440-1660
or (703) 440- Plus Extension
fax: (703) 440-1599

Office Hours: 8:00 a.m. - 4:30 p.m.

Eastern States
Milwaukee District Office
310 W. Wisconsin Ave., Suite 450
(P.O. Box 631 53201-0631)
Milwaukee, Wisconsin 53203
phone: (414) 297-4450
fax: (414) 297-4409

Associations, Publications, etc.

American Fisheries Society
PO Box 1278
Elkins, WV 26241
phone: (304) 636-6586
fax: (304) 636-7824

Trout Unlimited West Virginia Council
637 Grand Street
Morgantown, WV 26505-6911
phone: (304) 293-7749

Federation of Fly Fishers
http://www.fedflyfishers.org

West Virginia Bass Chapter Federation
12 N. Kawawha Street
Buckhannon, WV 26201
phone: (304) 472-3600

The American Bass Association of
West Virginia
2620 Fairmont Ave., Ste. 110
Fairmont, WV 26554
phone: (304) 366-8183

Kelly Creek Flyfishers

Gary Lang
Rt. 1, Box 328-41 • Elkins, WV 26241
phone: (304) 636-7642

West Virginia is overlooked by most Eastern flyfishers. While we have some fairly high country, our latitude saddles us with several weeks of 80-degree daytime temperatures in midsummer. For this reason, many of the area's stocked streams suffer from significant trout mortality.

The majority of our summer fishing is for native brook trout on small headwater creeks. There are now several high-quality catch and releases areas established on larger streams which maintain a carryover fishery. It is on these headwater creeks and catch and release areas where we guide.

With the benefit of our crew's combined 75 years' experience, a fishing vacation in West Virginia rivals anything in the East.

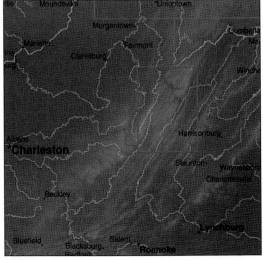

Wyoming

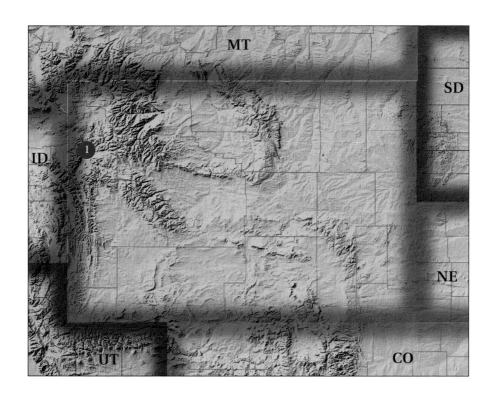

Outdoor Professionals

1 John Henry Lee Outfitters, Inc.

License and Report Requirements

• State requires licensing of Outdoor Professionals.

• State requires that Big Game Outfitters file a "Year-End Report".

• Fishing Outfitters need to get a permit to fish on BLM land.

• Outfitters and Guest/Dude Ranches must file a "Use" or "Day Report" with the Wyoming Forest Service if they Fish, Hunt or Raft on Forest Service Land.

Wyoming

State and Federal Agencies

Wyoming Dept. of Commerce
Board of Outfitters
1750 Westland Rd.
Cheyenne, WY 82002
(800) 264-0981
phone: (307) 777-5323
fax: (307) 777-6715

Wyoming Game & Fish Dept.
5400 Bishop Blvd.
Cheyenne, WY 82002
phone: (307) 777-4601

Forest Service
Intermountain Region
Federal Building
324 25th Street
Ogden, UT 84401-2310
phone: (801) 625-5306
TTY: (801) 625-5307

Bridger-Teton National Forests
Forest Service Building
340 North Cache
PO Box 1888
Jackson, WY 83001
phone: (307) 739-5500
TTY: (307) 739-5064

Bureau of Land Management
Wyoming State Office
(serves Nebraska also)
Information Access Center
5353 Yellowstone
P.O. Box 1828
Cheyenne, WY 82003
phone: (307) 775-6BLM or 6256
fax: (307) 775-6082
Office Hours: 7:45 a.m. - 4:30 p.m.

National Parks

Grand Teton National Park
PO Drawer 170
Moose, WY 83012
phone: (307) 739-3610

Yellowstone National Park
PO Box 168
Yellowstone National Park, WY 82190
phone: (307) 344-7381

Associations, Publications, etc.

Trout Unlimited Wyoming
PO Box 1022
Jackson, WY 83001
phone: (307) 733-1530

Federation of Fly Fishers
http://www.fedflyfishers.org

Wyoming Bass Chapter Federation
106 Folsom Drive
Rock Springs, WY 82901
phone: (307) 382-4742

Wyoming Outfitters & Guides Assoc.
PO Box 2284
239 Yellowstone Ave., Suite C
Cody, WY 82414
phone: (307) 527-7453
fax: (307) 587-8633

Jackson Hole Outfitters & Guide Association
850 W. Broadway
Jackson Hole, WY 83001
phone: (307) 734-9025

John Henry Lee Outfitters, Inc.

John Lee

Box 8368 • Jackson, WY 83001

phone: (800) 352-2576 • (307) 733-9441 • fax: (307) 733-1403

Come and experience a float-fishing trip with breathtaking views of the Teton Range and the serenity of the wilderness.

We offer guided fishing trips on the Snake, Green and New Fork rivers. In addition, we offer guided walk-in trips to Yellowstone with fishing on the Madison, Firehole, or Yellowstone River.

Backcountry fishing trips vary from seven to ten days in Yellowstone National Park or in the Bridger Teton Wilderness. These areas are considered by many to be the best cutthroat trout fishing in the world. Fish the headwaters of the Yellowstone or Thoroughfare River for an experience you'll always remember.

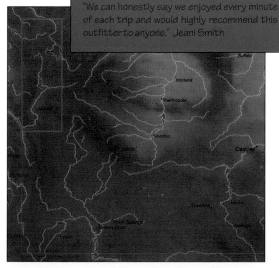

"We can honestly say we enjoyed every minute of each trip and would highly recommend this outfitter to anyone." Jeani Smith

Canada

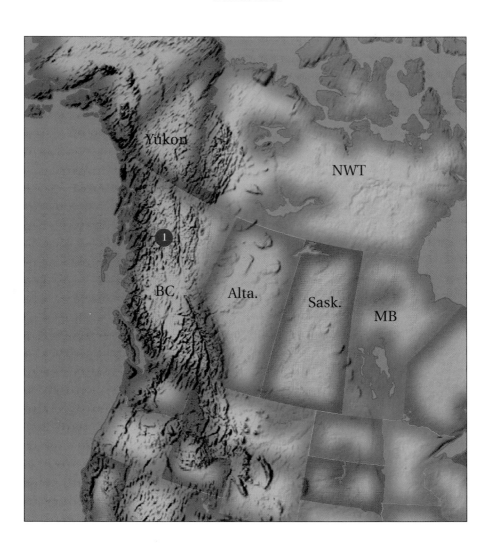

Outdoor Professionals

1 Love Bros. & Lee, Ltd.

Canada

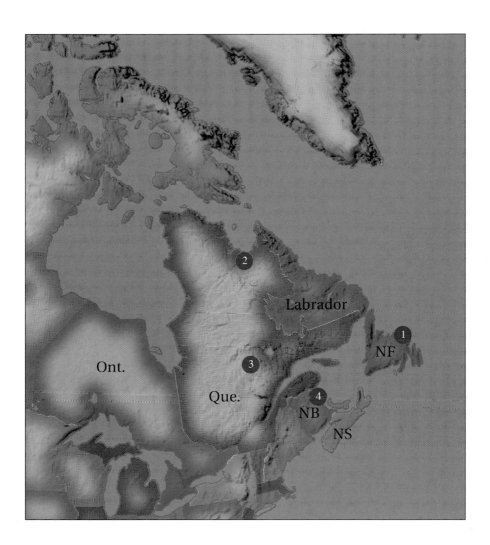

Outdoor Professionals

1. Gander River Outfitters, Inc.
2. George River Lodge, Inc.
3. Les Enterprises du Lac Perdu, Inc.
4. M&M's Whooper Hollow Lodge

Useful information for the provinces of
Canada

British Columbia:
Ministries and Agencies

Department of Fisheries & Oceans
200 Kent Street
Ottowa, Ontario Canada K1A 036

Ministry of the Environment
810 Blanshard St., 4th Floor
Victoria, B.C. Canada V8V 1X4
phone: (604) 387-9422

Ministry of Small Business Tourism &
Culture
1117 Wharf St.
Victoria, B.C. Canada V8V 2Z2
phone: (604) 387-1683

Associations, Publications, etc.

Federation of Fly Fishers
http://www.fedflyfishers.org

Guide Outfitters Association of British
Columbia
PO Box 94675
Richmond, B.C. Canada V6Y 4A4

New Brunswick:
Ministries and Agencies

Dept of Natural Resources & Energy
PO Box 6000
Fredericton, NB Canada E3B 5H1

Dept. of Fisheries & Oceans
Gulf Region
Bernard LeBlanc
Box 5030
Moncton, NB Canada E1C 9B6
phone: (506) 857-7750

Huntsman Marine Science Centre
Brandy Cove
St. Andrews, NB Canada E0G 2X0
phone: (506) 529-1200
fax: (506) 529-1212

Associations, Publications, etc.

Federation of Fly Fishers
http://www.fedflyfishers.org

Useful information for the provinces of

Canada

Newfoundland:
Ministries and Agencies

Department of Fisheries & Oceans
200 Kent Street
Ottowa, Ontario Canada K1A 036

Department of Natural Resources
PO Box 8700
St. John's, NF Canada A1B 4J6
phone: (709) 729-4715

Wildlife Division
PO Box 8700
St. John's, NF Canada A1B 4J6
phone: (709) 729-2817

Newfoundland Labrador Wildlife Fed.
phone: (709) 364-8415

Department of Tourism, Culture &
Recreation
PO Box 8730
St. John's, NF, Canada A1B 4J6
phone: (709) 729-2830
fax: (709) 729-1965
email: info@tourism.gov.nf.ca

Associations, Publications, etc.

Federation of Fly Fishers
http://www.fedflyfishers.org

Québec:
Ministries and Agencies

Department of Fisheries & Oceans
200 Kent Street
Ottowa, Ontario Canada K1A 036

Dept. of Recreation, Fish & Game
Place de la Capitale 150 Blvd.
Rene-Levesque Est, Québec
Canada G1R 4Y1
phone: (418) 643-6527

Associations, Publications, etc.

Federation of Fly Fishers
http://www.fedflyfishers.org

Federation of Québec Outfitters
2485 Boul Hamel
Québec, Canada G1P 2H9
phone: (418) 877-5191

Gander River Outfitters, Inc.

Terence D. Cusack, President

P.O. Box 21017 • St. John's , Newfoundland, Canada AIA 5B2
phone: (888) SALMON3 (752-6663) • (709) 753-9163 • fax: (709) 753-9169
email: flyfish@netfx-inc.com • www.netfx-inc.com/flyfish

Gander River Outfitters, Inc. offers a quality fishing experience from its camp on the lower Gander River. Angling has been very good and stock counts have shown our salmon population increased from approximately 7,500 in the early 1990's to annual runs of nearly 27,000 in 1993-95. The stock counts are up and are expected to increase the next few years.

The camp has a capacity of 10-12 rods and is reached by riverboat from Gander Bay. The camp has indoor plumbing, showers, electricity and refrigeration. Our uniformed guides are all well-trained and highly motivated, and our chef will delight you with a variety of excellent meals served on our Portmeirion "Compleat Angler" china.

We consider quality and service to be conditions of doing business. We are sure that you will enjoy the experience with us and we would be happy to discuss arranging a trip to meet your needs. We also offer hunting for Eastern moose and black bear.

"Top of the line gear. Excellent guide, catered to any kind of food. Best spot in Labrador/Newfoundland." Terrance Giblingham

George River Lodge, Inc.

Pierre et Jean Paquet

C.P. 88 • St. Augustin, Québec, Canada G3A 1V9
phone: (800) 473-4650 • fax: (418) 877-4652
email: norpaq@qbc.clic.net • www.promosit.qc.ca/norpaq

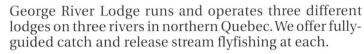

George River Lodge runs and operates three different lodges on three rivers in northern Quebec. We offer fully-guided catch and release stream flyfishing at each.

George River provides opportunities to catch Atlantic salmon, brook trout and lake trout. Club Chateauguay has two camps to cover 50 miles of stream for big brook trout and lake trout. The Whale River Camp is situated on the headwaters of the river for land-locked salmon, brook trout, northern pike and huge lake trout.

All destinations are top-notch for fly fishermen and offers some of the best flyfishing in the world because of its remoteness.

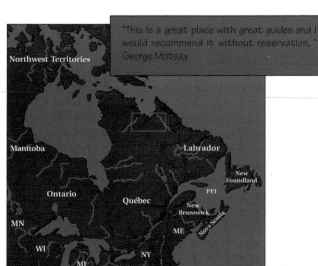

"This is a great place with great guides and I would recommend it without reservation."
George Motsay

Les Enterprises du Lac Perdu, Inc.

Michel and Mary-Anne Auclair

3, rue Zurich, Ste-Brigitte de Laval • Québec, Canada G0A 3K0
phone: (418) 825-3500 • fax: (418) 825-2113
email: Mauclair@lac-perdu.qc.ca • www.lac-perdu.qc.ca

Yes, we found the lost lake, north of the 50th parallel, deep in the heart of the Quebec boreal forest, in a savage and unchartered region.

Magnificent Lake Perdu, 12 miles long, overlooks an exclusive territory spanning more than 150 square miles, midway between Lake Mistassini and the Manic 5 hydro project.

We have been operating since 1980 and we guarantee that a stay at our lodge will provide you with the fishing thrills of a lifetime. We offer excellent trophy fishing locations for the serious angler interested in native speckle trout, lake trout, great northern pike and white fish. Our hunting and fishing lodge sits in the middle of a vast territory that will meet your highest expectations.

"A wonderful fly-in experience!! Plenty of trouts on dry flies." Ray Scott

Love Bros. and Lee, Ltd.

Ron Fleming and Brenda Nelson

RR#1, Kispiox Rd. • Hazelton, British Columbia, Canada V0J 1Y0
phone/fax: (250) 842-6350

Experience a flyfishing trip of a lifetime in northwestern British Columbia. Our remote wilderness camp is accessible by float plane only.

We offer guided flyfishing for wild rainbow or guided hunting for big game in an exclusive wilderness area, 165 airmiles north of Smithers, British Columbia.

Accommodations are fully-equipped log cabins. A shower is also available.

To ensure you have a personalized quality adventure, we take a maximum of four guests per week.

"Over the 12-13 years with Love Brothers & Lee, my experiences have been great... Brenda and Ron Fleming are the greatest." Sandy Wilkinson

M&M's Whooper Hollow Lodge

Martin and Marie Budaker

108 Fulton Ave. • Fredericton, New Brunswick, Canada E3A 2B6
office/fax: (506) 472-6391 • lodge: (506) 627-9391

M&M's Whooper Hollow Lodge is nestled in a field sloping to the shores of beautiful and legendary Dungarvon River, a tributary of the main Southwest Miramichi. Our lodge features delicious home-cooked meals and accommodations for nine guests with full bath. We take pride in our professional hunting and fishing guide service. We welcome mixed groups and are pleased to package and store your fish and game trophies.

Atlantic salmon are usually present in the Dungarvon from mid-June to mid-October. Angling packages feature one guide for every three anglers.

We accommodate a maximum of six guests for a minimum three-day stay. Book early for prime dates.

"The location of the Lodge is for those truly looking for the 'out of the way' adventure, located looking over the river. I have been several years and plan to keep going back. The food is always homecooking and in plenty. The family as a whole really enjoys our trips to Whooper Hollow Lodge." Paul Arnold

Top Rated Fly Fishing Photo Album

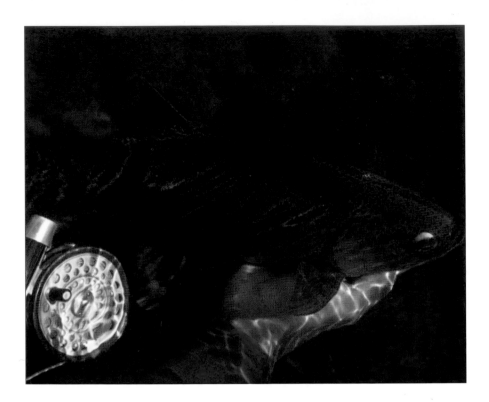

126

Photo Credits

Appendix

&

Questionnaire

&

Indexes

APPENDIX-FISHING

This is the list of **ALL** the fishing Guides, Captains, Lodges and Outfitters that we contacted during the compilation of our books. In all more than 11,000 just for fishing!

We invited them to participate in our survey by simply sending us their complete client list.

Some replied prizing the Picked-By-You idea, but decided not to participate in our survey. Their main concern was the confidentiality of their client list. We truly respect their position, but we hope to have proven our honest and serious effort. We are sure they will join us in the next edition. Some did not respond.

Others participated by sending their complete list of clients, but did not quality for publication. In some cases because of a low score, and in other instances because of an insufficient number of questionnaires returned by their clients.

The names of the Outdoor Professionals published in this book who have qualified with an A rating from their past clients are **bolded** in the Appendix.

Manuel Aaron	Ronald L. Appelbee	Capt. Clarence Bartlett	H. "Bick" Bicknell	Hal Borg
Chuck Abbott	Thomas April	Norman W. Bartlett	Fred M. Biddlecomb	Daniel G. Bork
Gregg W. Abel	Gloycie Ard	Frank Barton	Eric Bigler	Edward E. Born
Jim Abers	James Arden	Jack Lee Barton	David R. Bihlman	Don Boshoven
Frederick R. Abner	Ron C. Armalost	Billy Bass	Emer W. Billings	Capt. James Bostic
Capt. William Adair	Charles H. Armendariz	Jerry Bass	Farrell Billings	David W. Boudreaux
Terry L. Adair	David Armocido	Shannon Bassham	Bob Bingle	Wallace C. Boulden
Ben Adams	Robert V. Armstrong	Dennis E. Bassinger	Robert H. Bingle	Brady C. Bounds, III
Daniel Ray Adams, II;	Gary Arnett	Peter Basta	Garry Biniecki	Joe Edgar Bounds
Danny & Todd Adams	Donald R. Arnold	Bruce Batchelder	Darrel Binkley	Edmund J. Bowen
Darryl W. Adams	Kay C. Arnold	Todd Bather	Harry J. Biondi, Jr.	Albert W. Bowers
Glen Cody Adams	Richard R. Arnold	Steve Batka	John M. Biondo	Capt. Robert Bowers
Grover C. Adams	Ross P. Arseneau	Frederick W. Bauer	Capt. Richard Bird	Charles Bowers
Jay Lauren Adams	Michael Arujo	Mike Baxter	Douglas S. Bird	James M. Bowes
Ricky Dan Adams	John J. Asanovich	Edward Bayghan	Sherman Birdsong	Mark C. Bowes
Stephen H. Adams	Gary S. Ash	Ronnie H. Bayles	Bert F. Birdwell	Robert H. Bowes
Todd N. Adams	David A. Ashcraft	Rick J. Baze	John W. Birdwell	Dennis Bowlby
Kenneth G. Addington	Sid Ashton	John B. Beach	E. R. Biship	Sterling L. Bowles, III
Tracy Addison	David H. Askew, Jr.;	Donnie A. Beale	Daniel H. Bishop	Darrell W. Bowman
Robert J. Adelman	Barry Aspenleiter	Charles B. Beamer	James Bishop	Julian T. Bowman, III
William Adelman	Tom J. Aston	Jerry D. Bean	Jimmy Bishop	Capt. Richard Bowser
Donald Adkerson	Frank Atkins	Robert Bean	Richard Bishop	Gary Boyd
Gerald C. Adkerson	James D. Atkins	William H. Bean	William H. Bishop	Jordas B. Boyd
Paul W. Adolph, Jr.	James O. Atkins	Eddie D. Beard	Capt. Tony Biski	Larry Boyd
Roger B. Adrian	Thomas W. Atkins	Jerry T. Beard	Herschel D. Black	Lee Boyer
Roger W. Adrian	Clarence G. Atwood, Jr.;	W. C. Beard	Jerry Black	Yancy D. Brackin
William J. Agisotelis	Capt. Chris J. Aubut	Robert Bearding	Danny R. Blackburn	David M. Bradburn
Maria Luis Aguilar	Ted J. Auer	John S. Beardmore	Harry L. Blackburn	Marvin H. Braden
John J. Aho	Gregory K. Ault	Ralph Beatty	Carl A. Blackledge	Capt. Bramblett Bradham
Ernie Ahr	Louis Austin	James E. Beauchamp	Gary L. Blackmore	Erval M. Bradley
Marion T. Akers	Stephen S. Austin	Danny Beck	Capt. Claudette & Bart Blaha, Jr.	Loren E. Bradley
Mathew D. Alaniz	Vincent E. Austin, Jr.	James B. Bedlion	William C. Blake	Steven D. Bradley
Sonny Alawin	Clarence Auston	Bonefish Bednar	James M. Blakesley	Ted Bradley
Bart Albright	Ron Babbini	Capt. Michael Bednar	Stephen Blakley	Jeffrey S. Bradshaw
Corbet A. Albright	Victor Babbitt	Dan Beeler	Paul A. Blalock	Victor K. Bradshaw
Terry Alcorn	David J. Baca	Edward M. Beeson, Jr.;	Michael D. Blanchard	Willis Bradshaw
John Alelus, Jr.;	David S. Badalamente	Ronnie W. Behnke	Truman Bland	Jim Bradwell
Pete Alex, Jr.	Mitchell W. Bademan	Kurt Belcher	Billy G. Blankenship	Dayne A. Brady
Larry Alexander	Larry Badgett	Louis E. Belcher	Byron W. Blansett	Benny Bragg
Norman J. Alexander	David Anthony Badwak	Nick Belkofer	Frank Blawton	William T. Bralley
Justin D. Alford	Gary H. Baggett	Andy R. Bell	Michael R. Bledsoe	Harry E. Bramel, III
Charles R. Allard	Lonnie D. Bagwell	John Bell	William B. Blevins	Eugene D. Branch
Charles Allen	Dana Allan Bailey	Justin J. Bell	Capt. Jerry Bley	Kelly John Brandt
Gregory W. Allen	Robert H. Bailey	Raymond Bell	Steven Block	R.J. Branham
Ken Allen	Roy F. Bain	Ross Bell	Capt. Jimmy Bloom	Russel J. Branham
Mark Allen	William M. Bain	Michael Bellenir	Dennis Blue	Will R. Branscum
Randy R. Allen	Charles A. Bair	Gary Belletini	Capt. Dennis Bluhm	Scott Branyan
Robert W. Allen	Barbara A. Baird	Kenneth T. Beloskur	Thomas R. Bly	Tommy W. Bray
Thomas D. Allen	Carl G. Baker	Roger Belter	Blue Fin Charter Boat	Russell O. Breckenridge
Wayne E. Allen	John Baker, Sr.;	Elvin C. Beltz	Gregory H. Bock	Bruce C. Breisch
Richard Allenbrand	Paul F. Baker	Ralph O. Benefield	Herbert W. Bode	Tim Brendel
Wendell S. Allman	Phil Baker	Don Benick	William O. Bodeker	John M. Brennan
Kenneth T. Alt	Robert H. Baker	Michael A. Benjamin, Sr.	Capt. James Boehlke	A. Bresnahan, Jr.
Jim H. Alter	Thomas G. Baker	Jim Bennett	John A. Boender, III	Capt. Edward Brewer
John Alvarez	Edward (Skip) Baldwin, Jr.	Larry Bennett	Warren E. Boerum	Kenneth J. Brewer
Juan Alvarez	Geoffrey L. Baldwin	Richard T. Bennett	Angus Boezeman	Richard K. Brewer
George A. Amadei	Barry L. Bales	William K. Bennett	Gerald G. Bogan	Michael L. Bridges
Gary G. Amboyer	Ed Balfour	Capt. Rich Bensen	Capt. Clyde Boger	Rex M. Bridges
Roy Amburn, Jr.	Kirk Balke	Capt. Larry Benson	Tom S. Boggess III	Walter L. Bridges
Gary S. & Scott A. Amerman	Capt. Terry Ballard	Charles W. Benson	Michael E. Bogue	John S. Briggs
Neil Amundson	Samuel A. Balsano	Craig Bentley	Eric M. Bogy	W. C. Briley
Philip Anastasia	Mark Banister	Donald A. Bentley, Jr.	Greg R. Bohn	James C. Brincefield, III
Randy Andersen	Capt. Robert Banjoff	Paul T. Benton, III	William L. Bohunnon	Martin Bringhard
Don Anderson	Roy Bryan Bankston	Lou Bentsen	Bill Boice	Earl R. Brink
Bob Anderson	Bill J. Bannister	John Berezoski, Jr.	Alan E. Boland	William G. Briscoe
Eric A. Anderson	Eddie B. Bansemer	Steven Berg	Capt. Ross Boland	Jimmy Ray Britt
Ernest F. Anderson	Mike Barats	Capt. Dennis Bergeman	Frank C. Bolbecker	Randy Broadworth
Gregory John Anderson	Donald Barber	Christie D. Berger	Capt. Jack Bolduan	Rodney E. Brock
J. Scott Anderson	George Barber	Raymond E. Bergman	Capt. Carl Boley, Jr.	Dale A. Brockway
Joseph M. Anderson	Marvin E. Barber	Victor Bergstrom	Paul Lynn Boli	Ed Broderick
M.D. Anderson	John E. Barbree	William F. Bernhardt III	Dennis C. Bolton	Roger Lee Bronkhorst
Ray Anderson, Jr.	Capt. James Barcus	Howard L. Bernth	Capt. Andrew Bomba	Robert Brooks
Rodney F. Anderson	James E. Barker	Capt. David·Berry	John V. Bonander	Randy Brott
Tom Anderson	Robert Law Barker	Dan A. Berry	Jeffrey R. Bond	Capt. Larry Brown
William P. Anderson, Jr.	Travis D. Barker	Jim Berry	Steve Bond	Chanda Brown
James D. Anderton	Jack W. Barkley	John R. Berry	William L. Bone, Jr.	Charles E. Brown
Kenneth W. Anderson	Dan Barnes	Nelson B. Berry	Tex R. Bonin	Charlie F. Brown
Jeffery Andreen	John R. Barnes	Gerald R. Bertagna	Bucky Bonner	Dale W. Brown
Aubrey M. Andreson	Larry Barnes	Leroy Bertolero	Capt. James Bonner	Dale W. Brown
Albert L. Andrews	Sonny Barnes	Steve L. Bertrand	James D. Bonner	David C. Brown
Leonard Andrews	Wesley G. Barnes	James M. Berwick	Jason A. Bonner	Ed Brown
R. L. Andrews	Allen & Leslie Barnett	Joseph E. Besche	Weldon R. Bonner	Jeffrey C. Brown
Robert Andrews	Dan Barnett	Howard H. Bethune	Robert H. Bonslett	Joe Brown
Wyatt A. Andrews	Gerald Barnett	Gerald B. Bettendorf	Robert E. Booher	Mark J. Brown
Wallace D. Andrzejewski	Mike Barnett	Chuck Bettinson	Gordon W. Boomer	Mike C. Brown
Everglades Angler	Lyman T. Barney	Dennis Betz	Lance Booth	Randall E. Brown
Tropical Angler	John P. Barnhill	Capt. Richard Beverly	Capt. James Borcherding	Robert B. Brown
Brian C. Annan	Eddie Barr	James R. Beyers	Bradley H. Boreaux	Robert S. Brown
James Apata	Gilberto O. Barrera	Michael Bias	E. P. Borel	Stevenson E. Brown
Jim H. Apel	Blair Barrows	Harold Wad Bibbee, II;	Scott Boren	Terry M. Brown
Capt. Tim Apolito	Capt. Mike Bartlett	David Bickerstaff	Bill Boresek	Thomas A. Brown

Milton F. Browning
Frankie Broz
Capt. William Brubaker
Neal T. Brube
Mike W. Brumley
Timothy Bruning
Capt. Robert Bruns
Harvey F. Van Brunt
John E. Brust
Joseph A. Bryan
Ted Bryant
Joseph F. Bryer
Marsel Bryson
Jason Buchanan
Jeffrey Buchanan
Charles R. Buchen
Glen E. Bucher
Dennis A. Buck
Steve Buckingham
Milburn A. Buckler, III
Patrick T. Buckley
Rocky Buckner
Charles R. Bujan
Gary Wayne Bullion
Barry E. Bullock
Will Bullock
R. A. Bumbaugh
Charles F. Bump
Donald W. Bunch
Capt. James Bunn
John H. Bunting, Jr.
John Buoscio
Jack A. Burbridge
Craig W. Burch
Gary T. Burch
Clyde W. Burchard
John E. Burchell
James O. Burden
James R. Burdett
Capt. Ronald Burdette, Sr.
George L. Burdick
Stanley Burgay
Ronald Burget
Robert A. Burk
Kenneth R. Burkey
Rachael Burks
Edwin S. Burlarley
Kevin W. Burleson
John T. Burllile
Daniel E. Burns
Carl Burris
John True Burson
Steven D. Burt
Charles R. Burton
Jimmie D. Burton
Pat Burton
Brenda L. Burtrand
Bill Burwell
Dana Burwell
Jim Busch
Louis Butera
James M. Butler
Jeffrey T. Butler
Robert L. Butler
David A. Butterfield
Frederick J. Buttrum
Virgil F. Buttrum
Larry R. Butts
Cecil Ray Byars
Jerry D. Bynum
David Byrd, Jr.
Doug Byrd
James M. Byrd
Robert F. Byrd
Ronald G. Byrd
Capt. William Caban
Michael G. Cade
N. L. Cade
George E. Cadle
John D. Cagle
Capt. Mark Cahlik
Doyal W. Cain
Jess Cain
Bill Cairns
Chris L. Caldwell
Larry C. Caldwell
Kent Calhoun
Capt. Thomas Call
Robert W. Callahan
Sean Callahan
Kevin W. Callam
Alexander Callander
Robert D. Calli
John Calvin
Gilbert Camargo
Dewey J. Cameron
Joe N. Camp
Lake Seminole Fish Camp
Norfleet Fish Camp
Oak Haven Fish Camp
Bruce Campbell
Chris C. Campbell
Edward B. Campbell
Fred P. Campbell
Gene Campel
George Campbell
Johnny M. Campbell
Terry Lee Campbell
William L. Campbell
Sidney S. Campen, Jr.
Louis M. Canalito
Calvin E. Canamore
William L. Cannan, Jr.;
Capt. Thomas Cannon
Ronald G. Canon
Dennis R. Canoda
Harry C. Cantreall, Jr.;
John Cantrell
Matt Cantwell
Ralph Walter Capasso
David E. Capps
Lynn Capps

Capt. Jim Capucini
Capt. Louis Capucin
Dominico Carchidi
Bill Carey
Jerry H. Cariker
Steven E. Carle
Ed Carlee
James Carleton
Robert A. Carlisle
Daniel Carlson
Jennifer B. Carlson
Monty Ray Carlton
William P. Carnazzo
Carl Kent Carnes
Brett H. Caron
Richard H. Carpenter
David B. Carr
Carl M. Carrillo
Ben Carroll
Floyd J. Carroll, Jr.;
John Carroll
Randy Carroll
Christopher M. Carson
Garold Carson
Daniel J. Carter
Hellen J. Carter
Jason Carter
John P. Carter
John E. Carter, Jr.
John R. Carter
William R. Carter
Pedro Cartwright
Francis W. Carver, Jr.
Greg Cash
William E. Cashin, III;
David Castellanos
Mark A. Castillo
Olin E. Castleberry
Dominick Castoro
Joseph A. Catalano, Jr
Paul J. Catanese
Capt. Terry Cater
Connie Cates
Philip H. Cathell
Arlie D. Caudill
Kurt A. Caudill
Ben Causey
George Cavazos
Edward G. Cave
Ron Cervenka
Steven D. Chafin
James W. Chaires
Gary Chamberlain
John I. Chamberlain
Arthur W. Chamberlin
Tim A. Chambers
Terry C. Chandler
Richard H. Chaney, Jr.
Rick L. Chaney
Ronald W. Chaney
Bruce Chankler
Jack Chantler
Ed S. Chapko
Charles R. Chapman
Roy E. Chapman
John R. Chargulaf
John P. Charles
Bruce Charleston
Flyliner Charters
Bendback Charters, Inc.
Hamilton Fishing Charters, Inc.
Ralph R. Chatelain
Bobby D. Cheatham
Bobby J. Cheek
Eldred W. Cherrix
Allen Ross Chesney
James R. Chestnut
Capt. J.M. (Red) Childers
John M. Childers
Mark A. Childress
Daniel Chimelak
George C. Chimelak
Joseph Chimienti
John F. Chippi
Clifford L. Chism
James G. Chism
Keith Chism
Arthur R. Chmielewski
Mark Chmura
Kent W. Choate
Raymond Choate
Henry J. Chojnacki
Glenn L. Chonoski
Lori Chouinard
Allen M. Christenson, Jr.;
Ron Christenson
Capt. Fred Christian
Mark R. Christian
Thomas N. Christiana
Keith Christianson
E. Wayson Christopher
Capt. Patrick Chrysler
Dale R. Church
Anthony D. Cianciarulo, Jr.
Sam Ciaramitaro
David Cibulka
Raymond Cichocki
Neal G. Cissel
Douglas W. Clapson
Dennis L. Clark
Duanne Clark
Eugene C. Clark
Frank E. Clark
Gary L. Clark
George J. Clark
George Clark
Gerald R. Clark
James D. Clark
Jim Clark
Kevin D. Clark
Robert L. Clark

Rodney P. Clark
Roger R. Clark
Roy E. Clark
Russ A. Clark
Russ A. Clark
Tony D. Clark
Walter J. Clark
Charles F. Clarke
Capt. Lynn D. Clarridge
Bob Claunch
Donald C. Clauser
Robert A. Claypole
Jonathan C. Clayton
William J. Clayton
Howard E. Cleaver
Allen Dale Clement, III;
Capt. Chris Clemons
Capt. Barry Clemson
James L. Van Cleve
Brian Cleveland
Capt. David Clevenger
James W. Cliburn
Dorance K. Clifton
Lloyd M. Cline
Tim H. Cloe
Gary Ray Clouse
Deep Water Cay Club
Allen Clyde
Mike Cnudde
Douglas R. Coar
Lesley D. Cobb
William A. Cobb
Capt. Henry Cocain
Steve Cockerel
Benjamin A. Cockrell
C. A. Coder
Laurence D. Coder
Norman W. Coffman
Gregory Coffren
Dale Lynn Cogburn
Michael D. Cogburn
Carmine C. Coiro
Charles J. Coiro
B. J. Coker
Joe Coker
Paul H. Coker
Darr A. Colburn
Richard E. ColburnCasj ColbyBobby
Lee Cole
Douglas Cole
Steven N. Cole
Edwin D. Coleman
Richard L. Coleman
Capts. Sharon & Robert Collins
Donald E. Collins
Ernest G. Collins
Mel S. Collins
William Collins
William E. Collins
Don Collis
Rick Collis
John H. Collison, Jr.
Joe A. Collum
Wade F. Collum
Norman E. Colson, Jr.
Ron G. Colvin
Paul W. Combs
Walter Compton
Edward T. Concilla
Jeff L. Condery
William C. Conlee
Henry H. Conley
John E. Connelly
Claude L. Conner
James R. Conner, Jr.
Michael R. Connolly
Dan B. Conoly, Jr.;
Stephen J. Conover
John Conway
Gary W. Cook
Harvey C. Cook
J. Paul Cook
Penalope D. Cook
Rodney S. Cook
Russell H. Cook
William R. Cooksey
Marvin D. Coombe
Harold Walter Coombs
David Coon
Cecil R. Cooper
Donald A. Cooper
Gary N. Cooper
Joe Cooper
Larry E. Cooper
Michael W. Cooper
William H. Cooper
Craig Coover
Jim Cope
Robert L. Copeland
Joseph P. Copland
Darius A. Copley
Douglas R. Copperno11
William M. Copsey
Larry E. Corbett
George T. Cord, Jr.
Gary Corson
Lex Costas
Luis G. Costas
Raymond F. Cotnoir
Paul Coughlin
Back Country, Inc.
Tommy W. Countz
Francis D. Courtney, II
Eddie Covington
Randy Coward
Ronnie E. Coward
Calvin R. Cowart
Earl L. Cox, Jr.;
Frank M. Cox
Frankie J. Cox
Huey Cox
James R. Cox, Sr.

L.R. Cox
Lonnie L. Cox
Lonnie B. Cox
Nathan W. Cox
Nathan W. Cox
Raymond D. Cox
Rodger D. Cox
Danny Crabbe
Warren Crabtree
Edward M. Craft
Charles G. Crafts
Bob Cramer
Capt. Robert Cramer
Bernard W. Crandall
Bandit Crane
Donald D. Cranor
Tom Cravens
Alan R. Crawford
Alfred E. Crawford
Darwin Crawford
Norman G. Crawford, Jr.
Richard Crawford
W.A. Crawford
Bob Creel
Charlotte Cregger
Frank Cresswell
Gary & Scott Cresswell
R.G. Creswell
Anthony C. Crilley
Michael R. Crisenberry
Jeffrey E. Crites
David L. Crockett
Jeff Crockett
George R. Crosby
Toby A. Crosby
Capt. Larry Croskey
Amos C. Cross
Capt. James Crosthwaite
James Crosthwaite
Frederick T. Crouch
Alfred L. Crounse
Jim Crouse
Richard E. Crow
Don Crowe
James Crownover
Lance E. Crowther
Dan Cruchon
Robert B. Crumpler
Elmer Crumpton
Wayne D. Crumpton
Bob Crupi
Mark E. Crutcher
Roy M. Cryer
Bobby F. Cudworth
Patricia Culleeny
James H. Cullison, Jr.
Sullie Culpepper
R. Andrew Cummings
J. A. Cunningham, III;
Jenise Cunningham
Chris D. Curley
Rex A. Curley
William R. Currie
James E. Curry
Danny L. Curtis
Jimmy D. Curtis
Theodore Morrison Curtis, Jr.
Timothy C. Curtis
Ronald Cushman
Ralph Cutter
Steven Cyr
John D. D'Angelo
Daniel C. Daffin
Stephen K. Daffron
John C. Dahl, III
Clifford Dahlquist
Paul H. Daisey
Gary C. Dale
Jerome A. Daley
John Dall
John R. Dall
Charles P. Dalton
Darol Damm
Frank Danford
James W. Danford
Dwight H. Daniel
Rodney J. Danielson
Randall P. Darington
Leo P. Darr, Jr.
Tom W. Darr
Ed Darrach
Edwin M. Darwin
Lionel W. Daugherty
Cheryl Davenport
Edward L. Davenport
Haywood B. Davenport
Tony Davenport
Bill A. Davidson
Perry R. Davidson
Shane L. Davies
Alvin R. Davis
Bob Davis
Brad Davis
Charles S. Davis
Edison R. Davis
Gary R. Davis
Gerald D. Davis
Inky Davis
James Roy Davis
Jasper G. Davis, Jr.;
Michael B. Davis
Michael P. Davis
Sherman L. Davis
Vernon L. Davis
William L. Davis
Capt. Joseph Dawson
Charles W. Day
Michael L. Day
Gregory A. Deaderick
Gilbert C. Dean
Louie P. Deane
John E. Dear

John D. Dearmore
Danny E. Deatherage
Irvin & Richard B. Deatley
Leroy H. Deboer
Glenn A. Debrosky
Dennis L. Debuysser
David L. Deen
John S. Deering
Robert Deeter
Phil Defenbaugh
William R. Dega
Capt. John DeGirolamo
David J. DeGrow
Harold D. Dehart
Harold J. Deibler
Richard J. Dein
George L. Dejavier
James R. DeKam
Fred R. Dell
Mark Delnero
Elliot P. Dematteis
David Demoss
Brian Dempsey
Gerald Denison
Gene Dennis
William Dennis
Jack Denson
Billy Roy Denton
Joseph W. Denton
Robert A. Denyer
James D. Deordio
Randy Depee
John DePonte, III
Wayne A. Derby
Paul O. Descoteaux
Alan D. Devine
Henry E. Devito, Jr.
Richard A. Devivi
Hope P. Devlin
V.E. DeWitt
Matthew J. Deyo
Donald R. DeYoung
Paul A. Dhane
John D. Diaz
Ray Dickerson
Rutherford Dickinson
Steve R. Dickson
Dave Diffely
Stanley Dignum
Darren Dilday
David C. Dillman
Robert J. Dillman
Jerry W. Dilts
Jim Dinsmore
Gary Distefano
Frank A. Ditmars
Foster M. Divis
Capt. Paul Dixon
Dan R. Dixon
John W. Dixon, Jr.
John W. Dixon, III
Lawrence D. Dixon
Robert L. Dixon
Stephen A. Dixon
William M. Doak
John Dobis
Dennis A. Dobson
Russell L. Dobson
Gary W. Dodd
Ira Dodson
John P. Doetzer
Dave & Kent Dohnel
Stefan Dollins
Charles E. Donaldson
Frank Donaldson
Terry E. Donaldson
Walter L. Donaldson, Jr.
Walter L. Donaldson, III
Andrew R. Donato
Charles Donham
Jim Donich
James P. Donovan
Robert E. Dooley
Richard Doran
Thomas E. Doran
Randy V. Dorman
Jerry D. Dorsey
M.R. Dorsey
Vincent A. Dortenzo
Thomas H. Dosier
James R. Douglas, Jr.;
Mitchell G. Douglas
Tommy Dowdy
Charles B. Downey
Roger Doyle
Parker L. Dozmier
Jeremy Drakeford
William L. Draper
Timothy W. Drewry
Lloyd Dreyer
Willard L. Driesel
Donald Drose
Carey Drumheller
James O. Drummond
Kenneth R. Drummond
Meredith A. Drummond
William T. Drummond
Donna & Gregory L.Drury
Thomas R. Drury
Capt. Gary Drwal
James R. Dryden
Robert Lyn Dryden
Frank C. Duarte
Harold Dubay
Donald Dubois
Ron Dubsky
William Duckwall
Richard A. Duckworth
J. Wayne Dudley
Jerry D. Dudley
Andy Due
Jackie D. Due

James P. Due
Leon W. Due
Tommy G. Due
Danny Duff
Jimothy J. Duff
John A. Duffy
Edgar B. Duggan
Chuck Duke
Robert T. Dukehart
Douglas Dumas
Stephen E. Dumler
Jack R. Duncan
James R. Duncan
William F. Duncan, Jr.
James D. Dunlap
Billy G. Dunn
Chris J. Dunn
James A. Dunn
Jerry Dunn
Terry W. Dunn
Kit Dunnam
Brian Duplechain
James R. Dupnik, Jr.;
George V. Dupoy
Capt. Jim Dupre
G. R. Dupuis
George A. Durand
Jay Durkin
Glynn Durrett
William F. Dusterhoft
David B. Duvall
Capt. Ronald Duvve
Frank Duxstad
Victor Dwyer
David J. Dybowski
Steven E. Eager
Paul Eakins
Dale E. Ealy
David C. Eanes, III
Ervin R. Earl
Gary Early
John S. Earman
Dennis W. Eason
Paul C. Eason
Mickey Ray Eastman
Paul D. Eberly
Paul B. Ebert
Ronald Ebert
Paul Eccleston
James M. Eckelt
Randy P. Eckley
Capt. Norman Ecksmith
Danny Eddins
Terry L. Edelmann
Charles F. Eder
Travis S. Edgar
Steve R. Edgmon
Bradley K. Edwards
Cammeron Edwards
Henry G. Edwards, Jr.
Larry Edwards
Terry G. Edwards
William Egge
Edward R. Eichbrecht
Ron L. Eichelberger
Greg Eide
Gary L. Eikey
Gary Einkauf
Capt. Harry Eisman
Jan Eitelman
Robert E. Ekrut
Peter M. Eldridge
Ronnie Elkins
Dave H. Elling
Stephen C. Ellingson
Ralph Elliott
Ralph C. Elliott
Richard Elliott
Robert H. Elliott
Bobby L. Ellis
Capt. Edward Ellis
David J. Ellis
John Ellis
Charles W. Ellison
Nathan E. Ellison
Kenneth S. Elrod
Allen D. Elzinga
Douglas B. Embler
Michael J. Empey, Sr.
Byron P. Empson
Capt. Larry Endsley
Chistopher A. Engel
Robert J. Engel
Donald G. Englebrecht
E.S. English
Frank D. English
Jeffrey S. English
Robert C. Ennis
Maynard M. Enos
Milton E. Ensor, Jr.
Scandia Enterprises
James R. Epps
Capt. Mel Erb
David A. Erickson
Capt. David Ernsberger
Leon C. Erwin
Wendyl Erwin
Isael Espinosa
Corwin E. Estes
John M. Estevez
Miles S. Etchart
DeWayne L. Eubanks
Capt. Charles Eulitt
Capt. Joe Evans
Robert D. Evans
Roy Lee Evans
William A. Evans
Eddie W. Eversmeyer
Edward J. Ewers
Mark Ewing
Mark D. Excine
Capt. Jon Fails

Jay Fair, Sr.;
Randal Fair
Michelle E. Fales
James M. Fambro
Joe A. Farkas
Gary Farley
Gerald W. Farmer
Ralph Farmer
Richard K. Farquhar
Gerald W. Farrar
Michael J. Farris
Bobby D. Feagin
Leroy M. Fegley
Carl B. Felger
Douglas E. Felker
Capt. Melvin Fenger
James L. Fenner
Barry D. Fenstermache
Marc Fenton
Theodore A. Fenwerda
Joan Ferguson
Kenneth D. Ferguson
Fermin Fernandez
Dwight D. Ferrell
Frank D. Ferry
Walter N. Fields
Raymond R. Fifarek
Fish Finder
John Y. Findleton
Edgar Findley
David Finn
Daniel F. Finucan
Brian J. Firestine
Capt. Floyd Fisher
Michael Fisher
Neal L. Fisher
Robert L. Fisher
Doug Swisher Fly Fishing
Edward J. Fitch
Walter W. Fithian
William Fitspatrick
Jerry Lynn Fitts
Arthur M. Fitzgerald
Daniel L. Fitzgerald
John P. Flaherty
James L. Flaig
Rick Flamson
R. L. Flanagan
Harry & Jennie Flechsig
Bettie Fleenor
Christopher J. Fleetwood
Clifford D. Fleming
Leon D. Fleming
Bill W. Fletcher
William P. Fletcher
Gary E. Flippin
Michael R. Flippin
Robert L. Flippin
Russell L. Flippin
Donald Flournoy
King S. Floyd, Jr.;
Rodney W. Fluharty
Bobby J. Fly
Robert E. Flynn
Charles L. Fobbs
Capt. James Fofrich, Sr.
Clayton A. Folden
Richard H. Folden
Robert G. Foley
Michael T. Folkestad
Larry E. Folkner
Ramon D. Foltz
Noson E. Fontenot
James W. Forbes
Michael J. Forchini
Darin K. Ford
James E. Ford
Monte R. Ford
Steven C. Fore
Charles A. Foreman
Roger D. Foreman
Richard K. Forge
John M. Forrest, III;
Louis K. Forrest, Jr.
Dave Forster
David Fortner
Thomas G. Fossen
Charles H. Foster, III
Dave Foster
Dave Foster
Dudley D. Foster
Gary T. Foster
James B. Foster
John F. Fouch
Bobby Fowler
Ed Fowler
Forrest J. Fowler
Gary R. Fox
James Fox
Paul K. Fox
Stephen M. Fox
Garry Frahm
James E. Fraize
J. Naudain Francis
Richard I. Francis
Ronald L. Frank
Tim Wade Frank
Jerry W. Franklin
Bob Franks
Mark J. Fransen
Odis Frazier
Ralph E. Frazier, Jr.;
Pauline "PS" Freberg
Capt. David Fredericks
Jeff & Pam Fredericksen
Dennis Fredrickson
Capt. Larry Freeland
Anthony T. Freeman
Charles W. Freeman
George R. Freeman
Dennis L. Freeze
Paul A. Freitas

Richard E. French, III;
Jim & Ben Friebele
Blaien S. Friermood
Capt. Pasqual Friscone
William C. Fritz
Leonard J. Fritzley
George A. Fromm
Charles Fulghum
Phillip K. Fulghum
Capt. George Fuller
David Fuller
Jeffrey Paul Fuller
Charles Fullerton
Dale Fulton
Greg Fulton
Capt. Mark Funderwhite
Michael Funke
Fredrick W. Funkey
Tony Furia
Bob Fuston
Roger Futch
Joseph C. Fyvie
Richard W. Gaines
Michael Joe Gale
Patrick Gallagher
Richard Galland
Gary Gamble
Steve Gappa
Pedro Garcia, Jr.;
Blake H. Gardner
Mike Gardner
Rick Gardner
Robert H. Gardner, Jr.;
Wayne C. Gardner
Bobby G. Garland
Mike Garner
Danny Garrett
Dwayne L. Garrett
Richard A. Garrett
Albert A. Garrison
John Garrison
Ronald J. Garrison
Cameron Garst
Carroll T. Gartrell
Russell Garufi
Andrew Garza
James A. Gasch
Billy Gaskins
Henry L. Gassaway
Gregory L. Gates
Wayne C. Gatling
Greg Gatz
Randy Gatz
Donald K. Gauger
Perri R. Gaustad
Darryl C. Gay
Leo A. Gayan
Danny Ray Gaydos
David W. Gee
Wallace R. Gee
William Gee
Joseph P. Geipe, Jr.
Gary L. Geis
Steven M. George
Thomas H. George
Richard P. Gerber
Charles M. Gerek
Alfred Gereng
Stanley W. Gerzsenyi
Capt. Joseph J. Gibbs
Charles L. Gibbs
Michael B. Gibbs
Howard E. Gibson
Jack W. Gibson, Jr.;
Shane H. Gibson
Charles P. Gilbert
James S. Gilbert
Myron W. Gilbert
Scott Gilbert
W. T. Gilbert
Wiliam L. Gilbert
Gaylen Gilbreath
Gary A. Gilchrist
Rob Gilford
Cooper Gilkes
Rick A. Gillespie
Dwight Gillette
William T. Gingell
David N. Ginn
Tony Giorgi
Phillip A. Gladden
Robert A. Glameyer
Eric M. Glass
John Glass
Hayden A. Glatte, III
Jeff Glavaris
John D. Gleason
Tommy Gleason
James W. Glenn
Daniel E. Glines
Rube C. Glover, Jr.;
Mike Gnatkowski
Lawrence G. Godwin
Willis H. Godwin
Liam I. Gogan
Bobby J. Goins
Dennis C. Goins
Kenneth W. Gold
Curtiss W. Golder
Donald Goldner
James D. Goldsmith
Robert H. Goldsteen
Ronny Goldwin
Roy L. Golightly
Herb Good
John W. Goodell, III;
James R. Goodpasture
Charles I. Goodwin
John B. Goodwin, Jr.
Roger Goodwin
Philip H. Gootee
Fred Gordon

Maurice B. Gordon
James W. Gore
Michael T. Gorgas
Dennis L. Gorsuch
Wayne Goss
James Gotcher
William A. Gottleid
Melvin R. Gough
Robert L. Gover
Robert E. Gowar
Brent Goyen
Dan Goyen, Jr.;
Richard M. Grabein
William D. Grace
Dan Gracia
Stan T. Graf
C. Fred Graff
Jerry G. Gragg
Darryl Graham
David R. Gramza
Dean Granger
Bruce E. Grant
Capt. Robert Grant
Wesley M. Grant
Greg Grantland
Robert J. Grantland
David R. Granza
Peter A. Grasso
Floyd Graves
Jonathon S. Graves
Ken Graves
Dennis J. Gray
Douglas V. Gray
Francis J. Gray, Jr.
Gary Gray
Gaylord Gray
James R. Gray
Mark Gray
Pete N. Gray
Preston D. Gray
Lynette Gray-Branch
Charles M. Green
Charles E. Green
David Green
Ivan Green
Joseph Green
Robert L. Green
Russell M. Green
Bill M. Greene
Herbert R. Greene, Jr.;
Eldred W. Greenwell
Albert (Skip) Greenwood
Conlaw E. Greenwood
Douglas C. Greenwood
Todd W. Gregorio
Morris G. Gregory
Robert Lee Gregory, Jr.;
Steven K. Gregory
Thomas Gregory
David P. Grein
Orville L. Gren
John E. Gresham
Marc Grieve
William M. Grieve
Danny Griffin
Frederick R. Griffin
Kenneth L. Griffith
Josef F. Grigar
Bernard L. Grimes
Harry S. Grimes
Richard H. Grimes
Edwin Grimsley
Dennis L. Grinold
Dennnis L. Grinold
Charles Grisham
Paul D. Grissom
James R. Griswold
John P. Groch
Robert Gronowski
Ralf R. Gross
Ardie R. Grubaugh
Merritt Grubb
Neal T Grube
Thomas A. Gruber
Fred A. Grueber
D. Russell Grumbles
Jay D. Gudermuth
Darren Guernsey
Capt. Richard Guest
J.D. Guffin
Ken Burnette Hunting & Fishing Guide
Machala T-N-T Guide
Richard G. Guidry
Larry A. Guile
Capt. Dale Guiley
Bobby Fox Guinn
Bronko B. Gukanovich, Sr.
Joseph L. Gukanovich
Jeffrey M. Gunn
Roy Tate Gunn
Terry C. Gunn
Gary E. Gunsolley
Lloyd Gunsolus
Stephen Gunther
Wansley C. Gustafson
John G. Guy, Jr.
Capt. David Gwin
Marvin H. Gwin
Jason J. Haas
Duane E. Hada
Capt. Norman Haddaway
Michael L. Haddaway
Thomas L. Hadley
Larry H. Haeger
Charles G. Haegerich, Jr.
Donald K. Hagen
Randall Hagerman
Bryan W. Hague
R. W. Hague
L. A. Hagy
Edward G. Hahn

James E. Hahn
Capt. Don Haid
B. L. Haines
Brian Hair
C. B. Haire, Jr.;
Rusty Haire
Buddy Haislip
Ben Hald
Van D. Hale
Clinton J. Hall
Doyle Hall
Gregory A. Hall
James Hall
John T. Hall
Michael J. Hall
Randle D. Hall
Ronald D. Hall
Roy J. Hall
Thoms E. Hall
Tim R. Hall
Tom Hall
William F. Hall
Thomas L. Hallum
Robert N. Halmi
Joe Haltom
Bruce D. Hamby
Richard D. Hamel
Bobby Hamilton
Homer W. Hamilton
Robert Hamilton
Robert A. Hamilton
Steve Hamilton
Jack Hamlin
Richard Hamlin
Jon C. Hamm
Capt. Robert Hammer
Gary Hammes
Alfred O. Hammett
Calvin Z. Hammett
Grape Hammock
Capt. Herbert Hammond
Sammie R. Hammontree, Jr.;
Alton Hancock
Don Hand
Capt. Don Hand
Bradley L. Haney
David Haney
James E. Haney, Sr.
Jim J. Haniotis
Donald Ray Hanselman, Jr.
Peter Hansen
Eric Hanson
John S. Hanson
Steven A. Hanson
Adam F. Hardcastle
Thomas E. Hardegree, III;
Terry S. Hardesty
Glen Hardin
John Hardin
Manuel R. Hardwick
James D. Hardy
Albert Harless
Charles S. Harman
E. V. Harmon, IV;
Tommy Harmon
Capt. Ronald Harper
Harry Harper
Robert E. Harper
Alvah Harriman
Bob Harrington
John S. Harrington
Britton L. Harris
Capt. George Harris
James D. Harris
James Harris
Leveta Joy Harris
Michael W. Harris
Mike Harris
Norman E. Harris
Stanley B. Harris
Alan S. Harrison
Charles Harrison
Gary D. Harrison
Herman R. Harrison
Jack L. Harrison
William Harrison, Jr.
William Sanford Harrison
John Harsin
Claude A. Hart
Gary W. Hart
Ronald W. Hart
Vernon L. Hart
W. D. Hart
W. Preston Hartge
Ronnie D. Hartsfield
Wood W. Hartwell, II;
Bobby L. Harvey
Richard E. Haslett
Kenneth B. Hastings
Michael L. Hastings
Roy Hathcock
Willy Haurtmann
Robert E. Hauser
Christopher M. Haussmann
William L. Havard
Michael A. Haveland
Bailey Ray Hawley
Allen M. Haws
Billy A. Hawthorne
Jeffrey Hawthorne
Neal Hayden, Jr.;
George Hays
Michael L. Hays
James L. Hazlitt
William T. Heacock, Jr.
Jackie E. Headrick, Jr.;
Daniel A. Hecker
Gary C. Heckler
Capt. Charles Heckman
Jack A. Hedgcoxe
Walter Hedges
Wesley M. Hee

Dean Allen Heffner
Jack Hegdahl
Jeffrey K. Heimann
Capt. Mike Heinberger, Sr.
Wilmer Heishman, Jr.
W. D. Heldenfels, Jr.;
David L. Helder
Anthony J. Helfrich
James D. Helfrich
Arthur G. Helgesen
Capt. Ronald Helm
W. R. Helm
Capt. Roosevelt Helms
Carolyn S. & Donley G. Helms
Hebert L. Helms
Rick E. Helmus
Homer E. Helmuth
Clifford L. Hembree
Larry Hemphill
Capt. Frank Henderson
Greg A. Henderson
James E. Henderson
Jeffrey B. Henderson
John Henderson
Steven D. Henderson
Robert T. Hendricks
Frank M. Hendrickson
Mike S. Hendry
Aaron T. Henker
Charles W. Hennage
Capt. Donald Henry
Dwight Henry
Howard Henry
Hugh H. Henry
Mark J. Henry
Stevie D. Henry
John Hensel
Calvin Hensley
Capt. Philip Hepkema
Barry Herbster
Capt. John Herl
Capt. James Herl
Donald L. Hermance
Mark Hermon
Arthur L. Herndon
Capt. Bill Herold
Bill Herring
Raith Heryford
George Herzog
Mark Heskett
Greg Hess
Mike Hester
Robert W. Hester
Capt. Thomas Hetzel
Bill F. Heuel
Jeffrey M. Heuman
Joe E. Heuseveudt
James A. Hewitt
Rex Hewitt
Thewalt J. Hibbard
Jamie Hickman
Scott Alan Hickman
Robert E. Hickox
Daniel C. Hicks
Danny Hicks
Kevin Hicks
Steven Hicks
Tim Kostur & Tim Hiett
David Higginbotham
Glenn C. Higgins
Kevin Higgins
Scott Higgins
Gene Highfill
Robert Hightower
Edward G. Hilario
Doug Hill
James Hill
Louie F. Hill, Jr.;
Perry D. Hill
Phillip R. Hill
Harry L. Hilton, III
Frank E. Hinds
Bill and Kim Hines
Greg H. Hines
Kenneth Hines
Robert Hinesley
James G. Hinkle
Rene Hinojosa
Darrell Hipp
Marcellus L. Hippert, III
Capt. Willard Hipsher, Jr.
Capt. James Hirschy
Donald H. Hislop
Capt. Michael Hluszti
Paul J. Hobel
Leon Hobgood
Gerald Way Hobson
John E. Hobson
Roy C. Hobson
Jon E. Hockema
David W. Hodder
Wallace Hodges
Charles B. Hodgson
John W. Hoffman
Larry T. Hoffman
Michael R. Hoffman
William R. Hoffman
Oliver D. Hoffmann
James J. Hogan
Rick A. Hoistad
James C. Hoke
Capt. Daniel Holan
Douglas L. Holcer
Michael Holcer
Raymond P. Holcomb
Brian R. Holden
Robert A. Holden, Sr.
Wayne K. Holeton
Herman Henry Holl
Edgar G. Holland, III;
Gary L. Holland
Travis A. Holland

William M. Holland
Steven W. Hollensed
Gerald Holliday
Paris L. Hollins
Bernard C. Hollis
Clay Hollistar
Capt. Joseph Holly
Capt. Carol Holly
Wayne Holmes
Thomas L. Holmquist
Capt. Jon Holsenbeck
Gordon L. Holt
Jack D. Holt
Kenneth G. Holt
William L. Holt
Harold Honeycutt
John E. Honeycutt
Ted C. Hood, Jr.
Bill Hooker
Larry Hooks
Peter Hooks
Weldon C. Hooper
Wilburn H. Hooten
Donely R. Hoover
Lloyd G. Hoover
Jack J. Hopaluk
John P. Hope
Dolf A. Hopf
Gordon S. Hopkins
Ted A. Horechka
Capt. Steve Horn
George K. Horn
Ray Horn
Capt. Forrest Hornbeck, Sr.
Marvin M. Horner, Jr.;
Robert L. Horsmon
Reece D. Horton
Ronald L. Horton
Ronald Horton
Jon Van Hoskins
James W. Houchin
Capt. Byron Hough
Charles B. Hough
Cecil D. Howard
Frederic H. Howard
Jon K. Howard
Rick Howard
Bill D. Howe
James R. Howe
Jonathan K. Howe
Kathleen L. Howe
David R. Howell
John Roy Howell, Jr.;
Charles T. Howes, Jr.
Charles R. Hoyt
Capt. Michael Hritz
Lyle E. Hubbard
Tommy Lee Hubbard
Don Hubert
Capt. Scott Hubert
John M. Huck
Jason Hudgens
Steve Hudgens
Elton B. Hudson, Jr.;
Roger Huelsberg
Niles Huey
Bruce P. Huff
James Lynn Huffman
Terry Huffman
Bruce S. Hughes
Bryan W. Hughes
Capt. Ed Hughes
Maple C. Hughes, Jr.;
Robert Hulen
George Hull
Otis Humphrey
Dennis W. Hunerberg
Kenten H. Hunnell
Pat Hunt
Thomas A. Hunt
David J. Huntress
Robert D. Hurley
Donald W. Huskin
George Husted
Capt. Jack Huston
David Roy Huston
John C. Hutchins
Bart Huthwaite
John E. Hutter
Paul S. Hyland
Peter Ide
John D. Ihnat
Jeff Iid
John P. Ingram
Phyllis Ingram
William L. Ingram
Danny P. Inskeep
Helen's International
Ben Iradi
Thomas H. Ireland
Henderson's on Lake Istokpoga
Richard Iverson
Richard H. Ives
Hugh Ivey
James A. Jachim
James D. Jackman
Bryon Jackson
George C. Jackson
James K. Jackson
Maurice L. Jackson
Paul Jacobs
Thomas M. Jacobs
John Jacobson
John David Jacoby
William D. Jacoby
Charles Jacquette
Patrick F. Jaeger
James D. Jahn
Joseph F. James
Randy Jameson
Richard B. Jankowski
George W. Janssen

Gordon D. Janssen
James O. Jarboe
Marty Jay
Peter A. Jay
Richard C. Jay
Jackie L. Jefferson
Lawrence D. Jefferson
Capt. Clyde Jeffries
Kevin G. Jeffryes
Robert J. Jenereski
Capt. James Jenkins
Edward D. Jenkins
Robert R. Jenkins
William Jenkins, Jr.
William P. Jenkins
Lloyd D. Jennings
Capt. Gary Jennrich
James B. Jensen
John R. Jensen
Joe Jesmer
Mike Jespersen
William W. Jespersen
Charles Jeter
Thomas L. Jeter
William R. Jett, Jr.;
Gregory B. Jetton
Kenneth R. Jewett
Mark O. Jimenez
Harry Jioras
Tim Johansen
Brent Johnson
Brett R. Johnson
David L. Johnson
David Joseph Johnson
Eddie Dean Johnson
Edward E. Johnson
Floyd Lee Johnson
Francis Johnson
J. C. Johnson
J R Johnson
James D. Johnson
Jimmy L. Johnson
John Johnson
Kerry S. Johnson
Larry Johnson
Larry Johnson
Marijo Johnson
Pat Johnson
Randall H. Johnson
Royce R. Johnson
Russell W. Johnson
Sandy K. Johnson
Terry Johnson
Thomas L. Johnson
W.R. Johnson
Stephen W. Johnston
Theda A. Johnston
H. R. Joiner
Thomas R. Jolin
Malcolm Carter Jolley, Jr.
Robert B. Jolliff
Alan E. Jones
Alfred R. Jones
Billy D. Jones
Capt. Arthur Jones
Capt. Earl Jones, Jr.
Capt. Edward Jones
Carl H. Jones
Charles E. Jones
George L. Jones
Gerald D. Jones
Harvey Jones
Jack Jones
James L. Jones
Jewel R. Jones, Jr.;
Kenneth W. Jones
Len T. Jones
Leonard R. Jones
Loren D. Jones
Montie P. Jones
Phillip N. Jones
Richard S. Jones
Robert S. Jones
Roger Jones
Russell C. Jones
Steven R. Jones
Travis W. Jones
James A. Jordan
Larry G. Jordan
Steve Jordan
Richard Jorgensen
Roy L. Jorgensen, II;
John K. Josenhans
Adrian L. Joy
Jimmy Joy
Perry E. Joy
Capt. Ralph Joyce
Michael R. Joyce
Joseph Juckel
Howard L. Judd
Ralph R. Judd
Alexander M. Judice, Jr.;
John E. Judy
Floyd Juern
Capt. George Jumper, Jr.
Stephen R. Jusseaume
Charles O. Justice
Stephen N. Justice
K, S, Brown, Jr.
Mark Kaesemeyer
William Kaht
Robert D. Kalbitz
John Kalbmach
William R. Kampfert
Pal B. Kamprath
John M. Kane
Michael Kane
Jimmy Lee Kanetzky
Mike L. Kanppel
Les Karaffa
Cameron W. Karber
Raymond J. Karboske

Walter R. Karboske
Daniel F. Kardash
Rick W. Karpuik
Jim J. Karr
Chuck Kashner
Joe B. Kasper
Harris Katchen
Clayton O. Katski
Marion N. Kaufman
Nick Kautt
Charles V. Kayser
Kenneth Keating
Robert M. Keehne
John M. Keehnel
Jerry Keeler
Roger Keeling
Harry M. Keene
John E. Keiser
Richard H. Keitt
Capt. John Keki
Capt. Pat Keliher
Donald J. Keller
Edwin F. Keller, Jr.;
Ashley A. Kelley
Chad E. Kelley
Pat Kelley
Walter J. Kellmer, Jr.
William M. Kells
Capt. Wallace Kelly
Michael D. Kelly
Michael E. Kelly
Wallace E. Kelly, Jr.;
Danny B. Kelsay
Russell F. Kenaston
Harry D. Kendall
Kevin L. Kendall
Capt. Larry Kennedy
Eamo B. Kennedy
Richard T. Kennedy
Roy Lee Kennimer, Jr.;
Don M. Kennon
Fred A. Kenny
Paul Kenny
John M. Kernan
John E. Kerr
Keith F. Kerrigan
Rickey D. Kersey
George L. Kesel
David Kessel
Capt. Vernon Ketcham
Jonathon L. Kibler
Billy Kidd
Craig Clay Kidd
Patrick D. Kilgallon
Jerry D. Killebrew
Vaughn Killebrew
Travis H. Kilpack
David Kimar
Ronald Kimball
Jay Kimberly
Joseph E. Kimsey
Bernard M. King, Sr.
Calvin King
Capt. Roger King
Gary L. King
John E. King
Kenny M. King
Larry B. King
Troy Wayne King
Daniel L. Kingery
Steven D. Kinierim
Robert H. Kinniburgh
Lee Kinsey
John Kipp
Clifton R. Kirby
Ellis Kirby
Jack E. Kirby
Jack Kirby
Steve Kirby
Monty D. Kirk
Willard Kirkpatrick
David Kistle
Walter A. Kittelberger
Harold J. Owen, KK;
John M. Klar
Gary A. Klein
Harry Ol. Klein
Robert E. Klein
William L. Klemin
Darian F. 'Buzz' Kleven
Capt. Allen C. Kline
Kenneth D. Kloostra
James D. Klusman
Arnold Knight
Capt. Eugene Knight
Daniel P. Knight
George L. Knight
Joe Knight
John L. Knight
Richard K. Knight
Ronald L. Knight
Todd Knight
George T. Knighten
Charles Knipschild
William W. Knott
William R. Knox
David A. Kobasic
Louis J. Kocurek, Jr.;
Mark A. Koehler
Capt. Ronald Koenig
Shane R. Kohlbeck
George Kohler
Douglas A. Kolb, Jr.
Dennis Kolender
Stephen Koler
Mark David Koliba
Ron Kolodziej
Capt. Joseph Kostura
William E. Kouba

William Kouba
George A. Koumonduros
John F. Kowalsti
Bob Kowell
Chuck Kraft
Richard Kraklau
Floyd L. Krank
David M. Krawczyk
William P. Kremer
Dennis Kreutzer
Doyle S. Kridelbaugh
Stanley J. Krol, Sr.
Greg Kroll
Elroy Krueger
Robert T. Kruft
Capt. Kenneth Krul
Donald F. Kruse, Jr.
Jerry Kruse
Albert Krzyston
Louis L. Kubica
Thaddeus E. Kubinski
Gary R. Kubowitz
Elaine C. Kuchenbecker
Preston Kuks
John O. Kunkel
Leigh K. Kunnam
Robert S. Kunowsky
Michael C. Kurtz
Eric Kurz
Jeffrey A. Kush
Tim W. Kutzkey
Bryan A. Kwiatkowski
Albert W. Laaksonen
Capt. Ed LaBounty
Richard T. Labbe
Michael L. Lacey
Richard T. LaChance
Don L. & Eddie D. Lack
Lonnie S. Lack
Troy Lackey
Capt. Paul LaCourse
David K. Lacy
Lloyd Leon Lacy
Washington Lacy, III
Kevin W. Ladden
Marianne Ladzinski
Tom Laffey
Terry A. LaFuze
Charles L. Lagana
Luigi G. Laghi
Roberta C. Lagomarsini
David B. Laine
Steven M. Laing
Thomas J. Lake
Capt. Bob Lamb
Stephen J. Lamb
Capt. Earl Lambert
Capt. Edward Lamhart
Brent F. Lamm
Frank Lammens
Capt. Ronald LaMont
Danny A. Lampe
Lowell Lamy
Rip Lance
Norman K. Land
Harry E. Landers
Charles H. Landon, Jr.
James Landon
Paul Lane
Richard V. Lane
Larry Langford
Jack D. Langley
Phil L. Langley, Jr.
Roger W. Langley
Anthony Langston
Dennis N. Langston
Jimmie D. Langston
Mark C. Lanham
F. H. Lannom
Michael J. Lantzy
Larry Large
Richard C. Larkin
William A. Laroche
Harry W. Larrimor
Ronne T. Larson
Theodore K. Larson
Dennis N. Lary
Capt. Leroy Lasher
Lloyd L. Lassiter
Gerald Lastfogel
Roy H. Latham
Mark Lathrop
Ricky W. Latimer
Peter R. Latvala
Dennis J. Lautner
William E. Lavender
Roy W. Lavinder
Bill Law
Jerry G. Lawrence
Jerry D. Lawrence
Jerry G. Lawrence
Jess W. Lawrence, Jr.;
Mike Lawrence
Capt. Robert Lawson
Ken Lawson
John Stuart Lax
Robert E. Layne
Martin Lazar
David Leal
Robert Leard
Dick F. Leavitt
James E. Leavelle, II;
Joe LeBlanc
Keith LeClair
Dave Ledwa
Jeffrey C. Lee
Jerry Lee
Mark E. Lee
Robert M. Lee
Robert R. Lee
Stewart M. Lee
Charles H. Leflore

Colin J. Leflore
David A. Lehan
Capt. Patrick Leibje
Jim G. Leishman
Dave Lekin
Michael J. Lemke
George O. Lening
Capt. William Lenner
Capt. Kenneth Lennox
Eugene Lentz
Tony Lenz
Frank Jose Leoeffler, IV;
Gary Leon
John G. Leonard
Thomas Leonard
Walter D. Leonard
Alexander Lesh
David Lessner
Camp Lester
Eddie D. Lester
John J. Leuy
Ronald E. Levitan
Arthur Lew
Arland Lewis
David W. Lewis
David Lewis
Elroy M. Lewis, Jr.
Henry Lewis, Jr.;
Marion B. Lewis
Thomas G. Lewis
Wally J. Lewis
Greg Lfoulk
Victor G. Liebe
Daniel G. Liechty
David Liedtke
Richard A. Lillard
Rick Lillegard
Capt. Carl Lillis
James R. Lilly
David W. Lincoln
John R. Lindenau
James C. Lindquist
Peter J. Lindquist
James R. Lindsey
Gary Lindstrom
Todd B. Linklater
James A. Linn
Jimmy W. Lipscomb
Michael J. Lipski
I. C. Little
Burt B. Llewellyn
Dwayne A. Lloyd
Gary W. Lock
Greg Lock
Gary W. Locker
Freeman P. Lockhart
Mike Lockyer
Big Bass Lodge
Calusa Lodge
Flamingo Lodge
Kenneth N. Loeser
John Lohrey
John P. Loman
Herbert London
B. J. Long
Gary W. Long
James S. Loop
James Loosey
Jon Edwin Loring, Jr.;
Edward A. Loughran
Dick Lounsbury
James R. Love
Jeremiah S. Love
Benjamin R. Loveland
Douglas W. Lovell
Ted Allen Lovell
Capt. Raymond Lowe
Capt. Terry Lowe
Curgus Lowe
James B. Lowe
Ronald R. Lowe
Michael J. Lowenstein
Dwayne A. Lowery
Joe Wayne Lowery
Joseph L. Lowery
William L. Lowrie
Douglas C. Lowry
Capt. Russell Loyd
Edward J. Lozowski
Mike W. Luark
Stephen M. Lucarelli
Mike Lucas
Peter J. Lucia
William J. Luckey
Daniel R. Luckman
Christopher L. Ludlow
David J. Lueck
Paul L. Luedtke
Joseph P. Lugar II
Frankie W. Luker
Robert D. Lutz
Larry Lybrand
David E. Lynch
John R. Lynch
Matt Danny Lynch, III; -.
Capt. Leslie Lytle
Steve Lytle
Alfred MacDonald
Glenn E. MacDonald
Wayne P. Mace
John C. & Kenneth W. MacEwen
Capt. Bob MacGregor
Camp Mack
David MacKenzie
Kenneth F. Mackert
Patrick S. Macy
Gregory N. Madjeski
Stephen F. Madjeski
George Magnanelli
Capt. Gene Magni
John W. Mahaney
James M. Maki

Steven G. Malaer
Joseph Malatesta
Donald L. Malcom Jr. Malesic
Michael G. Mallamo
William D. Maloney
Gregory D. Mangus
Rudolph E. Manili
Ted Maniurski
Joseph Mann
Larry Mann
Perry Mann
Samuel L. Manning, Sr.
Terry W. Manthey
Dean Mantle
David Maraccini
Paul A. Marcaccio
Daniel Marchi
Capt. Dennis Marek
Larry Lee Marek
Jeffrey E. Margenroth
Angler's Marina
Cypress Isle RV Park & Marina
Uncle Joe's Marina
Cherster L. Marion
John L. Markham
Gary S. Marks
Capt. John Markwica
Donald P. Markwith
Harold B. Marlin
Kimberly H. Marowski
William A. Marr, Jr.
Dudley Marschall
Brian E. Marshall
David E. Marshall
James Marshall
Monte B. Marshall
Monte Marshall
Ronald W. Marshall
Wallace E. Marshall
William R. Marshall
Winfield L. Marshall
Aaron Martens
Linwood Martens
Albert T. Martin
Dan Martin
Donald D. Martin
James P. Martin
Jeff Martin
Jerry Martin
Joey Martin
Mark E. Martin
Mark Martin
Richard D. Martin
Richard Martin
Steve Martin
Steven T. & Arthur T. Martin
Terry W. Martin
William D. Martin
Ludwig Martinson
James C. Marton
John Mason
Lawrence W. Masoner
Alton Matchett
Dan Matchett
Thomas A. Mathena
Capt. John Mather
William B. Mathers
Gregory Mathews
Johnnie M. Mathews
Willie Mathis
Capt. David Matta
Capt. John & Louise Matta
Capt. Michael Matta
Bill Matthews
Capt. Michael Matthews
David G. Matthews
Jack Matthews
John Matthews
John E. Matthews
Larry S. Matthews
James F. Mattis
Frank Mattison
Mitchell K. Mattson
Albert J. Matura
David Maxwell
Kenneth H. Maxwell
Robert A. Maxwell, Jr.;
Derald R. May
F. Dale May
John B. Mayer
Wally Mayer
Greg W. Mayfield
Ronny Maynard
Nial Maytubby
Capt. Bob McAdams
James M. McAlexander
Capt. John McArthur
Burl L. McBride
William H. McBurney
Kramer L. McCabe
Russell McCall
Charles R. McCallum
Lucian A. McCallum
Joel W. McCandless
Joseph W. McCarthy
Patrick McCarty
Richard T. McCarty
James K. McCasland
Scott McClary
Paul D. McClure
Capt. Jerry McClurg
Kim McCluskley
Ronnie Ray McComic
Douglas W. McCormick
James E. McCowen
Jeffrey F. McCoy
Paul G. McCoy
Randel A. McCoy
Robert F. McCready
George A. McCullough
Joe M. McCullough

Earl McDaniel
James M. McDaniel
Mark McDole
Charles M. McDonald
John H. McDonald
Daniel D. McDougal
Bryan S. McDowell
John W. McEachern, Jr.;
Walter McEntyre
Sonny McFadden
Del D. McFarland
Monte McFarland
Robert A. McFarlane
Joseph L. McGahey
Rodney J. McGarrie
Kenneth McGaughey
Charles G. McGonagill
Clyde McGowan
Charles G. McGowen
Lloyd McIntosh
Michael McKay
David R. McKee
Donald T. McKellup
John W. McKinley
David J. McKinnon
John W. McKnett
Brian R. McKnight
H. Turney McKnight
Robert F. McLain
Todd G. McLean
Mike V. McLucas
Daniel P. McManman
Eddie McMillion
Merl S. McMullin
Curtis McNabb
Larry J. McNair
Ralph D. McNair
James McNey
Willis McQueen, Jr.
Raymond McReynolds
Jim D. McSwain
Steve A. McVay
Henry L. McWilliams, Jr.;
Paul E. McWilliams, Jr.
Denise Mead
Ronald F. Meadows
Roy M. Meadows
Brad H. Medlock
Carl E. Meeks
Capt. Bill Meier
Gerald V. Melton
Michael Wm. Melville
Joe D. Mendez
John Mendleski
Craig A. Mercier
Patricia A. Mercier
Thomas J. Mercier
Victor P. Mercogliano
Charles A. Meredith
Eldridge C. & Tyrone A. Meredith
Harley F. Meredith
Don Merki
Bill Gablehouse & Ron Merritt
Edward Q. Merritt
Arthur Meru
William W. Messick
Capt. William Meszaros
Russell C. Metcalf
Vern A. Metz
Lyle Meyer
Capt. Jerry Meyers
Robert C. Meza
Bernard V. Michael
Dean R. Michael
Charles P. Michalk
Frank Michelfelder
Bernard H. Michels
James L. Michols
Ronald S. Mickele
Jerry Mickey
Everett G. Middleton
Mark Middleton
Richard B. Mikuska, Jr.
Alvin R. Milam
Frank Byro Milam
Ken Milam
Louis Milani, Jr.
Christopher Miles
Frederick J. Miles
Wayne D. Miles
John Milina, Jr.;
Mark V. Millar
Bobby J. Miller
Daryl D. Miller
David C. Miller
G. A. Miller
James C. Miller
Johnny Lee Miller
Jon K. Miller
Phillip D. Miller
Steve Miller
William O. Miller
Billy D. Mills
Ray Mills
Robert Mills
Wayne A. Mills
William A. Mills
Wynn Millson
Randal W. Milner
Charles A. Minnick
Alfred J. Minns, Jr.;
Ed Miranda, Jr.
John H. Miskelly
Kenneth Mitchell
Michael L. Mitchell
Pat Mitchell
Patrick C. Mitchell
Gary R. Mitzel
Robert R. Mixon
Raymond O. Mobley
Edward R. Mock
Raymond Mock

Capt. Bruce Moewe
Russell P. Mogel, Jr.
Henry R. Mojeske
John S. Molner
Gary Monical
Augustine Monjaras
Troy Monjaras
Billy Dean Monroe, II;
Michael Monroe
Stewart Monroe, III
Corey Montgomery
John A. Montgomery
Kingsley V. Montgomery
Tom R. Montgomery
William A. Montieth
Sandra C. Moon
Patrick Mooney
Andre Moore
Clark Moore
D. W. Moore
Donald Moore
Edward Moore
Gary Moore
George Moore
James H. Moore
Jeff Moore
Jerry Moore
Michael & Lillian Moore
Michael W. Moore
Paul J. Moore
Roger R. Moore
Ronald L. Moore
F. Marty Moran
Capt. Wanda Morehead
Don Morgan
Eric Morgan, Sr.
Greg W. Morgan
Michael G. Morgan
Michael Morgan
Ronald A. Morgan
David A. Morgans
David P. Morlan
Frederick H. Morosky
Capt. William Morris
Glenn D. Morris
Jim Morris
Robert A. Morris
Terry L. Morris
John W. Morrison
Mark R. Morrison
Capt. Douglas Morrow
Chuck B. Morrow
Douglas D. Morse
Capt. Lex Moser
Jack F. Moses
Clifford Mosley
Joe M. Mosley
Donald S. Moss
Richard L. Mossholder
David C. Motes
Michael H. Mottlage
Keith L. Mount
Robert J. Mudd
Danny C. Mulder
Terry L. Mulkey
Billy L. Mullen
Larry Mullinnix
Robert Glen Mullis
Tammie J. Mumma
Paul E. Munarriz
James M. Munoz
William C. Munroe
Clyne John Murphy, Jr.;
Daniel A. Murphy
Dick Murphy
Francis L. Murphy, Jr.
Gerald L. Murphy
James R. Murphy
Matt E. Murphy
Michael A. Murphy
Patrick E. Murphy
Richard C. Murphy
Robert A. Murphy
Samuel T. Murphy
Stephen D. Murphy
Hal H. Murray
Jimmy H. Murray
John E. Murray
Jonathan T. Murray
Patrick Murray
John L. Murter
Kerry R. Muse
Jerry E. Myers
Jimmy Nail
Mark P. Naillon
Charles R. Naiser, Jr.;
William Nakaki
William Nancollas
Louis G. Napfel, Jr.
John M. Nash, IV;
Joseph Nassar
Harrison C. Nauman, Jr.
Leland Nave
Ross L. Nave
David Wade Neal
Terry Neal
Joel K. Neely
Capt. William Neer
Dan H Negus
Michael Neher
Eugene Neiderlander
Kenneth E. Neidlinger
Donald K. Nelson
Gary Nelson
Jack Nelson
Jack Nelson
John W. Nelson
Steve W. Nelson
William D. Nelson
David W. Nesloney
Francis L. Neve, III;
Steve Neverick

Wes I. Newberry
Steven C. Newbrey
Ron R. Newcomb
Capt. Charles Newman, Jr.;
Dan Newman
Floyd D. Newman
William M. Newman
Damon M. Newpher
Charles M. Newton
Mason A. Newton
Roscoe H. Niblack
John Nicholas
Don Nichols
David Nichols
Patrick A. Nichols
Raymond C. Nichols, Jr.
Rodney C. Nichols
Vicki Nichols
Wallace S. Nichols
Wallace R. Nichols, IV;
Charles Nicholson
Robert A. Nicholson
Capt. Robert Nickel
Capt. John Nickell
Don T. Nicoles
Buddy R. Nicosia
Jerry Nied
Terry Nied
Verron L. Nieghbors
Rick Nielsen
Raymond P. Niemi
Nelson Niemhuis
Capt. Thomas Niese
Felix Nieves
Richard L Niffenegger
Kurt W. Nilsson
Marc Nimitz
Skip Ninninger
Chris Nissman
John Noe
James D. Nolder
Donald R. Noles
Lucy L. Noonan
Paul Nordrum
Dale L. Norman
Robert M. Norman
Michael W. Norrell
George W. Norrington
Lionel G. Norrington
Jerry Norris
Joseph J. Norris
Jody Norsworthy
Capt. Jeff A. Northrop
Jerry W. Norton
Linda J. Norton
Robert G. Norton
Ervin E. Nothnagel
Dennis L. Notson
Darrell T. & Jeffrey T. Nottingham
Richard E. Nottke
Ray J. Novack, Jr.
Ray Novack
Charles M. Novak
Terry L. Novak
Richard N. Novotny
Capt. Michael Nowaczyk
Ken Nowazzyk
Capt. Raymond Nowak
Michael Nowicki
James W. Nowlin
Timothy Nuber
Michael D. Nugent
Alfred D. Nulisch
Capt. Charles Nutter
Boyd M. Nutting
Pat Nye
Capt. George Nyerges
Edward A. O'Brien
Francis J. O'Brien, III;
John P. O'Brien
Patrick J. O'Brien
Charles D. O'Brien
Gilbert R. O'Connor
Michael D. O'Connors
Steve F. O'Dell
Michael J. O'Halo
Brian O'Meara
Capt. David O'Neal
Roger O'Neal
Richard A. O'Neale
Chris O'Neill
The Oasis
George J. Oberdin
Scott C. Ocacio
James J. Ocker
Bill Ockerhausen
Kent Nischman
Lowell L. Odom
Steven J. Oeller
John B. Ogden
John T. Ogle
Randy Oldfield
M. Don Oliver
Larry E. Oliver
Chris Olsen
Herbert Olsen
Brian F. Olson
Kurt J. Olson
Richard T. Olson
Jennifer Olsson
Scott Oman
James C. Onderdonk
Capt. Jeffery Opelt
William L. Oppelt
Donald L. Orcutt
Kenneth R. Orr
Capt. James Osborn
Kenneth G. Osborn
Eugene T. Osborne
Mike W. Osborne
Capt. Raymond Osolin
Steven Osterman
C. C. Oswalt

Michael D. Oswalt
Steve Otterbein
Lake Erie Outfitters
Dane S. Ovalls
Harold E. Owen, II;
Charles E. Owens
Kevin Owens
Michael L. Owens
Robert D. Owens
Steven R. Owens
Donald W. Oxford
Walter E. Oxley, Jr.
Gregory L. Oxner
Jackie W. Pace
Rod Pacheco
Capt. Paul Pacholski
Jodie Pack
Mark Pack
Tracy B. Pack
Greg Packer
Andy Packmore
Andy J. Packmore
Marvin PadierLarry E. Page
Richard S. Painter
Peter Palajac
Dennis Palla
Billy W. Palmer
Michael W. Pancratz
Terry Panknin
Ronald Pannell
Glen Papez
Jerome A. Papineau
Martin M. Papke
Charles F. Paradoski
Henry I. Parker
Jeffrey L. Parker
Jesse Parker
Lloyd W. Parker
Mark Parker
Robert J. Parker
Scott Parker
Tony L. Parker
Winston Parkinson
Kelly D. Parks
Robert W. Parks
Thomas A. Parks
Capt. Kendall Parsley
Delbert J. Parsons
John Paslaqua
Pete Paszli
Capt. John Patrick
Charles L. Patrick
Louie Patrizi
Hargis & Janet Patroni
Alvia E. Patterson
Buddy M. Patterson
Clifford L. Patterson, Sr.
Herbert O. Patterson
Randy Patzkowsky
Barbara Payne
Bary A. Payne
Clayton L. Payne
Don R. Payne
Leon Payton
Richard L. Peabody
Richard C. Pearce
Arlen Pearsall
George B. Peat
James H. Peck
Donald L. Pedro
Capt. Russ Pellow
Oscar L. Pence
Wayne Pennell
Capt. Thomas Penny
Kenneth Penrod
Ed Peplinski
Lillymae Pepper
Dwight O. Peppler
Todd Percival
James M. Perdue
Patrick A. Perdue
Dennis Perea
Capt. Jon Perette
Fredrick Perkins
Andy Peroulis
Capt. James Perrine
Bruce Perry
James M. Perry
Richard E. Perry
Alfred S. Perryman
Michael N. Perusse
Charles M. Peters
Keith D. Peters
Lee R. Peters, Sr.
Michael J. Peters
Fritz Peterson
James W. Peterson
Robert K. Peterson
Francis A. Pettolina
Freddy Petty
Janie Petty
R. J. Petty
William P. Petz
Mick Pfeiffer
Ronald E. Pfeiffer
Capt. Ronald Pflug
Steve Pfuntner
Jerry Q. Phelps
Arthur A. Phillips, Sr.
Capt. Danny Phillips
Carl E. Phillips
Doug R. Phillips
Frederick A. Phillips
Jimmy L. Phillips
Rod R. Phillips
Walter Phillips
George W. Philpott
Capt. James Phipps
Jason Phipps
Capt. Lou Pieczonka
Gene Piel
Joseph D. Pieratt

Steve Pierce
Theodore W. Pierce
Capt. Ron Pierson
George J. Pierson
Stephen C. Pilant, Sr.;
Robert W. Pilger
Jack Pinch
David G. Pingree
Fred 'Fritz' Pinkerman
Clarence Pinkerton
Mark Pinto
William Pipkin
Laren M. Piquet
Frank R. Pisciotta
Gregory R. Pishkur
Kim D. Pitner
Eugene Pittman
Bruce Pitzer
John R. Pizza
James Plaag
Paul Bruce Place
Al Plath
Daniel Plescher
Alvin E. Pletzke
Robert Plitko
Ronald C. Plosnak
Rodney L. Plummer
William Plunkett
Capt. Jeff Poe
Galand S. Poe
Charles Pokorny III
Capt. Keith Poland
John Eddy Polhemus
Frederick S. Polich
Ervin Polishuk
Charles S. Polityka
Michael S. Polk
Capt. Thomas Polta
Capt. Bernard Pompiley
Harold Ray Ponder
Harlin D. Ponnell
Leonard H. Poole
Gerald W. Pope
Alexander Porter
Samuel J. Porter
Richard D. Portz
Tina Posey
Robert S. Potesham
A. Dee Potter
Mark L. Pounds
Charles E. Powell
Jeffrey W. Powell
Jerry Powell
Joe W. Powell
Phillip P. Powell
James M. Powers
Walter M. Prather
Harry Pratley
Joseph B. Pratt
Dan Prause
Kenneth R. Preder
George A. Prenant
Norman I. Presson
Gene W. Prevette
Cid A. Price
Duncan PriceGary Price
Larry C. & Michele M. Price
Richard Price
Thomas R. Price
Sorin S. Pricopie
Wayne E. Priddy
Frank N. Prim
Preston O. Prince
Pete Pritchard
Daniel G. Pritchett
Johnny E. Procell
Robert Cole Proctor
Terry Promowicz
Penny L. Prough
Charles Pruitt
John Pryor
Gerald D. Puckett
James B. Puckett, Jr.;
Alan D. Pullin
David Pulsifer
Peter Pumphrey
John Punola
William Pustesovsky
Harry A. Putney
Joseph H. Quade, Jr.
Jeffery S. Qualls
Thomas B. Quimby
Lloyd B. Quinby, II;
Billy J. Quinn, Sr.;
Rick L. Quinn
Ron Rabun
William Boyd Radford
David B. Ragin
Ed Ragsdale
James H. Ragsdale
Roger Raines
Bill Rainey
Charles S. Rains
Don Ralph
Curtis B. Rambo, Sr.
Del E. Ramesbothom
Ricardo Ramirez, Jr.;
Marlon R. Rampy
Stephen B. Ramsey
Tommy Ramzinsky
Don R. Rand
Capt. Stephen Randell
Oscar B. Randles, III;
Garry L. Randolph
Leonard Randon
Thomas W. Ranft
Richard L. Rang
Richard M. Rangel
Jerry Rankey
Rickey L. Ransom
Christopher Rash
Harold Raskey

Capt. Jon Rasmussen
David E. Rasmusson
Lawrence K. Raum
Terry L. Raven
James L. Rawls
Bill Rawson
Bryan D. Ray
Darrell Ray
Douglas Ray
Lynn Ray
Ralph V. Ray, Jr.;
William L. Ray, III
Beryl A. Rea
Andrew D. Read
Joseph Read
Joseph L. Reagan, Jr.;
James H. Reaneau
Robert A. Reavis
Doug Reckling
Tim Redden
Arlie N. Reece
James B. Reece
Phillip B. Reed
Ronnie S. Reese
Shawn O. Reese
Wayne Reeser
Harold R. Reeves
Virgil M. Reeves
Richard J. Regula
Frank Rehak
Charles T. Reichert, Jr.
Robert E. Reid
Thomas A. Reid
Ernest Neal Reidhead
Al H. Reinhart
Gail T. Reininger
Capt. Leonard Reino
Raymond F. Rende
L. W. Renner
Mossy Cove Fishing Resort
River Ranch Resort
Roland Martin's Lakeside Resort
Nate's Restaurant
Edward Retherford
Dale Rexroat, Jr.;
Richard D. Rexroat
Gary L. Reymann
Jeff Reynolds
Leslie E. Reynolds, Jr.;
William T. Reynolds
F. Mark Rhoades
Newell L. Rhodes
John C. Rhyne
Thomas E. Rials, Jr.
Michael E. Rice
Joe Richard
David Richardson
Fredic J. Richardson
Jack Richardson
Ricky Joe Richey
Thomas F. Richmond
Leroy Richter
Robert L. Rickerson
Steven Ricks
Larry W. Riddle
Michael L. Riddle
Mitchell R. Riddle
Aaron V. Ridgell, Jr.
Charles E. Ridgell
Walter J. Riedel
Randolph Rigdon
Louis D. Riggs, Jr.;
Stephen Riha
Michael Riley
Robert F. Rillings
Larry D. Ring
Leroy S. Rippy
Donald D. Risner
David W. Ristow
Johnny Rivers
Capt. Jim Roach
Steven R. Robards
Robert Robbins, Jr.;
Ted Robbins
Sammie E. Roberson
Dale E. Robert
Lindy M. Roberts
Richard J. Roberts
Gene S. Robertson
John C. Robertson
Billy T. Robinson
Delane Robinson
Eddie Robinson
John E. Robinson
Raymond M. Robinson
Ricky Robinson
Russell K. Robinson
Terry A. Robinson
Tom Robinson
Mark N. Rochester, III;
John Rockwood
William Charles Rode, Jr.
John R. Rodgers
Michael D. Rodgers
Tommy N. Rodgers
Daniel Rodriguez
Capt. Larry Roe
Gerald N. Roebuck
Clement V. Rogers
Clinton B. Rogers
Daryl Rogers
Dean C. Rogers
Henry C. Rogers
Randy W. Rogers
Richard L. Rogers
Rick Rogers
Robert R. Rogers
Michael R. Rogge
George R. Rohe
Dean Rojas
Dennis Rollan
Robert Romanishin

Richard Rombal
Ron Romig
Carrol E. Rommell
Robert W. Rommell
Willie D. Ronshausen
Randall R. Rooks
Joe A. Rosania
Ronald D. Rosborough
Gerald D. Rose
Jack T. Rose, Jr.
Jimmy Rose
Mickey D. Rose
Capt. Gary Rosebrock
Dana Rosen
Bryan D. Rosenquist
Sue Rosenwinkel
Alvin L. Ross
David Ross
John Ross
Jonathan M. Ross
Robert F. Ross
Christian Roth
Mike Roth
Christopher P. Rothes
Randall R. Rouquette
James W. Rouse
Martin Rovenstone
Donald C. Rowand
Darin M. Rowe
David M. Rowe
Fred Rowe
Glenn Rowe
Henry G. Rowe, Jr.
Tracy H. Rowell
Capt. Albert Rowh
Gary Rowland
De Lyle Rowley
Darrell Roy
Louis A. Royal
Purdy James Royce
John T. Ruben
Peter Ruboyianes
Henry Rucker
T. M. Rucker
Dewey S. Rudolph
Jerry C. Ruehle
Joel Ruiz
Billy D. Rule
George W. Rule
Richard A. Rule
Allan W. Rumball
Charlie Z. Rumfield
Zachary S. Rumfield
Randall E. Rumrill
Gordon Runyon, Jr.
Janet L. Rupp
Joseph F. Rupp, III
Stanley J. Rura
David E. Rusch
L.B. Rush, Jr.
Billy Rushing
C. L. Rushing
Denmark S. Rushing
Capt. James Rushworth
Joe Rusnak
Annette Russ
Bill Russell
Robert Russell
Scott C. Russell
Scott Russo
John H. Rust
Dale Rutherford
Ed Rutledge
Raymond R. Rutzen
Capt. Dean Ryberg
Paul M. Saba
Jan Sabin
A. Sachs
A. R. Sachtleben
Claude W. Sacker
Capt. James Sackett
Capt. David Sackett
Gary L. Sacks
Joseph W. Sadler, Sr.
Ron S. Saiki
Frank S. Saksa
Anthony J. Salamon
Capt. Jack Salisbury
Charles Salmon
Ted Salzman
Merle J. Samakow
Ted Samford
Jim Sammons
Mark Sampson
Don J. Sanders
Jim E. Sanders
Jimmie D. Sanders
Barbara Sanderson
Larry Sanderson
James E. Sandlin, III;
Paul S. Sandlin
James L Sandusky
Joseph M. Santone
John K. Sasser
Rickey P. Sattenwhite
George Satterfield
Hector Saucedo
Michael D. Saverino
Terry F. Sawyer
J. Elwood Scaggs
Capt. John Scaife
Bobby Joe Scarberry
Gary Bob Scarberry
Chuck & Lynn Scates
David Schachter
Capt. Daniel Schade
William H. Schadler
David C. Schaefers
Capt. Park Schafer
Capt. Roger Schaffer
Jim W. Schaffer
Larry R. Scharich

Vernon A. Schatz
David A. Schauber
John A. Schaul
Robert Scheer
Andrew F. Scheible
Bruce Scheible
Douglas W. Scheible
Michael O. Schelsteder
David B. Schemenauer
Jerome R. Schiller
Patrick Schiller
Rocky L. Schippa
Tom L. Schippa
Andrew C. Schipul
Ronald D. Schlabach
Capt. Daniel Schlegel
Robert Schlitts
William J. Schnabl
Ronald J. Schneider
Todd L. Schneider
William A. Schneider
Randel K. Schoen
David W. Schoenfeld, Jr.;
Capt. Thomas Schofield
Yarri Schriebvogel
Donald L. Schroeder
Larry T. Schubert
Curtis L. Schuenemann
Bill Schultz
Craig R. Schultz
Dan E. Schultz
Donald K. Schultz
George G. Schultz
William J. Schultz
Carl W. Schumann
Roy M. Schuster, II;
Max Schwab
Richard K. Schwalm
Cliff Schwark
Allen V. Scott
Carl Scott
John E. Scott
Regan I Scott
Ronald L. Scott, Jr.
Warren J. Scott
Capt. David Screptock
Richard J. Scriven
Robert Scrogin
John A. Scypinski
James R. Seaboldt
Carl E. Seago
James D. Seaman
J. A. Searcy
Charles E. Secoy
Capt. Lynn Seery
Richard O.Seiferlein
Irwin S. Seigel
Ed Sekula
Ray L. Self
John Sellers
Bob Semanski
Thomas J. Semeeal
LeRoy G. Senter
Raymond Serfass
Martin D. Serna
Lloyd B. Service
Capt. Mathew Severns
John L. Seymour
David P. Shafer
Jerry C. Shafer, Jr.;
Patrick Shafer
Scott A. Shafer
Michael E. Shaffner
Stephen R. Sharp
Phil F. Sharpe
Jerry C. Shaum
Danny r. Shaw
Jack E. Shaw
Jerry D. Shaw
John J. Shaw
Perry Shaw
Robert D. Shaw
Steve W. Shawl
Bernard F. Shea
Kevin P. Shea
Michael Shearer
Ronnie J. Sheeon
Robert M. Sheets
William A. Sheka, Jr.
A. L. Shelby
Dennis J. Sheley
Bernard Shellman
Gary Shelton
Jackie R. Shelton
Les R. Shelton
Dennis B. Shepherd
Ray Shepherd
Raymond W. Shepherd
Harry E. Sheppard, III
Patrick H. & Janet L.Sheridan
Bink Sherman
Roger W. Sherman
Charles W. Sherry
George D. Sherwood
Capt. Robert Shetenheim
Charles L. Shipley
Randy Shipp
Jerald Shoemaker
Tom Shones
Otis Shook, Jr.
Jeffrey N. Shores
Jack Short
Egene R. Shropshire
Robert L. Shuler
Brandon J. Shumake
Brian L. Shumaker
Capt. Bruce Sibbersen, Sr.
William M. Siematel
Allen Sifford
Thomas A. Sifford
Thomas I. Sigler

James Sigman
Don R. Simic
Jerry Simmons
Murray M. Simmons, Jr.
Rhandy Joe Simmons
Charles H. Simms
Mark Simonds
Greg Simonson
Roland M. Simounet
Albert W. Simpson
Jerry E. Sims
Marvin C. Sims
Michael Simunoil
Randall Singleton
Virgil P. Sipes
Soren Siren
Robert S. Sirvello
Lee G. Sisk
Charles R. Sisson
Robert E. Sivinski
Dale D. Skiles
Darrell L. Skillern
Charles D. Skinner
Gene Skinner
John D. Skrobot
Mark T. Slack
Robert Slaff
Robert A. Slamal
James Scott Slaughter
Mike Slavin
Ernest D. Slessman
Bruce Slightom
Lyndal Van Sloan, Jr.
Jesse Sloss
Capt. Robert Slye
Jack Smack
David Small
Timothy C. Small
Alton L. Smith, Jr.
Arden T. Smith
Brett Smith
Buddy Smith
Don C. Smith, Sr.
Carl S. Smith
Cary C. Smith
Charles B. Smith
Charles C. Smith
Christopher T. Smith
Daniel N. Smith
Frederick W. Smith
James L. Smith
James C. Smith
Jason E. Smith
Jimmy G. Smith, Jr.
Jody G. Smith
Lonnie D. Smith
Lynn Vess Smith, Jr.;
Michael D. Smith
Nick D. Speicher & Sam Smith
Paul Smith
Perry J. Smith
Peter M. Smith
Phil S. Smith
Robert M. Smith
Ronald D.Smith
Sandy G. Smith
Stanley M. Smith, Sr.
Stephan I. Smith
William R. Smith
William F. Smith
Zeke Smith
R. J. Smithey
Ronald Smyer
Jack B. Smythe, Jr.;
Lawrence F. Snead
M. M. Snell
Edward H. Snelson
Steve E. Snopek
Capt. Ottie Snyder, Jr.
James F. Snyder
James G. Snyder
Jeffrey R. Snyder
John E. Snyder, Jr.;
Terry L. Snyder
Thomas Snyder
Earl Soderquist
Scott Soisson
Jack D. Solanik
Robert T. Solinski
Jeffery S. Solis
Gary L. Somers
James T. Somerville
Leon H. Sommerville, Jr.
Jay R. Sorensen
Stephen Sorensen
Rick Soto
Dallas F. Southard
James T. Southard
Paul J. Souza
Ronald M. Sowa
John A. Spangler
Robert E. Spani
Pete J. Sparacio
Paul L. Sturgis
Timothy Sparks
William A. Sparks
Michael Spaulding
Johnny C. Spear
Robert E. Spearman
Gregory J. Spears
Stephen W. Spedden
Harold Speed, Jr.;
John L. Spencer
Garry N. Sperry
Robert P. Spezio
Elmer Spicer
Dennis D. Spike
Lowell E. Spitzer
Rodney C. Spivey
Carl R. Spongberg
Sportfishing
World Wide Sportsman

Paul Spracklen
Joel Springer
Tal W. Sprinkles
Chris F. Spurry
Steven Spurry
John St. Beverly
Gary St. Martin
Michael A. St. Pierre
Terry W. Stacy
Bill Staff
Audie J. Stafford
Dick Stafford
Jack Stafford
Kerry W. Stafford
James M. Staight
Gary F. Stamm
John C. Stanley
Arthur L. Stanton
Bonita Staples
Ron L. Stark
Ronald Stark
John McMahon Starkey
Michael O. Starrett
Dennis J. States
William F. Statler
Daryl Stauffer
Capt. Jerry Stayer
James A. Stayer
Robert B. Staysa, Jr.
Capt. Marvin Stechschulte
Capt. Richard Stedke
Charles G. Steed
Gary L. Steed
Gordon Steele
Jeffrey R. Steele
Robert A. Steele
Capt. John Stefano
Michael K. Stegall
George L. Stelmach
Del L. Stephens
Glen W. Stephens
Kevin K. Stephens
Robert L. Stephens
Virgil Stephenson
Butch Sterling
Donald K. Steussy
Howard E. Steussy, II;
Marsh Alan Steussy
Riles C. Steussy
James Stevens
Scott W. Stevens
Robert M. Stevenson
Charles R. Stewart
David N. Stewart
David O. Stewart
Gary Stewart
James Stewart
Larry W. Stewart
Michael P. Stewart
William R. Stewart
William L. Stickley
Darryl Stiers
John Q. Stine
Mary Carolyn Stine
Jackie Stinnet
Larry W. Stinson
Roman Stockton
Russell Stockton
Ronald L. Stokes
Robert F. Stoner
Paul Storm
Gary Stott
David W. Stover
Charles C. Stowe, III;
Charles C. Stowe
Edward Stowe
Michael Stowe
George F. Strader
Samuel D.Strahan
George J. Stransky, Jr.
Robert J. Strathmann
David L. Streeter
Jeffrey M. Streett
Durwood Strickland
Charles Stringer
Paul L. Strobel
Capt. Karl Stroh
Terry L. Strom
David Strong
Dale H. Stroschein
Bobby G. Strother
Claude Stroud
Gregg Strouse
Stevie Lee Strunk
Douglas W. Strzynski
Michael W. Stuard
Jolley J. Stuart
Michael R. Stuart
Daniel M. Stucky
Eric W. Stuecher
Captain Richard C. Stuhr
Lenwood Sturdivant
Peter Sturges
Paul L. Sturgis
Capt. William Sturm
Bob Stuvek
Robert F. Sugar
Carolyn Sullivan
Christopher G. Sullivan
Herman J. Sullivan
Randall E. Sullivan
Russell Sullivan
Lee Roy Summerlin
Travis O. Summerlin
Capt. Robert Summers
Marion R. Sunday, Jr.
Capt. Matthew A. Supinski
Thomas D. Sutton
Carl J. Svebek
James E. Swagler
Michael A. Swaney
James S. Swanezy

Jeffrey J. Swanson
Robert Swantek
Chuck Swartz
Dan Swartz
Jimmy D. Sweat
Jimmy L. Sweat
Eric T. Swedman
David Sweeney
Howard F. Sweet
Barry Franklin Sweitzer
Ora Swick
Doug Swisher
Otis D. Swisher
Dennis F. Swope
Johnny Sword
James E. Sykes
Wayne J. Syn
Adam F. Szczypinski
Fernando C. Tabor
Henry E. Tabor
Richard Taddei
Hitoshi Takahashi
Norman W. Talbert
James Talbot
Frank V. Talbott
Philip M. Talbott, III
Otis Tally
Timothy N. Tanis
Carroll Tanner
John Clark Tanner
Robert C. Tanner
Zolan Tanner
Arnold Taratuta
George W. Tate
Charles N. Tawes, Jr.
George D. Tawes
Harry L. Tayloe
Capt. Edward Taylor
Charlie Taylor
Clifford E. Taylor
Dennis Taylor
Garlin Taylor
Jerry R. Taylor
Matthew Taylor
Melvin D. Taylor
Mitchel B. Taylor
Neal A. Taylor
Richard Taylor
Robert Taylor
Robert L. Taylor
Aaron B. Teague
Jimy R. Teague
Daniel Tebo
Phillip M. Tedder
Donald E. Teeple
William M. Tenison
Capt. James Tennant
Michele Tennies
James B. Tennyson
Edward J. Tercoe
Butch Terpe
Daniel Terrell
Donald E. Terrell
Capt. Austin Tester
William A. Theisen
Charles R. Thetford
F. William Thim
Charles F. Thomas
Larry C. Thomas, Sr.
Lawrence Thomas
Richard W. Thomas
Tommy's Thomas
Ann Thomasson
Capt. Dean Thompson
Charles Thompson
David W. Thompson
E. J. Thompson, Jr.
Janet & William R. Thompson
Jim Thompson
Johnnie J. Thompson
Ralph L. Thompson
William K. Thompson
James R. Thorne
W.D. Thornhill
Marvin W. Thornton
Jim P. Thorwarth
Mark V. Thow
Glen S. Thurman
Michael G. Thurman
Kelly Thurow
Delbert Thyarks
Billy W. Tidball
Tommy Tidwell
Michael J. Tihila
Elmo Tilley
Greg W. Tilley
Jimmy Tilley
Lonnie Tilley
Randy D. Tilley
Capt. James Tillman
Damon R. Tillman
Harry L. Tillolson
Charles K. Tilton
Lawrence D. Tippett
Brent R. Titus
Joy B. Tlou
George L. Todd, Sr.
Carl M. Toepfer
David Tokay
Don Tollison
Bobby L. Tolliver
Rang G. Tolliver
Jeremy R. Toman
Jerry G. Toman
Carl Ray Tomlinson
George F. Tompkins
Jean T. Toney
Capt. Michael Topp
Richard D. Tortelli
Hector V. Torres, Jr.;
Capt. Dennis Toth
Jackie L. Touchstone

Rick Toumey
Peg Leg II Tours
Capt. Randy Townsend
Eldon O. Townsend
Capt. Dave Tracy
James L. Trahan
Eddie G. Trapp
Harley E. Travis
Jim Traweek
Jim Traylor
Winfred O. Traywick
James J. Tresch
Robert L. Tribble
David Trimble
Donald J. Trimble
Neil Trimble
Noble D. Trimble
Lisa B Fish & Dive Trips
Harold F. Trivitt
Kenny Trivitt
Capt. Ronald Trogdon
Jeff Tropf
Robert L. Troup
Douglas M. Trouten
Capt. Bob Trozel
Brian K. Truax
James Truesdale
Gerald Truesdell
Robert S. Trull
Dale Tucker
James C. Tudor
Patrick T. Tully
Donald F. Turner
Gregory R. Turner
Louis M. Turner
Mark Turner
Ray Turner
William Edward Turner
William L. Turner
John I. Turney
Tom A. Turney
David E. Turowski
Capt. Edd Twigg
Edward R. Tworek
Richard Tworek
Dudley L. Tyler
James K. Tyler
Tommy T. Tyler
Laurel A. Tyrrell
Thomas W. Uhls
Dave Unger
Lon J. Unger
Capt. Keith Unkefer
Paul Updike
Thomas J. Upshir
Pete Uptmor
Terry J. Upton
Charles A. Uzzle
Robert G. Vail
Capt. Frank Valencic
Ruth VanAtter
David H. Vance
Capt. Mitchell Vanch
Ricky D. Vandergriff
Richard L. VanderWest
Tom Vanderwest
Brad W. Vanderzanden
Charlie VanDusen
Edward A. VanDyke
Thomas N. VanItteersum
Jack G. VanLoon
William VanLuven
Carl B. VanNetter
Bernard L. Vannoy
Preston Vanshoubrouek
Victor Vardenega
Nicholas E. Varga
Capt. Raty\\ymond Vargo
Capt. David Vargo
Gilbert Vasquez
David H. Vassallo
Scott Vaughan
Craig Vaughn
Palmer Veen
Douglas Veihl
Gilbert C. Vela
Gary E. Verstuyft
Rocky Vertone
Mark L. Veurink
Patrick C. Vick
Robert K. Vickey
Stephen L. Vierkorn
Rene Villanueva
Emilio Villarreal
Gerald F. Vindick
Ed Viola
John H. Viser, III
Tim Voaklander
Claude Vogelheim
Dan Voiles
Capt. Edward Volan
A. D. Volk
Richard Vollmer
Jeffrey A. Voss
Richard Voth
Perry Voyles
Andrew Vrablic
Randall K. Wade
William G. Wade
Willie W. Wade
Richard C. Wader
John Wagenhals
Capt. Ron Wagner
David A. Wagner
Charles F. Wagnon
Eldawan Wagoner
Mick Wagoner
John A. Wahler
Edward R. Waits, III
Mark Wakeman
Kenneth L. Waler
Hiram I. Walker, Jr.

John Walker
John W. Walker
Phillip Walker
Richard J. Walker
Steve Walker
Terry A. Walker
Bobby Ray Wall
Donnie L. Wallace
Miles E. Wallace
Murray R. Wallace
Normal L. Wallace
Russell Wallace
William N. Wallender
Samuel E. Waller
Jimy W. Walling
Steven B. Walser
Larry Walsh
Richard J. Walsh
Sid Walsh
Terry R. Walsh
Lee Walter
Patrick Walter
Henry Walters, Jr.
Bob Walton
John I. Waner
Jim Wann
Phil Wantland
David J. Warcham
Bernie Ward, Jr.
Bernie Ward III
Claude E. Ward
James C. Ward
Jamie L. Ward
Jeffrey Ward
Robert W. Ward
Robert S. Ward
Willard C. Ward
Howard D. Wards
Carroll Ware
Calvin D. Warner
James F. Warner
Kelly Warner
Robert H. Warner
G.H. Warren
Joseph A. Warren
Robert C. Warren, Jr.
David L. Washington
Dewey H. Waters
Capt. Gary Watkins
Haron H. Watkins
Jay Watkins
Rex M. Watkins
Stephen P. Watkins
James Thomas Watkinson
Christopher D. Watkowski
John E. Watson
Jonathan D. Watson
Michael J. Watson
Richard Watson
Donald G. Watts
Jerry D. Watts
Thurl L. Watts
Howard J. Waugh, Jr.;
Jerry Weakley
L. C. Weatherford
Billie Weaver
Billy Weaver
Elvin L. Weaver
Randall L. Weaver
James T. Webb, Jr.
Mark Webb
Richard J. Weber
Bob Webster
Edward T. Webster
Nick Weeks
Chris Weems
Mark Lee Weems
Capt. Thomas Weese
William H. Weigele
William Weiland
Patrick S. Weir
Randy Weir
Richard G. Weir
Arthur Weiss
Rodney Weiss
Bill Welborn
Capt. John Welch
Thurman Welch
Frank A. Welles
Gerald L. Wellman
Craig S. Wells
Terry W. Wells
Vere C. Wells
Capt. Dan Welsh
Jerry Welton
Carl Elmer Wentrcek
Dennis H. & David L. Wessels
Craig West
Jerry L. West
George E. Westcott
Todd Andrew Wester
Mark E. Westmoreland
Edward L. Weston
Ronald Westrate
James R. Wetzel
Joe D. Whaley
David L Wheat
Mike Wheatley
Calvin Wheeler
Gary P. Wheeler
Jerry Wheeler
Michael r. Wheeler
Michael P. Wheeler
Steve Whinnery
Carl J. Whisenhunt
Bruce A. White
Byrd E. White III
Charles G. White
Chris A. White
Elbert D. White
James White

Jerry W. White
Mark White
Peter J. White
Richard E. White
Robert White
Roy White, Jr.;
Slim R. White
Lance J. Whiteaker
Gary M. Whitehair
John L. Whitehead
R. W. Whitehead
Robert Whitenberg
Jerry Whitfield
Ronald H. Whiting
J. D. Whitley
Wendell A. Whitloch
Thomas D. Whitlock
William Whitlock
Willliam G. Whitlock
Mark David Whitman
Jodey C. Whitmire
Dale L. Whitmore
Ken Whitney
Paul D. Whitney
Capt. Phillip Whitt
Jim T. Wiebe
Capt. Anthony Wieczorek
Ralph Wiegand
Capt. Thaddeus Wierzba
Robert L. Wigal
F.W. Butch Wiggs
Matt Wilbur
Bill Roger Wilcox
Timothy P. Wilcoxson
Theodore J. Wiley
Michael R. Wilkerson
David G. Wilkes
Don Wilkey
Judith Wilkie
Clifton M. Wilkins
Russell L. Wilkins, III
John F. Wilkinson
Charlie E. Willet
George G. Willett
Wayne Willett
Capt. Jeff Williams
Charles C. Williams
Clifton H. Williams
Gary R. Williams
J. M. Williams
James R. Williams
James E. Williams
John E. Williams
Julian B. Williams, Jr.
Ken Williams
Larry Williams
Leland C. Williams
Mark A. Williams
Paul D. Williams
Roland R. Williams
Thomas E. Williams
Timothy E. Williams
Walter C. Williams
Wayne L. Williams
William P. Williams
Dan Williamson
Ricky E. Williamson
Wade Williamson
George Willing
Lyle Willmarth
R. B. Wilshire
Bo Wilson
Choice D. Wilson
Dale Wilson
Gary Wilson
Henry Wilson
Herbert W. Wilson
Jerry Wilson
Kalen Wilson
Merle G. Wilson
Morris E. Wilson
Ralph L. Wilson, Jr.
Robert M. Wilson
Stephen C. Wilson
Thomas W. Wilson, Jr.
Dennis Winchester
Chris Windram
Jerry S. Windsor
Stuart L. Windsor
Curtis L. Wing
Jim Wingard
Wesley W. Winget
Arvle L. Winkler
Christopher L. Winslow
Robert C. Winters
Ronnie L. Wipff
Tommy W. Wisdom
Capt. David Wise
Capt. Bernard Wise
Raymond S. Wise
Capt. Barry Witt
Lorrie Witt
John Henry Witte
Clyde W. Wofford
James E. Wohlford
Darren Ray Wolf
Richard F. Wolf, Jr.
Capt. Clark Wolfe
Lloyd C. Wolfe
Murrey E. Wolfe
Murrey Wolfe
Wally L. Wolfe
William F. Wolfe, Jr.
Joe Wolff
Billy E. Wolford
Gary J. Wolgamott
Judy L. Wong
Capt. James Wood
Charles A. Wood
Dale R. Wood
Donald Wood
Larry L. Wood

Cris E. Wooden
Phillip D. Woodford
Gus Woodham
Mark Woodruff
Robert E. Woodruff
Arthur G. Woods
James Woods
Morrell J. Woods
Randy L. Woods
Carl J. & David Wooten
Christopher L. Wooten
John Wooten
John E. Wooton, Jr.
Robert Bruce Wootten
Bill H. Workman
W. D. Workman
Mike Wornom
James Worster
Curtis L. Wortman
Don Wouda
Anton R. Wratney
Raymond Wray
Bobby R. Wright, Sr.
Charles D. Wright
Dan Wright
Francis J. Wright
Montro Wright
Percy L. Wright
Roy B. Wright
William C. Wright
William G. Wright
Mike Wurm
Donald R. Wurz
Charles T. Wyatt
Donald E. Wyckoff
Gary T. Yamaguchi
John D. Yarbrough
Ken Yarnelle
Paul B. Yeager
Raymond Yeager
Todd R. Yeatman
Barry E. Yeatts
Ken Yee
Jerald D. Yensan
Capt. John Yingling, Jr.
Thomas A. York
Capt. Robert Young, Jr.
Chris D. Young
Joseph E. Young
Ray V. Young
Robert H. Young
Timothy J. Young
Dusty Youren
J. M. Zamora
Wally W. Van Zandt
Jose R. Zapata
Danny Zarlengo
Edward C. Zeerip
Jeffery R. Zennie
Craig R. Ziegler
Michael Zielinski
Henry K. Zimmerman
Joseph R. Zink
Capt. Robert Zvosec
"Caps" Tundra Time Adventures
Chriss D. Hurley
"Deputy Dawg's" Fishing Adventures
Ed Weldon
"Farr-Out" Charters Capt. Ron Farr
"Fish On" Fishing Adventures
Frank Carter
"Must Be Nice" Drift Co.
Tom Cutmore
"Think Fish"Kenneth Gammill,Jr.
#1 Guide Service
Capt. Scott Corbisier & N Outfitters
Timothy Henley McCollum
2-E Fish Company Michael Tuhy
20 Mile Lodge Bruce Leadman
24 North Outfitters Phil Chalifour
2V Outfitters, LTD.
Stephen Greenway
3 Mile Bay Tent & Trailer Park
Vern & Helen Phillips & Family
31 Ranch Joe Kyle Parker
4-Winds Capt. Mauri Pierce
4 Corners Outfitting
Dwain Lee Gibson
4 UR Ranch, Inc. - Rock Swenson
4 W Air/JustinTyme Guide-Bill Woodin
4C's Guides & Outfitters-Chet Connor
5 Springs Ranch Guide & Outfitter
Louis Rabin
5/S Outfitting & Guide Service
Glenn E. Smith
58 22' North Sailing Charters
Delbert & Wayne Carnes
580 Outfitters Ron Girardin
62 Ridge Outfitters
Ken & Elizabeth Smith
7 Seas Charters Marvin M. Miller
777 Ranch Kevin Christiansen
7C Quarter Circle Outfitters
Dennis P. Chatlain
7M Guide Service - Seven Mazzone
7W Guest Ranch - Russ Papke
9T9 Ranch
A'Vanga Capt. Byron Smith, Jr.
A-1 Adventures/Mauer's Charter
Serv.Capt. James Mauer
A-1 Fishing Craig Renfro
A-1 Mauer's Charter Service
Capt. Pete Mauer
A-Able Fishing Charters
George Goggins
A-Coho-Motion Charters/Lodge
Capt. Brian Neal
A-Float on the River Larry Nelson
A-Hook Charters
Myron Craig McDonald
A-M Charters
Melissa Sherman Allan

A-W Wilderness Outfitters
Sandy Podsaid
A-Ward Charters
Robert, Sandra & Alexandria Ward
A&A Fishing Charters-John Armstrong
A&J Trophy Charter-Capt.Jerry Gurske
A & M Charters-Allan Sherman
A Charter You'll Never Forget
Gregory L. Trigg
A Cross Ranch Chuck Sanger
A Gateway Sport Fishing Charter
Rose Lohman
A Hot Lady Sport Fishing Charters
Capts. Peter R. & Cecilia M. Budge
A J Brink Outfitters
James D. Brink
A J Charters
Steve & Andrea Torok
A Lazy H Outfitters- Allen J. Haas
A Seagull Sport Fishing Charters
Capt. Stephen Cedarburg
A SmartCharter-Gerald & Cathy Smart
A. Helfrich Outfitter Aaron D. &
Jonnie F. Helfrich
A. McMillan Outfitter-Andrew G.
McMillan
A. Otto Greene - Otto Greene Guide
A.J.'s Outdoor Services
Aaron Parker, Sr.
A.J. Charters Capt. A. J. Johnson
A1 Charters-Capt. Glenwood Zellmer
AAA Charters -Capt. Ron Langevin
AAA Halibut & Salmon Charters
Jeff & Myrna Rogers
AAA Unpredictable Charter
Capt. Jerry L. Eichmann
Aberdeen Lodge
M. Nevakshonoff
Abitibi-Temiscaming Fly Fishing, Inc.
Lou Cote'
Abram Lake Park-The Pizziols
Absaroka Mountain Lodge
Absolut Charters David Worgum
Absolute Charters-Sean McLean
Absolute Sport Fishing
Access - Alberta Outfitting & Guide
Service Michael Terry
Access to Adventure Ace Charters
Steve Merritt
Ace Sportfishing
Ace Whitewater, Ltd.
Jerry Cook & Ernest Kincaid
Aces of Angling Dennis Gerke
Aces of Angling Chris Tarrant
Acord Guide Service Greg Acord
Action Hunts Charles Loeschen
Action Jackson & M & M
Mkell Welsh
Action Jackson Charters
Charles Jackson
Action Marine Adventure-Jim Frary
Action Outfitters Arvin Stroud
Adair's Outfitting Larry D. Adair
Adirondack Bass & Camping
Mark PeDuzzi
Adirondack Canoes & Kayaks
Harry Spetla
Adirondack Fishing Adv./Beaver
Brook Pete Burns
Adirondack Fishing Adventures
Adirondack Fly Fishing Guide Service
Wes Cunningham
Adirondack Foothills -Sonny & Sheila
Young
Adirondack Guide Service
William Faelten
Adirondack Guide Service
Daniel Josephson
Adirondack Wilderness Experiences
Michael J. Olivette & Craig L. Tryon
Admiral Halibut Charters
William T. Jones
Admiralty Island Charters
Matt Kookesh
Adobie Sport FishingAdriondack Zak
Guide Service James L. Zak
Adventure Bound Alaska
Steven & Winona Weber
Adventure Center
Kirby & Minette Schmidt
Adventure Charter-Brad R. Kimberlin
Adventure Connection- Nate Rangel
Adventure Experiences, Inc.
Tim Kempfe
Adventure Guide Service/O.J. Sports
O.J. Chartrand, Jr.
Adventure Guides of Vermont
Graydon Stevens
Adventure Guiding George Ortman
Adventure Lodges, Inc.
Gerry Pritchett
Adventure North, Ltd.
Bill Murphy
Adventure Northwest Bill Tait
Adventures Afloat
Francis A. & Linda C. Kadrlik
Adventures, Inc. Eddie Lilly
Aerial Adventures
Barry & Lana Prall
Aerial Sportfishing
Affordable Charters-Capt. Rick Lesch
Afognak Wilderness Lodge
Roy & Shannon Randall
After You, Too Capt. Frank Blume
Agape Outfitters & Guide Service
Donna & Wayne Peck
Agassiz Taxidermy & Outfitting
Rick Liske
Agency Bay Lodge Ron/Sharon
Palmer
Aggipah River Trips Bill Bernt
Agimac River Outfitters

Harold St. Cyr
Agnew Lake Lodge Ltd.
Robert & Marlene Kennedy
Ahmic Lake Resort Verna & Rob
Hibbert
Ahukini Fishing For Fun
Aikens Lake Wilderness Lodge
Turenne & Lavack
Air-Dale Flying Service Ltd.
Air Adventures Robert Brouillette
Air Adventures Matt Kimball
Air Adventures Mike McBride
Air Adventures Jeremy Schimmel
Air Kenda Roy & June Bennett
Airboat Charter Clarita B. Fears
AJ's Gun Club Anthony J. Kippes
AK Panhandle Charters
Val Tibbetts
AK Quigley Sport Fishing Charters
James Quigley
AK Recreational Services
Jack Willis
AK Scenic Charters Mike & Ellen
Williams
AK Trophy Hunting & Fishing
Mel Gillis
AK Wilderness Trips Clark &
CherylWhitney
AK. Pac. N.W. Fish Adv.
Jack Oneil
Akers Ferry Canoe Rental
Aksarnerk Adventures
Randy & Donna Lee Bean
Al's Charter Service Al Turner
Al's Charter Service Al Tyrrell
Al's Four Season Taxidermy
Al Gadoury's 6X Outfitters
Allan W. Gadoury
Al Troth Fly Fishing Guide Service
Alfred C. Troth
Al Wind's Trout Futures
Alan Wind
Alagnak Lodge Vin Roccanova
Alameno Outfitting & Guide Service
Frank Alameno
Alan W. Coe
Alani Moku Corp.
Alaska's Cook Inlet Lodge
James Yancy
Alaska's Enchanted Lake Lodge
Dick Matthews
Alaska Fish & Trails Unlimited
Jerald D. Stansel
Alaska's Lost Rainforest Guide
Lavern R. Beier
Alaska's Valhalla Lodge
Capt . Kirk
Alaska's Wilderness Lodge
Tim Cudney
Alaska Ridge Riders, Inc.
Sharon Kanareff
Alaska Adventure Charters
John Padilla
Alaska Adventure Company
Mark Underwood
Alaska Adventures Allen Miknich
Alaska Adventures Charles & Eric
Miknich
Alaska Angler
Chris & Adela Batin
Alaska Anglers David Fandel
Alaska Anglers Ed Tompkins, Sr.
Alaska Angling Adventures
Rafi Jeknavorian
Alaska Angling, Inc. Kent A. Brekke
Alaska Aquamarine Experience, Inc.
Johny Gilson
Alaska Blue Water Roger &
Elizabeth Watney
Alaska Bound Adventures
Robert & George Wagner
Alaska Cast & Blast Kenneth Darrell
McDonald
Alaska Charter Service
Julian J. Gustin
Alaska Clearwater Charters
Tom Standerwick
Alaska Clearwater Sportfishing Adv.
Daniel R. Myers
Alaska Coastal Airlines, Inc.
Dave Brown
Alaska Coastal Outfitters
Brad A. Dennison
Alaska Commercial Emmet
Heidemann
Alaska Connections/Sherlter Lodge
Richard Yamada
Alaska Dawn Charters
Donald R. Byrd
Alaska Deep Sea Adventures
Dustin W. Clark
Alaska Deshka Landing Charters
Gerald Gange
Alaska Dream Charters
Alaska Dream Fishing
William Byrnes
Alaska Drift Boaters Ken & Tim
Robertson
Alaska Farwest Fish Camp
Peter F. Hanson
Alaska Fish Andrew Szczesny
Alaska Fish-N-Fun Charters
Anthony L. & Debra L. Azure
Alaska Fish 'n Fun Charters
Rhon & Sandra Lyons
Alaska Fish Guides George B.
Webster IV
Alaska Fish Tales
Burl D. Weller & Robert Bailey
Alaska Fishing Centre
Raymond Pelland
Alaska Fishing Charters

Delfin Cesar
Alaska Fishing Expedition
John Hart
Alaska Fishing Guide Service
Michael & Jeanne Allen
Alaska Fishing Safaris-Merle R. Frank
Alaska Fishing with Terry Adlam
Alaska Flaggs Kenai-Luren Flagg
Alaska Fly Fishing Safaris
Rolf Sandberg
Alaska Flyfishing Expeditions
Thomas & Virginia Leroy
Alaska Freshwater Safaris
Roger A. Denny, Jr.
Alaska Girl Adventures
James & Joy Baldridge
Alaska Guides Herman Fandel
Alaska Gulf Coast Adventures, Inc.
George Davis
Alaska Holiday Charter Company
Victor Johnson
Alaska Hunting & Fishing
Meryl & Beverly Wolford
Alaska Hunting Co.-Gary Thompson
Alaska Jetboat Charters
James & Lori Kedrowski
Alaska Midnight Sun Charters
Douglas Judge
Alaska Native Charters
Wayne Kvasnikoff
Alaska Native Charters
William Kvasnikoff
Alaska Northern Adventures
Thomas & Katie Prijatel
Alaska Northwind Charters
Donald D. Phillips
Alaska on the Fly
Jeremy Schimmel & Rene Wilson
Alaska Outfitters Bill Stevenson
Alaska Pacific M.W. Fishing
Adventures Jack O'Neil
Alaska Passages
Brian & Julie Hursey
Alaska Peak & Sea's Mark A. Galla
Alaska Premier Charters, Inc.
Theresa Weiser & Calvin Hayashi
Alaska Private Guide Donald Duncan
Alaska Professional Guides
C. Vernon Humble
Alaska Quest Gary Kroll
Alaska Rainbow Lodge
Ron & Sharon Hayes
Alaska Rainbow Unlimited
Clifford Pulis
Alaska River Adventures
George Heim
Alaska River Charters- Robert Krize
Alaska River Journeys-Steve Weller
Alaska River Pros-Kent & Paula Hueser
Alaska River Safaris-Ronald B. Hyde
Alaska Rivers Co.-Gary/ Leon Galbraith
Alaska Salmon Guaranteed Charters
Michael W. Miller
Alaska Saltwater Toney Hannah
Alaska Saltwater Charters
Dianne Dubuc
Alaska Se Air Adventures
Michael & Connie Mills
Alaska Sea Adventures
Robert L. Horchover
Alaska SeaHunter-Mark/Cathie Prindle
Alaska Seakatch Charters
James Van Der Sanden
Alaska Sheefish Haven Lodge
Gail & Robert Vanderpool
Alaska Skagway Outfitters
Chadd Harbaugh
Alaska Skiff Charters, Inc.
Mark & Michelle Kaelke
Alaska Sport Fishing Tours
Les Coates
Alaska Sports & Hobby Expediters
Gerald Silliman
Alaska Sunrise Fishing Adventures
Wayne Pulley
Alaska Tolovana Adventures
Doug Bowers & Kathy Lierniger
Alaska Trail & Sail Adventures
Clint Lentfer, Tadd Owens, Zach Steer
Alaska Travel Tim Montroy
Alaska Trophy Safaris, Inc.
H. Dennis Harms
Alaska Tropic Charters
Floyd M. Jones
Alaska Trout Outfitters
Richard Andres
Alaska Troutfitters
Curt Muse & Bob Andres
Alaska Tuff, Inc.
Charles McGurrem
Alaska Victory Adventures
Vickie Staples
Alaska Walkabouts- Ted Raynor
Alaska Waters Charters-Eric Morisky
Alaska Waters, Inc.-Jim & Wilma Leslie
Alaska Waterways- Don Reesor
Alaska West Air, Inc.- Doug & Danny
Brewer
Alaska Whitewater Kings-Dave Burk
Alaska Wild Salmon Charters
Jason Yeoman
Alaska Wilderness Expeditions
Kevin Fitzgerald
Alaska Wilderness Expeditions
Timonty D. & Marsha A. White
Alaska Wilderness Tours
Ty & Bill Newman
Alaska Wilderness Tours-Steven Parks
Alaska Wilderness Trips
Clark & Cheryl Whitney
Alaska Wildland Patrick Carr
William Fischer Robert Rees

Alaska Wildland Adventures
Kirk Hoessle & Fred Telleen
Alaska Wildlife Charters
Hans Zietlow & Paul Berg
Alaska Yacht Guides
Bob & Ann Widness
Alaska Yachting & Fishing
Dean Jaquish
Alaska/Idaho Fishing Guide
Steve Toth
Alaskan Ecoventures-Glen Tilghman
Alaskan Adventure- Pete Wedin
Alaskan Adventure Charters
Michael Hopley
Alaskan Adventures- Sean Barrow
Alaskan Adventures- Ray Crandall
Alaskan Adventures in the Wilderness
Chuck Hugny
Alaskan Angler Robert Johnson
Alaskan Angler Charters
Joseph & Cynthia Kilian, Jr.
Alaskan Angling Matt Dimmick
Alaskan Charters-Dale & Betty Tyree
Alaskan Combination Charters
Stewart & Jani Trammell
Alaskan Escapes-Kim & Sue Betzina
Alaskan Experience-Jim Bailey
Alaskan Fishing Eagle Charters
L. Tom Smotherman
Alaskan Game Fisher-Mel Erickson
Alaskan Great Adventure Guide
Service- Gregory Lee Franz
Alaskan Helicopter Fishing
John & Anthony Oney
Alaskan Helicopter Fishing
Tony Oney
Alaskan Mountain Safaris
Kenny Lake & Robert Fithian
Alaskan Outback Adventures
George R. Cambell
Alaskan Outback Outfitters
Alaskan Outdoor Adventures
Brad Adams
Alaskan River's & Sea's Fishing Guides
Melvin H. Forsyth, Jr.
Alaskan River Charters
Fred Rhoades
Alaskan Scenic Waterways
Ron Compton
Alaskan Silver Highlander
Dan Rawding
Alaskan Snow Bear-Patrick Grimm
Alaskan Sportfisher
Shawn Friendshuh
Alaskan Sports- Rodney J. Kelly
Alaskan Star Charters-Ken/Toni Wyrick
Alaskan Summertime-Jon/Tena Tippit
Alaskan Trophies-Mark Tuter
Alaskan Trophy Charters
Donald L. Erwin
Alaskan Wildlife & Fishing Adventures
Richard Baker
Alasking Charters-Michael Dick
Chad Thurman
Albany River Outfitters
Jerel & Sharon Johnson
Alberta Native Guide Services
Ken Steinhauer
Alcantara Outfitting Charles Bourque
Alconsen Fly-In Outpost Camps
Alex & Helene Bosse
Aledia Tush C.B.'s Saltwater Outfitters
Alexander Creek Lodge
Alan Budney
Alexander Creek Lodge
Kristi Sherwood
Alexander Creek Lodge, Inc.
Henry Budney Fred Sorensen
Alexander LakeLodge-Dr.Gunter Weis
Algoma Hardware & Sporting Goods
Algonquin Guides, Ltd.-Roy Earley, Jr.
Algonquin Outfitters The Swift Family
Alibi Sportfishing
Alie-Bob Charters-Robert P. Mattson
Alii Kai Sport Fishing Alkali Outfitters
Jerry Satterfield
All-Seasons Catalina Mako Charters
All Alaskan Adventures-Fred C. Heim
All Seasons Guide Service- Jack Smith
Allaman's Montana Adventure
Kenneth C. Allaman
Allanwater Bridge Lodge
Barney & Jane Jelinski
Allegheny Outdoors David L. Heflin
Allen's Diamond Four Wilderness
Ranch
Jim Allen
Allen's Guide Service
Don Allen
Allenberry Resort & Playhouse
Allison Ranch, Inc.
Harold Thomas
Almont Outfitters, Inc./Scenic River
Matthew L. Brown
Aloha Charters Gary Jarvill
Aloha Sportfishing & Charters, Inc.
Alpha-Con, Inc.
Alpine Adventures
Alpine Anglers Fly Shop & Boulder
Mountain Adventures
Rich and Lori Cropper
Alpine Angling & Adventure Travel
Anthony Fotopulos & Bruce Stolbach
Alpine Lodge Danny Stewart
Alpine Outfitters Chris Cassidy
Altenbern Hunting-Clay A. Altenbern
Altland's Kenai Guides
William & Sandy Altland
Alton Matchett
Alyce C. Sport Fishing
Amalijek Lodge Melvin Jeddore
Amaya's Alaska Adventures

Alvaro Amaya
Amber Dawn Charters
Capt. Gregory J. Meyers
Amberg Enterprises William Amberg
Amberjack Charter Boat
American Adrenaline Company, Inc.
Deb Wood & Steven E. Zettel
American Fishing Institution
Clif Paulin
American Hunting Services
American Outfitters James M. Knight
Amethyst Lakes/Tonquin Valley Pack
Trips Wald & Lavone Olson
Amorak Traders-Craig S. Loughran
Amphibian Lake Lodge
Peter & Geri Czorny
Anama Bay Tourist Camp
Alex Letander
Anasazi Angler
Anchor D High Mountain Hunts, Ltd.
Dewy Matthews
Anchor Inn Rodney Vollmer
Anchor Marine Charters
Richard Pendrey
Anchor Pass Charter Co.
Randy Spearing & Craig Trulock
Anchor Point Lodge Dean T.
Murayama & Matthew T. Sugal
Anderson's Guide Service
Ray Anderson
Anderson's Lodge
Dick Fahlman & Jackie Premack
Anderson's Yellowstone Angler
George R. Anderson
Anderson Charter Fishing
Lorry Anderson
Anderson Charters-Curtis Anderson
Anderson Creek Outfitters
Edmondson & Nanette M. Klingback
Anderson River Adventures
Robert D. Anderson
Andrea K.J. Olson
Dennis M. Olson
Andrew Lake Lodge Glen Wettlaufer
Andrew Lake Lodge & Camps
Andy Julius Outfitter & Guide
Leal Andrew Julius
Andy Lake Resort
Marc & Judy Bechard
Angel Haven Lodge Thomas Angel
Christopher Sopp
Angela Rose Adventures
Angell's Resort
Angle Outpost Resort
Paul & Diane Edman
Angler's Alibi, Alagnak River
John Holman & Karl Storath
Angler's Charter Service-Mike White
Angler's Covey, Inc.-Kent/Kurt Brekke
Angler's Edge Paul R. Rice
Angler's Guide Service
William N. Spellman
Angler's Inn Byron Gunderson
Angler's Inn Resort
Jerry & Marie Hemen
Angler's Lodge & Fish Camp
Patrick Tolar
Angler's Paradise-Kip Minnery
Angler's Trail Resort-Ivan/Elsie Fauth
Angler Choice Lodge-Doug Unruh
Angler Paradise - Kulik Peter Ball
Anglers Academy-Bob Sentiwany
Anglers Afloat, Inc.-David J. O'Dell
Anglers Emporium-Joe Dibenedetto
Angling Concepts-Mike Claffy
Angling Unlimited, Inc.
Angus Lake Lodge
Elizabeth & George Tamchina
Angus Wentzell's Hunting & Fishing
Camps Angus Wentzell
Aniak Air Guides- Rick Townsend
Aniak River Lodge-Sam Sudore
Anini Fishing Charters
Ann's Charters -David A. Bernhardt
Anna R -Capt. Franklin A. Rathbun
Another Adventures
Collette M. & Robert E. Golson
Antelope Valley Outfitters, Inc.
Harold E. Smith, Jr.
Antler's Kingfisher Lodge
Doug & Sandra Antler
Antsanen's Lodge-Peter Antsanen
Anvik River Lodge
Clifford Cheryl Hickson
Anytime Charters-Marvin H. Walter
Anytime Cruises, Inc.-James R. Chen
Apache Outfitters-Andrew Marshall
Apache Park Ranches-Erna Sears
Apostle Island Charter Services
Capt. Steve Prevost
Appalachian Backcountry Expeditions,
Inc.
Bill Handy
Apple Annie's Charters, Inc.
Apple Island Charter & Lodge
Dana Anderson
April Point Lodge Eric Peterson
Aquabionics, Inc.
Jack, Jon & Lois VanHyning
Ara Lake Camp Ltd.
Dick & Shirley Fayle
Arch Cape Charters Brenda Hays
Archery Unlimited Outfitters
Marshall Ledford
Arctic Alaska Hunts David S. Morris
Arctic Blue Adventures
Stephen W. Gierke
Arctic Fox Charters Larry E. Bass
Arctic Grayling Guide Service
Reed Morisky
Arctic Lodges Ltd.
Fred & Linda Lockhart

Arctic Maritime, Inc.
Darwom & Kay Waldsmith
Arctic Tern Charter
William Grasser Perry Flotre
Arctic Wilderness Charters, Inc.
Shawn Stephen
Arcularius Ranch- Bill & Diane Nichols
Ardison Charters Jason Young
Argo Charters -L. Branch, J. Long
Argyle Lake Lodge
Chuck & Joan Fernley
Ariola Catfish Farm
Arkansas River Fly Shop
Rodney A. Patch
Arkansas River Tours Robert Hamel/
Margie Geurs
Arnesen's Rocky Point
Edward Arnesen
Around the Bend Outfitters
Will D. Cole, et al
Arrick's Fishing Flies
Arrick Lyle Swanson
Arrow Lake Outfitters
Wayne Ewachewski
Arrowhead Camp Clyde Mason
Arrowhead Guide Service
R. Van Middlesworth
Arrowhead Lodge & Resort
Kathy Wilson
Arrowhead Outfitters, Inc.
Howard Tieden
Arrowhead River Adventures
Don L.Kirkendall
Artesian Wells Resort
Paul & Barb Scidel
Ashambie Outpost Ltd.
Scott & Lynda Marvin
Ashland Fly Shop Guide Service
Mark E. Swisher
Ashnola Guide Outfitters
Clarence Schneider
Ashuanipi Hunting Outfitters
Francis Rioux
Aspen Canyon Ranch, LLC
Steven Roderick
Aspen Lodge @ Estes Park
Tim Resch
Aspen Trout Guide & Outfitter, Inc.
Scott Alan Nichols
Aspen Wilderness Outfitters, Ltd.
Tim McFlynn
Assoc. Fishing Charters of Milwaukee
Astco Burr Henriksen
Astraddle A Saddle, Inc.
Gary Bramwell
At East Sport Fishing
Richard LaChance
At the Summit Outfitting Service
Athabasca Camps-Cliff Blackmur
Athabasca Fishing Lodges
Cliff Blackmu
Athabasca Lone Wolf Camps
Brian MacDonald
Athapap Lodge Stan Bowles
Atikaki Wilderness Camp
Bob Jackson
Atlantic Adventures-Brian McVicar
Atlantic Salmon Sports Fishing, Inc.
Bill Bennett
Augu Bassmasters-Scott Calhoun
Auke Bay Charters-Richard A. White
Auklet Charter Services-David Janka
Auld Reekie Lodge
Doug & Cathie White
Aune's Absaroka Angler- Scott Aune
Aurora Charters
Clifford Chamberlin,Carl & Kim
Hughes
Rodney W. & Stacey A. Mitchell
Aurora Sport Fishing & Tours
Austin's Alaska Adventures
Jerry & Clara Austin
Austin's Service Austin Tide
Autumn Brown Outfitting
Alvin Blakley
Avalanche Basin Outfitters
Douglas Caltrider
Aventure Excursions
Ralph & Lauren Mirsky
Avila Beach Sportfishing
Avon Outfitters
Robert D. Cunningham
Awesome Lake Lodge Len Rich
Aztec Curt Wegener
B-Bar-C Outfitters
Michael J. Stockton
B-Fast Charters
Mike Bartlett
B-Obe Charters
Robert Shepard
B & B Fishing Adventures, Inc.
E.F. 'Bus' Bergmann III
B & B Guide Service- Hal J. Borg
B & C Charters- Mary Baringer
B & D Outfitters- Robert D. Frisk
B & J Hunting Camp
Robert W. Wells
B & L Cabins & Outfitters Ltd.
Blaine & Linda Cunningham
B & R Drift Trips- Brian Greco
B & W Guide Service Lawrence
Beagley
B Bar B Ranch Inn
B Bar Two Outfitters
Lance C. Vines
B R Rhyne Guide & Outfitting
Bruce L. Rhyne
B&T Professional Outfitters
Thomas Barrett
B. Karklin Outfitter & Guide Service
Barry Karklin
B.K. Service's- Brian Kelley

BA Charters- Brett Aldridge
Babcock Creek Outfitters
Leroy E. Books
Babe Wojslaw-Michael Wojslaw
Baby J Fishing Charters
Tom & Darcy Stetson
Back 40 Wing & Clay, Inc.
Back Country Guides & Outfitters
William A. Yeagher
Back Country Logistical Services
Greg L. Finstad
Back Country Logistics
Richard Wysong
Back Country Outfitter & Charter
Elbert Loomis
Backcountry Angler Backcountry
Outfitter, Inc.
David L. Guilliams, Sr.
Backcountry Outfitters-Jeff Moore
Backcounty Angler-Gregg Jorgensen
Backlash Charters
Backwoods Adventures
Todd Braley
Badger Creek Outfitter-Joe E. Nelson
Bain Lake Camp
Beverly & Howard Dobbs
Bain Lake Lodge
Northwoods Angler Ltd.
Bait-Masters Hunting Camps
Brain E. & Sylvia Hoffart
Baja 31, Charter Boat Baja AirVentures
Kevin Warren
Baja Alaskan Experiences
Charles L. Chandler
Baker's Guide Service-Ray Baker
Bakers Crossing Ranch-Mary Hughey
Bakers Narrows Lodge Ltd.
Dave & Gene Kostuchuk
Bald Mountain Air Service, Inc.
Jeannie G. Porter
Bald Mountain Outfitters, Inc.
Terry Pollard
Bali Hai Sport Fishing, Inc.
Ballantyne's Indian Lake Lodge
Scott & Leigh Ballantyne
Bally Creek Camp
David & Cathi Williams
Balmy Weather Donald Tirrell
Banzai Capt. Ralph Miyata
Bar-B-Q Charters
Sandra K. Petersen
Bar-Lyn Charters Barry Wise
Bar-X-Bar Ranch Ed Pugh
Bar Diamond Ranch/Ferrier Outfitters
Dellis Ferrier
Bar Lazy L Family, Inc.-Gary Yeager
Bar S Harry Simon
Bar Six Outfitters
Terry D. Throckmorton
Bar T Outfitters
Mark, Phillip & Joanne Talmadage
Bar Z X Ranch & Lodge-Dean Lampton
Barbie Doll III & IV Charter
Capts. Dave & Lou Mayer
Barbless Hook Fly Fishers Guide
Jim Shuttleworth
Barker River Trips, Inc.
John A. K. Barker
Barking Trout Guide Service
John M. McClure
Barkwick Camp
Bill & Doreen Wickens
Barlow Outfitting
Robert L. Barlow
Barnes' Outfitters, Inc.
Barnes Brothers, Inc. Jack R. Joyce
Barney's Fishing & Tours
Barony Lodge - Hewitt Lake
Michael Barron
Barr Woods Resort-Burrows Family
Barrel E Steven Childs
Barrett Park Outfitters
Jack Steenbergen
Barrier Bay Resort-Kevin & Gail Nally
Barrier Beach Resort Scott O'Bertos
Barrier Dam Guide Service
Donald Glaser
Bartlett Creek Outfitters-Mike Smith
Bartley J. Spieth -Richard L. Spieth
Basin Outfitters Ken E. Wissel
Basket Lake Camp Olga North
Bass Adventures
Bass Fishing Charters-Jim Sweeney
Bass Fishing with Darl Ray Hagey
Bass Isle Resort
Bass Unlimited-Lawrence W. Burdette
Baston Catfish Farm
Bator Boy Outfitting Geraldine &
Michael Bator
Batten Kill Canoe, Ltd.-Jim Walker
Battenkill Lodge-Capt. Bob Storc
Battle Creek Outfitters-Ronald Gayer
Battle Creek Outfitters
Larry Richtmyer
Battle River Wilderness Retreat
Tim Conway
Bay Breeze Yacht Charter
Bill Allgaier,Harry Ashton,Ken Coffman
Bay Excursions Karl Stoltzfus
Bay Resort
Bay Run Charters
Capt. Matt Stevens
Bay Springs Marina
Bay Star Ventures
Paul A. Starner
Bay Store & Resort
Frank & Laura Walsh
Bay Street Outfitters Bayfield Fishing
& Sailing Charters
Bayfield Trollers Assoc.
Bayside Charters-Bert Stromquist
Bayside Inn James Hamilton, Jr. &

Mallory Darcey
Bayside Inn-Michael Massa
Bayview Camp & Cottages
Barb & Mike Batsford
Bayview Charters, Inc.-Danny Wilson
Bayview Lodge George Hardy
BB's Guide Service Robert Ball
BC Charters- Capt. Bill Crozier
BDS Investments-Bill Breedlove
Beabout- Dennis Beabout
Beachwater II Charter Boat
Beacon Landing Motel & Marina
David A. & Betty J. McCloskey
Beagle Charters-Leanne & Jeff Pilcher
Beam's On The Prairie-David J. Beam
Beamer's Landing/Hells Canyon Tours
Jim & Jill Koch
Bean Hole Bean Jim Guide Service
James Cunningham
Bear's Den Outfitters, Inc.
Bruce C. Delorey
Bear Basin Camp-Francis Fox
Bear Cat Outfitters-Seth E. Peters
Bear Country Sporting Goods
Bear Creek Guest Ranch
William Beck
Bear Creek Lakes
Bear Creek Lodge
Bear Creek Ranch- Edward Wintz
Bear Cub Adventure Tours
Gary Marchuk
Bear Guiding Service
Kim & Roxanne Molyneaux
Bear Lake Guides & Outfitters
Dirk & Traute Schuirmann
Bear Lake Lodge Sandy Beardy
Bear Mountain Lodge-Carroll Gerow
Bear Necessity Charters-James Davis
Bear Paw Charters-John/Denise Ogle
Bear Paw Guide & Outfitters
Dennis & Irene Smith
Bear Paw Lodge
Bear Paw Mountain Outfitters
Eric M. Olson
Bear Paw Outfitters Sam & Susan Ray
Bear Pw Lodge-Thomas Kreinheder
Bear Ridge Fishing Company
John & Lynn Pizza
Bear River Lodge, Ltd.-John Priebe
Bear River Outfitters, Inc.-Brad Ipsen
Bear Spring Camps-Peg/Ron Churchill
Bear Tracks Lodge-Randall McDuffie
Bear Trail Lodge
Charlie & Kristine Haussermann
Bear Valley Outfitters
Chris Switzer
Beardown Adventures
Neil Webster
Beardsley Outfitting & Guide Service
Tim Beardsley
Beartooth Flyfishing Daniel J. Delekta
Beartooth Plateau Outfitters
Ronnie L. Wright
Beartooth Ranch & JLX Outfitters
James E. Langston
Beartooth Whitewater-Randow Parker
Beartrack Charters
Todd Wich & William Helms
Beartrack Charters
Ken & Darlene Wicks
Beartrack Hunting Consultants
John Abernathy
Beartracks Lodge
Frank & Karetta Barrett
Beartracks Lodge
Frank Barrett & Dan Reiling
Beartrap Express
Johnny C. France
Beaten Path Outfitters
Jeffery Wayne Baylor
Beaufort Delta Tours
Willard Hagen & Dolly Carmichael
Beaufort Outfitting & Guiding
Services Tuktoyaktuk HTC
Beaver Canoe Rental, Inc.
Beaver Canyon Guide & Outfitter
Greg Pink
Beaver Creek Boat Dock
Everett Williams
Beaver Creek Stables
Steve Bruce Jones
Beaver Island Charters
Capt. Elwood V. Baker
Beaver Lake Trout Club
John Litwhiler
Beaver Lodge Fly-Inn Ltd.
Wellace & Elaine Johnson
Beaver Lodge Ltd.-Wayne Thomas
Beaver Mountain Lodge/Migules
Mountain
Dave Toms
Beaver Mountain Outfitters
C. Duain Morton
Beaver State Adventures
Robert L. Snook
Beaverfoot Lodge
Don Wolfenden
Beaverhead Anglers
Paul George Wiedeman
Beaverhead Outfitters
Jack Diamond
Beaverhead/Bighole River Angle
Shawn Lester Jones
Beaverkill Valley Inn
Darlene O'Dell
Beaverland Camp-The Dykstra's
Beavertail Outfitters-Dennis Rehse
Becca's Haven-Phyllis/Rick Flewelling
Becharof Lodge-Mark LaRae LaCrosse
Beck's Treks Robert H. Beck, Jr.
Becuna Charter Boat
Behram Outfitting-Russell Behrman

Belgian Queen-Capt. Rod Baudhuin
Belinda V. Charters
Shapleigh & Saundra Howell
Bella Coola Outfitting Co., Ltd.
Leonard Ellis
Bells Marina
Beluga Bob's Guide Service
Robert W. Honea
Ben Heilman Shady Oaks
Bequest Guide Service-Bob Sedlacek
Berean & Sons' Enterprises
William Berean
Berger's Trading Post
Elizabeth Lessard & Glennda Scott
Bergie's Guide Service-Bruce Bergman
Berglund's Outposts
Wayne & Carol Berglund
Bering Straits Exploration & Charter Serv.- Louis H. Green, Jr.
Bernie Fishing Charts-Bernard White
Bertrand Guide Service
Kenneth E. Bertrand
Besnard Lake Lodge
BEST Adventures-Bobby Lowe
Best Guide & Outfitters
Donald L. Ankrum
Betts Kelly Lodge-Keith Betts
Betula Lake Resort
Elmer & Yolande Bigelow
Beyer's Charter Service
Ronald R. Beyer
Beyond Boundaries Expeditions
Mike Trotter
Beyond La Ronge Lodge
Andy & Beatrice Fecke
Bienville Plantation-Steve Barras
Big-Un's Guide Service
Terry M. Brasel
Big Al's Charter Allen Clark
Big Bass Guide Service
Big Bay Marina & Fishing Resort
Kay Knierim
Big Bear Camp
Claude & Lucille Charbonneau
Big Bear Lodge, Inc. Alan R. Harris
Big Bird Charters
James T. Conder
Big Bite Charter Boat
Big Blue Charters
Michael R. Keating
Big Bluff Ranch
Big Bones Unlimited/Catspaw Ranch
Dennis E. Schutz
Big Boys, Inc.-Fred Pentt/Larry Carlson
Big Buffalo Resort- Lynette Ulrich
Big Cedar Lodge
Big Cimarron Outfitter
Matt Wade Munyon
Big Creek Lake Front Resort
Jim & Nancy Heintz
Big Dan's Cheap Charters
Dan Martin
Big Dick's Wild Alaskan Adventures
Richard L. Nadeau
Big Dipper Charters-Dave Minister
Big Dipper Guides-Joseph Hanes
Big Dog's Alaska Guide Service
Gary & Bev Lindstrom
Big Eddy Camp Solomon Carriere
Big Family Charters
Capt. Dick Lettenberger
Big Fish Charter Boat
Big Fisherman Charters
Thomas & Bruce Knowles
Big Foot Fly Shop
Big Foot Guide Service
Earl D. Lowe
Big Four Wilderness Camp
Stan & Joan Wilson
Big Gama Outfitters Ing. Carlos Gonzalez Hermosillo
Big Game Hunts, LLC
Ralph A. Babish
Big Grass Outfitters
Tom & Judy Usunier
Big Hole River Outfitters
Craig Fellin
Big Hook Wilderness Camp
Steve & Evie Hartle
Big Horn Outfitters
Lester Dean Hawkins
Big Horn Outfitters R. Vernon Mann
Big Horn River Lodge
Phil Gonzales
Big Horn River Outfitters-Gael T. Larr
Big Horn Trout Shop-Steve M. Hilbers
Big Indian Guide Service
Big Intervale Salmon Camp
Ruth Schneeberger
Big Jim's Charters-Jim & Jane Preston
Big John's Charter Service
John Malouf
Big Jon Pro-Team Charters, Inc.
Chrissie Hills
Big K Guest Ranch & Guide Service
Charles Kesterson
Big Mike's Charters-Michael Boettcher
Big Moore's Run Lodge, Ltd.
Big Netley Outfitters
George Walker
Big Nine Outfitters-Barry Tompkins
Big North Lodge-Alex & Pat Rheault
Big Northern Lodge & Outfitters
John Eisner & Ian McKay
Big Pond Sportfishing-Charles A. Hoff
Big Rack Outfitters-Eric Lee Hamilton
Big Redd's River Guide Service
William H. Harrison
Big River Camps, Inc.-R. W. Skinner
Big River Hunting Club & Kennel
Rich & Rose Baumgartner
Big Rivers Guide Service-Don Burks
Big Rock Hunting & Fishing Lodge
Gus Borkofsky
Big Rock Resort-Karl & Karen Kelnhofer
Big Salmon Outfitters
Richard Kehoe Wayman
Big Sand Lake Lodge
Don & Lynn McCrea
Big Sandy Lodge-Bernard Kelly
Big Sky Charter & Fish Camp
Joseph F. Connors
Big Sky Expeditions
Big Sky Flies & Guides
Gary McCutcheon
Big Sky Guide & Outfitters
Tom D. Brogan
Big Sky Overland Cruises
Big Smoky Outfitting, Ltd.
Gary & Ricki Kruger
Big Smoky Valley Outfitters
William A. Berg
Big T's Fishing Guide Service
Timothy W. Linngren
Big Trophy Outfitters-John Hatley
Big Vermillion Lodge
Jim & Doreen Kusick
Big Whiteshell Lodge
Henry & Diana Bergen
Bigfoot Campground Guide Service
Bighorn Angler Donald R. Cooper
Bighorn Angler-Mike /Tom McClure
Bighorn Country Outfitters
George J. Kelly
Bighorn Outfitters
George Butcher & Dave Melton
Bighorn Outfitting
Dan C. Cooper & Dan Moyer
Bighorn River Fin & Feathers
James L. Pickens
Bighorn River Lodge-Phil Y. Gonzalez
Bighorn River Shop/Lazy Boot Outfitters
Bighorn Trout Shop
Hale C. Harris & Steve Hilbers
Bighorn Troutfitters, Inc.
Joseph D. Caton
Bilak's Stillwater Adventures
Richard P. Bilak
Bill's Alaska Charters William Cox
Bill's Fishing Guide Service
William Deavilla
Bill's Guide Service-Keith Bockhahn
Bill Conley, Bill M. Matejka
Bill's Riverboat Service
William Bohlscheid
Bill Buster Charters
Bill Hedlund Guide Service
William E. Hedlund
Bill Johnson Outfitters
Bill Martin Fish Alaska, Inc.
William R. & Mary K. Martin
Bill Mitchell Outfitters, Inc.
William H. & Karen Mitchell
Bill Mueller Fishing Guide Service
Bill Mueller
Bill Roley Guide Service-Bill Roley
Bill Urie Guide Service-Bill Urie
Bill Zup's Camps-Mark & Kathy Zup
Billiken Charters
Frank & Linda Sheppard
Billingsley Ranch Outfitters
Jack Billingsley
Billup's Landing
H.D. "Smitty" Smith, III
Billy Goat's Bait & Tackle
Biloski Resort Bernie & Dorothy
Biltmore Resort Mrs. Jarvis
Bing Nelson Guide Service
Bing Nelson
Birch Bark Charters-Birch Robbins
Birch Creek Outfitters
William W. Galt
Birch Creek Outfitters
Laddie Peverley
Birch Creek Outfitters-Rick Peverley
Birch Grove Resort-Elaine Goodrum
Birch Island Lodge-Stephen J. Brooks
Birch Island Lodge & Air Service
Gary & Margo Schroeder
Birch Island Resort-Mike/Wendy Reid
Birch Knoll Ranch-Duke Hust
Birch Lake Lodge-Barry/ Edith Labine
Birch Point Camp-Lodge-The Greens
Birch Point Resort-June & Bob Gibbs
Birchy Point Lodge- Linda Mercer
Bird's Nest Lodge & Outfitters
Steve Gottschalk
Bird River Outfitters Ron Alexander
Biscotasing Sportsmans Lodge
Eddy & Terry Peters
Bit O Lab Kennels
James & Marilyn Bitney
Bitterroot Anglers
Andre August Carlson
Bitterroot Outfitters Thomas L. Henderson
BKD Guide Service-Capt.Kirby LaCour
Blachford Lake Lodge
Mike Freeland & Bob Stephen
Black's Camp Pam Blackmon
Black's Crescent Beach Resort
Jerry & Deanna Pekar
Black's Hunting & Fishing Camps
Juanita Black
Black-Jac Charters-Capt. Jack Swartz
Black Bear Camp-Vicki & Robert Lowe
Black Bear Island Lake Lodge
Earl Mockellky
Black Bear Lodge-Gilbert Pelletier
Black Bear Outfitter
Black Bear Outpost Camps
Mary & Walter Fleming
Black Brook Guides-Denni Aprill
Black Butte Outfitters
J.O. Hash, Jr.
Black Dog Fishing Guides
Patrick D. Carter
Black Elk Outfitters, LTD-Dell H. Bean
Black Farms
Black Fox Lodge
Nancy Conklinand, Eddie Metcalf
Black Fox Lodge/K and M Ventures
Kris Draper
Black Hawk II Capt. Peter Clark
Black Heart Charters Bill & Barbara Swearingiz
Black Island Resort-Mike/Barb Sergio
Black Mesa Lodge-Tom McLeod
Black Mountain Enterprises
Milt Sherman
Black Mountain Invest. Ltd.
Nowell R. May
Black Mountain Outfitters
Black Otter Guide Service
Duane Neal
Black Pine Beach Resort
Bob & Lynn Scharenbroich
Black Rapids Salmon Club
George Curtis
Black River Outfitters, Ltd.
William F. Drude, Jr.
Black Rock Resort
Sverre & Hildur Kjevik
Black Timber Outfitters
Carrol M. Johnson & Kent Fischer
Black Top Mountain Ranch
Eldon M. Berry
Blackbird's Fly Shop & Lodge
Blackhawk River Runs
Blacktail Ranch Sandra Renner
Blackwell's Guide Service
Mike & Joyce Blackwell
Blaine R. Southwick Outfitting, Ltd.
Blaine Southwick
Blake's Wilderness Outpost
John & Marie Blake
Bliss Creek Outfitters
Tim Doud & Doris Roesch
Bloodvein River Outfitters
Nick Arseniuk
Bloomfield's Ballantyne Bay Resort
George & Fran Bloomfield
Blue Bayou Charter Boat
Blue Bronna Guiding & Outfitting
Glenn Brown
Blue Chip II Charters
Capt. Ken "Cubby" Smith
Blue Eagle, Inc.-Russell & Gene Loomis
Blue Fin Charters
Capt. Joseph Anderson
Blue Fin Sport Fishing Charter
Terry Gray
Blue Fox Camp -Dr. Paul R. Morgan
Blue Hawaii Sportfishing
Blue Heron Charters James Hansen
Blue Jacket Enterprises
Peter Kimzey
Blue Marlin, Inc.
Blue Max Charters-Capt. Jim Hirt
Blue Mountain Lodge-The Malott's
Blue Mountain Outfitters
Shawn M. Bentley
Blue Nun Sportfishing
Blue Quill Anglers, Inc.
Mark A. Harrington
Blue Quill Fly Co.-Robert E. Krumm
Blue Raven Charters
Frank Demmert, Jr.
Blue Ribbon Charters
Richard D. Lindsey
Blue Ribbon Fishing Charters
Blue Ribbon Fishing Tours
Dale D. Siegle
Blue Ribbon Guide Service
Anthony A. Schoonen
Blue Ribbon Jewel Flyfishing Guide Service
Blue Ridge Angler
Blue Rivers Guide Service
Blue Sky Charter-Kevin C. Fromm
Blue Sky Charters-James Wilson
Blue Star Charters-Brett Stillwaugh
Blue Water Charter-Terrance L. Clark
Blue Water Fishing-Capt. Ken Mandy
Blue Yonder Charters
Capt. Dan Peterson
Blueberry Hill Outfitters
Ken & Lorraine Polley
Bluefish Services-Greg Robertson
Bluewater Charters
Blunt Mountain Outfitters
Norm Blaney
Bo's Fishing Guide Service
Raymond Ansel
Boardwalk Wilderness
Douglas Ibbetson
Bob's Guide Service-Robert F. Lipo
Bob's Guide Service-Robert Wigham
Bob's Tackle Box-Bob A. Cleverley
Bob's Trophy Charters-David Morris
Bob's Walkabout Fly Fisher's Guide
Robert P. Shafer
Bob-Kat Charters Tom Markley
Bob Baccus Guide Service-Bob Baccus
Bob Brown's Guided Sportfishing
E. B. Brown
Bob Claypole Guide Service
Bob Gross
B-C Guide Service
Bob Jacklin's Fly Shop, Inc.
Bob Jacklin
Bob Marino Outfitters-Bob Marino
Bob Marshall Wilderness Ranch
Virgil B. Burns
Bob Roberts Outdoors
Bobby L. Roberts
Bob Snyder's Web Page
Bob Stone's Guide Service
Robert P. Stone
Boggy Creek Outfitting
Maxwell Nemertchek
Bogie Mtn./Besa River Outfitters
Pal Gillis
Boiling Spring Resort
Gerald Koogler
Bojola Charter Boat
Bolhouse Charters
Gary and George Bolhouse
Bolin Sportfishin Charters
Bolinder's Country Store
Terry Bolinder
Bolton Guest Ranch Kay Bolton
Bolton Lake Lodge, Inc.
Brian Dick
Bon Chance-Menton "Bobby" Chouest
Bongo's Sportfishing Headquarters
Bonne Amie Charter Boat
Bonnet Plume Outfitters, Ltd.
Charlie Stricker
Bonnie Lake Camping
Tom & Paula Stephanie
Bonzo's Guide Service-Jeff Brennan
Booi's Wilderness Lodge & Outposts Ltd.-Jim & Tracy Booi & Family
Boomerang Resort-Debby Lindsey
Boomerang Sportfishing
Booth Trophy Fishing
David Booth
Borde Du Lac Lodge
E.K. & Maribeth Crowell
Border Outposts Dave Schneider
Border View Lodge-Mike Trueman
Borderland Lodge
Eric & Jan Thompson
Borderland Lodge & Outfitters
Boreal Camp Services
Morton G. Harbicht
Borealis Charters-Tom Cocklin
Boren Outdoor Adventures, Inc.
Elisabeth Boren
Borg's Guide Service -Hal L. Borg
Borgers Sport Fishing Charters, Inc.
Capt. Jaco Borger
Born 'N' Raised on the San Juan River
Tim R. Chavez
Bottom Line Charters
Capt. John Bartlett
Boulder Mountain Ranch
Boulder River Fly Fishing Company
Bounty Hunter Charter-Joseph Laba
Bow River Troutfitters-Bowes Ranch
Brabant Lodge
Brabazon Expeditions
Patrick & Kathi Pellett
Bracke's Guide Service-John Bracke
Brad Downey's Angler's Edge
Brad Garrett Guide Service
Brad Garrett
Bradford & Co. Guide Services, Ltd.
Myles Bradford
Brado's Fishing-Keith Brady
Brady Guide Service-Jeffrey L. Brady
Branch's Seine River Lodge
Carl & Joan Branch
Branch River Guide & Tour Service
Doreen & Walter Corcoran
Brandts' Resort-Wayne/Linda Brandt
Branson Hwy. K Marina-Lee Neary
Brant Oswald Fly Fishing Service
Brant Konrad Oswald
Bray's Charter Service-Tommy Bray
Bray's Island Plantation
Brazos River Ranch-Ron Prieskorn
Bread 'n Butter Charters
Kenneth R. & June A. Miller
Break Away Charter Boat
Breakaway Adventures
Eric Yancey
Breckenridge Outfitters
Crosby, Beane, Davis & Beane
Breken Guided Trophy Hunts
Ken & Brenda Maxymowich
Brereton Lake Resort-The Nedohins
Bressler Outfitter, Inc.-Joe Bressler
Bressler Outfitters-Gary Beebe
Brett's Guide Service-Brett Gianella
Bridger Mountain Guide Service
James R. Brogan
Bridger Outfitters-David B. Warwood
Bridger Teton Outfitters
Randy Foster
Briggs Guide Service-Jerry Briggs
Briggs Guide Service-Bret A. Clark
Brightwater Alaska, Inc.-Charles Ash
Brightwater House-RichardChesmore
Briska Charters
Bristol Bay Anglers-Chip Henward
Bristol Bay Charter Adventures
Patrick & Diedre O'Neill
Bristol Bay Coastal Charters
Anthony G. & Deborah A. Bartlett
Bristol Bay Lodge
Ronald & Margaret McMillan
Bristol Bay Outfitters
Robert Heyano & William Chaney
Bristol Bay River Charters
James V. Grimes
Bristol Bay Sportfishing, Inc.
Bruce Johnson
Bristol Charters-James Archer Corbin
Broad Ripple Bassmasters
James Wagers
Broken Antler Outfitters
Jacob H. Kauffman
Broken Arrow Lodge
Erwin and Sherry Clark
Broken Hart Ranch-Lee I. Hart
Broken Heart Guest Ranch
Bernard C. Nieslanik
Broken Horn Outfitters
Ken D. Murdoch
Brooks Cottages
Chris & Christine Brooks
Brooks Lake Lodge-Will Rigsby
Brookville Striper Federation
Richard Johnson
Brown's Clearwater West Lodge/ Outposts Barry Brown
Brown's Guide Service
Brown's Landing Perch Charters
Jerry Brown
Browner's Guide Service
Raymond G. Kitson/Hank Bevington
Brownie's Charters Wayne B. Brown
Bruce Brock Darrell Mittlesteadt
Bruce Nelson's Float Fishing Service
Bruce Nelson
Brunswick Lake Lodge
Marcel Dumais
Bruton's Guide Service
C. Warren Bruton
Bryan-Sherman Packing
Mike Bryan & Bink Sherman
Bryant's Hunting Adv.-Larry Bryant
Bryce Outfitting-Jim Bryce
BS Flies & Tackle-Bill Schiess
BSL Enterprises-Scott Taylor
Bubba Charters- Eryl J. Peterson
Buccaneer Charters-Arthur Myers
Buck's Guide Service-Roger Markham
Buck's TrophyLodge-Shelly Lawrence
Buck & Bingwood Cabins
Brock & Brenda Chisholm
Buck Horn Charters
Capt. Harris Quesnel
Buck Point Lodge & Resort
Jack & Margaret Weiler
Buckhorn Ranch Outfitters
Harry T. Workman
Bucks Livery, Inc.- Ben Breed
Bucksaw Point Resort & Marina
Gale Nichols
Buckskin Trails-Glenn W. Pritchard
Bud's Bait & Tackle-Curtis E. George
Bud Lilly's Trout Shop-Dick Greene
Bud Nelson Outfitters-Bud Nelson
Budd's Gunisao Lake Lodge
Jim & Brendon Budd
Buddy's Guide Service
Buddy Bradham
Buffalo Creek Outfitters, Inc.
Mike L. Prescott
Buffalo Horn Ranch, Inc.
James H. Walma
Buffalo Lake Outfitters
Brad Steinhoff
Buffalo Point International Resort
The Thunder Family
Buford Guide Service-Tom Tucker
Buggywhip's Fish & Float Service
Jim Blackburn
Bugle Masters Troy J. Hicks
Bugle Ridge Outfitters-John Keenan
Buglin' Bill Outfitters -Bill Allen
Bulchitna Lake Lodge
William Mazoch
Bull Moose Camp-Tom/SharaMetzner
Bull Moose Outfitters
Albert & Terri de Lighte
Bull Mountain Outfitters
Harry Wayne Garver
Bull Mountain Outfitters, Inc.
Vicki L. Hale
Bull Ridge Guide Service
Charles F. Marques
Bull Run Outfitters-Bud Heckman
Bullock's Gowganda Lake Camp
Dave & Mary Bullock
Burdick Guide Service
Shaun A. & Walter A., Jr. Burdick
Burnside HTA - Tundra Camps
Boyd Warner & Sam Kapolak
Burnsville Docks, Inc.
David Waldron
Burnt Land Brook Ltd.
Leroy G. Scott
Burntland Brook Lodge
Joan & Barrie Duffield
Burton Charters Hugh Burton
Burton Hunting Service
Kenneth D. Burton
Bush Fishing Perry S. Burress
Bush Guiding Bobby Kempson
Bush Ventures Peter Turcotte
Bush Wacker Fly Fishing Service John & Cidi Godsey
Buster's Guide Service
Buster Loving
Buzzy's River Adventures
Phillip Franklin
BW Guide Service, Inc.
Butch & Lance A.Wicks
By the Sea Enterprises
Avery G. Simmons
C-B Ranch-Sandy VanderLans
C-Cat Sportfishing Charters
C-Frog/Blackjaw Bandit Charters
Capt. Jim Dennis
C-Jo Charters-Joe R. Collins
C & D Guides & Outfitters
Charles Dickson
C & E Enterprises
Clifford & Ernestine Alexander
C & M Adventures-Ron Bloxham
Tim Crist,James - Ryan Miller
C & R Outfitters-Richard Bennett
C Activities
C Angel Charter Boat
C B Three Charters
Robert R. & Cheryl Wambach
C K Hunting & Fishing Camp
Darrell Copeland
C&J's Alakan Safaris
James & Connie Sargeant

C. C. Charters Chad Christoffer
C.C. Anderson Guide Service
Claude Anderson
Cabin Creek Outfitters-Tony Tingle
Cache Creek Lodge
Bonnie Hutcheson
Cache Creek Lodge-Robert Lane
Caddisfly Angling Shop
Brian R. Barnes, Jr.
Caddo Pass Lodge
Pershing & Marcille Hughes
Caddy Lake Resort
Wayne Mooney & Shirley Whitehead
Cadez Charter Service
Captains Phil & Mark Cadez
Cadisfly Angling Shop
Chris Daughters
Cail's Private Salmon Pools on the
Miramichi-Stephen J. Cail
Cal's Hunting & Fishing-Calvin White
Call of the Wild
Boyce D. "Bud" Rawson, Sr.
Call of the Wild Outfitters
Nick Gorda
Calumet Harbor Sport Fishermen
Dick Ruess
Camelot Farms-Danny Garrett
Cameron & Smith Fly Fishing
Cameron Guiding-Stew Cameron
Cameron Outfitters-Del Cameron
Cameron Wildlife
Sammie Faulk & Steve German
Camp Anjigami
George & Elizabeth Young
Camp Baker Outfitters
Donald W. Johnson
Camp Bendeleben-John Elmore
Camp Branch Marina-David George
Camp CanUSA-Nelson/Brenda Leudke
Camp Conewango-Doug Lynett
Camp Grayling-
Margy, Michel & Ed White
Camp Gutelius on Dog Lake
Mark & Marta Lamoureux
Camp Hide Away
Terry & Brenda Mihaychuk
Camp Horizon
Denny & Ruth Dusky
Camp Kinisoo Ltd
Christopher and Sheila Brown
Camp La Plage The Bedards
Camp Lochalsh Ltd.
Chris & Lynne Wilson
Camp Manitou-Jerry Kostiuk
Camp McIntosh-Jim/Madeleine Roger
Camp Midgard- Manfred Mueller
Camp Narrows Lodge-Tom Pearson
Camp Quetico-Marshall/Karen Manns
Camp Raymond-Fred & Barb Roth
Camp Richfield
Tom, Sharon & Charlotte Kmetz
Camp Wanikewin Lodge
Ken & Dee Baker
Camp Waterfall-Nancy/Rob Rummery
Camp Wenasaga Brian Pudil
Campbell's Cabins
Robert, John & Jay Handberg
Campbell's Fishing Charters
Clyde & Vicki Campbell
Campbell Air, Inc.-Kevin Campbell
Campfire LeRoy & Shelly Pruitt
Campfire Adventures
Camps of Acadia
James & Kathleen Lynch
Campsall Outfitters-Hank Campsall
Can-Am Outfitters Ltd.
Chris or Cindy Shea
Can-Do Fishing Charters
Rick V. Sauve
Canada North Lodge Ltd.
Mike & Julie Hoffman
Canadian Adventure Safaris
Odd Aasland
Canadian Fly-In Fishing, Ltd.
Jim Thomas
Canadian Northern Outfitters, Inc.
Bill Lynch
Canadian Trophy Lodges Ltd.
Enns & Keller
Canadian Whitetails Canadian
Wilderness Camps & Outfitters
Wolf & Gica Lehnhoff
Canadian Wilderness Outposts
Jordie & Mitzi Turcotte
Canadian Wilderness Travel Ltd.
Cannonball Charters-Foy Nevers
Canoe Arctic, Inc.-Alex Hall
Canoe Canada Outfitters & Outpost
Cabins-Bud Dickson & Jim Clark
Canoe Country Cabins & Campground
Bob Olson
Canoeing House/Blue Ribbon Guide
Allan L. Anderson
Canoose Camps
Thomas Mosher or Faith Sonier
Canterbury Hunting & Fishing
Shawn Collicott
Cantrell Canoes & Rafts/Ultimate
Rafting Richard Cantrell
Canvasback Charters Tim Fales
Canyon Marine Whitewater Exp.
Gregory Wright Felt
Canyon Outfitters, Inc.
George & Lynette Hauptman
Canyons Incorporated
Leslie W. Bechdel
Cap'n Patty Charters
Michael & Patricia Wing
Cape Codder Adventures
Bruce A. Reddish
Cape Lodge Donald E. Davis
Capital City Fishing Charters

Tracy A. Rivera
Capitol Peak Outfitters, Inc.
Steve Rieser
Capt Albert Ponzoa- Joe McNichols
Show & Tell Charters
Capt. Andrew Bostick
Mangrove Outfitters Guides
Capt. Andy Griffiths, Jr.
Capt. Barry Hoffman
Capt. Bill's Charters Bill VanLuven
Capt. Bill Walsh
Dawn Patrol Charter Fishing
Capt. Black Bart's Charters
James M. Cowan
Capt. Bligh's Beaver Creek Lodge
Clinton & Dolores Coligan
Capt. Bligh Beaver Cr.
Larry Wheat
Capt. Bob Marvin
Capt. Bob Prestyly
Affordable Fly Fishing
Capt. Bruce Foster
Capt. Bruce Miller
Grand Slam Outfitters, Inc.
Capt. Chris Dean
Capt. Dan Malzone
Capt. Dan Prickett
Capt. Daniel Ratliff
Capt. Danny Watkins
Capt. Darrick Parker
Capt. Dave "Flash" Eimers
Capt. Dave Prickett
Capt. Dennis Meehan
Reel Fun
Capt. Dennis Meehan
Happy Hooker
Capt. Denny McAllister
Capt. Dick Williams
Capt. Doug Hanks
Capt. Doug Swisher
Capt. Duane Baker
Capt. Frank Catino
Capt. Frank Garisto
Capt. Glen Puopolo
Mangrove Outfitters Guides
Capt. Hamilton M. Franz
Capt. Hunter Brown
Capt. Jack Lloyd
Capt. Jimbo Hail
Capt. Joe Wierback
Capt. John Carlisle
Capt. John Weeks
Capt. Jon Shaffer
A to Z Backwater Fishing
Capt. Larry Miniard
Capt. Linwood Martin
Judith M
Capt. Mel Dragich Fish On Charters
Capt. Mike's Charters
Michael & Mary Huff
Capt. Mike Lane's Charters
Capt. Michael Lane
Capt. Mike PattersonTuff Ship
Capt. Paul's Charter Fishing
Capt. Roger Voight
Capt. Paul Hawkins
Capt. Pete Greenan's Gypsy Guide
Service
Capt. Peter Taves Sea Squirt
Capt. Randy Hamilton
Capt. Richard DeVito
Capt. Robert Collins Mangrove
Outfitters Guides
Capt. Robert Nemson Rocket
Capt. Ron's Specialty Charters
Ronald W. Becker
Capt. Scott Kolpin Elusive Endeavors
Capt. Shaun R. Chute
Capt. Sophia Stiffler
Barron River Charters
Capt. Stacy Mullendore
Capt. Steve
Backcountry Specialty Charters
Capt. Steve Guinan BlackJack Charters
Capt. Terry Parsons
Capt. Tom Rowland
Capt. Wally Valleau
Capt. Wayne Whidden
Native Charters
Captain's Choice
Capt. Alan Artkop
Captain Angelo's Fishing Bug Charter
Capt. Angelo Trentadue
Captain Billy Spearin Billy Spearin
Captain Bob's Charters
Robert C. Crocker
Captain Brian's Bayou Adventures
Capt. Brian Epstein
Captain Brown's Sound Adventures
Grady Brown, Jr.
Captain Cal's S.E. AK Charter Service
Cal & Marie Schipper
Captain Chuck Chuck Wilkinson
Captain Cook Charters
Alfred M. Cook
Captain Dale's Lake Michigan Sport
Capt. Dale Coleman
Captain Dan's Charters
Dan Gagnon
Captain Don's Charter Service
Capt. Don Anderson
Captain Don's Charter Service
Capt. Don Hauke
Captain George's Charters
George Will, Jr. & Ann Dimmick
Captain Hook Charters
Capt. William Scheid, Jr.
Captain Jim's Great Alaska Charter
Co. Jim & Ruby Alexander
Captain Ron's Boat Charters
Ron Williams
Captain Trout Outfitter & Guides

Robert Coppock
Captain Wally's Charters
Capt. Wally Lindemann
Captain Wally Burbage Charters
Capt. Wally Burbage
Captain Willie Charter Boat
Capts. Al Helo, Tom Rizzo & J.
Boardman
Sanibel Light Tackle Outfitters, Inc.
Capts. John Dahl & George Stransky
Reel Suprise
Careen Lake Lodge
Jack & Eileen O'Brien
Cariboo Mountain Outfitters
Bradley Bowden
Caribou Country Adventures
Stan B. Suess
Caribou Creek Lodge Ltd.
Dwight & Bev Whitley
Caribou Lodge
Gervais & Martha Beaulieu
Caribou Pond Outfitting-Baxter Slade
Carl's Fishing Fiesta-Carl Ulrich
Carmuk Charters
Carla Szitas & Mike Norris
Carney's Fishing Adventues
David Carney
Carol Ann Charters-Carol/Jerry Crake
Carol Hooper
Richard Hooper
Carol Marie
Capt. Terry Thomas
Carolina Dorrington Hill Hunt Club
Carolina Fly Fisherman
Carpe Dien Charters-Robert W. Cowell
Carpenter's Clearwater Lodge &
Outfitters-Jim Lorden Doug Sangster
Carpenter's Mate Charters
Capt. Paul (Butch) Grasser
Carr's Wild Trout Adventures
Colin J. Carr
Carriere's Camp-Freda/John Carriere
Carte Court Motel/Resort
Mary Ann Veach
Casa De Kings-Steve Nowak
Casa De Kings Fishing Adventures
James, Phil & Earl Mertzweiller
Cascade Adventures Jeff S. Hennessy
Cascade Fishing Adventure, Inc.
Dana C. Bottcher
Cascade Guides & Outfitters, Inc.
Cascade Inn & Boat Charters, Inc.
Cascade River Tours Todd A. Flightner
Casey's Charter Service
Furman Casey, Jr.
Casey's Guide Service
Casey Malepsy
Cast-Away, Inc. Robin E. Moore
Cast & Catch Freshwater Bass Guides
Cast and Blast Outfitters
Curt D. Collins
Castaway Fly Shop Daniel Lee Roope
Castle Creek Outfitters & Guest Ranch
John D. Graham
Castle Mountain Fly Fishers
Dillon S. Dempsey
Cat Daddy Guide & Tour
Renne R. Shumway
Cat Island Lodge
Mike & Gaye Tamburrino
Cat Track Outfitters-Cal Thornberg
Catch'Em-Capt. Richard J. Siedzik
Catch-A-King Charters
Richard Manning & Paul Roop
Catch-a-Lot Charters
Robert & Kathleen Junglov
Catch 'Em Guide Service
Kenneth R. Hagen
Catch 1 Ronald Yagelski
Catch Master Charters
Rick & Teresa Versteeg
Catch Montana John N. Adza
Catchem 1 Sportfishing
Catfish Ponds
Cats on the Red-Stu & Dianna McKay
Caught A Big One-David Milton
Cavu Charter Boat
Cedar & Canvas Adventures
Cedar Breaks Guides & Outfitters
Monte Lew Miller
Cedar Breaks Outfitters
John A. Stuver
Cedar Creek Cove Resort
Ron & Gail Misek
Cedar Grove Camp
Bill, Nancy & Casey Goodhew
Cedar Grove Lodge-Gary Fleming
Cedar Island Lodge-Jim Moore
Cedar Mill Guide Service
John MacDonald
Cedar Mountain Guide Service
Daniel L. Weber
Cedar Point Lodge Ltd.
Pat & Sharon Hron
Cedar Shore Resort-Jennifer Redman
Cedar Shores Resort & Wilderness
Camps Bob Binkley
Cedar Springs Marina
Cee-Bar-Dee Outfitters
Darrell Weddle
Celebrity Charters-J. C. Morrison
Centennial Charter & Launch
George F. Zenk, Jr.
Centennial Outfitters
Mel W. Montgomery
Centerfire Outfitters, Inc.
Clay Woodward & Stan Rogers
Central Delta Guide Service
Romey Jones
Central Flyway Outfitters
John K. Kersten
Central IN Anglers Duane Strauch

Central Newfoundland Outfitters
Reg, Bev & Gord Robinson
Central Oregon Adventures, Inc.
Richard L. Wren
Centre Island Resort David Ballinger &
Laura St. John
Century Lodge Rich & Kay Tyran
Cetacea Enterprises Dan Garner
Chad Hopwood Construction
Chad Hopwood
Chaik George Charters
Garfield P. George
Challenge Outfitters-David L. Eider
Challenge Outfitters-Mike Martindale
Challenger-Capt. Bob Jenkins
Chama River Outfitters
Bob Ball
Chamberlain's Trout Dock
Chamberlain Basin Outfitters, Inc.
Tony & Tracy Krekeler
Champ Guide Service
Capt. Paul Boileau
Chan IV Charters-L.S. & Alvara Wright
Chan Welin's Big Timber Fly Fishing
Channing W. Welin
Chances R Charters-Ken & Lori Elliott
Chandalar River Outfitters
Keith C. Koontz
Change of Pace-Scott A. Bolka
Channel Islands Sportfishing Center
Chanty Cheryl Pritchard
Chaonia Landing Dave Bowman
Chapleau Air Services & Sunset View
Camp Lee Cole
Chapleau Lodge Resort
Bob & Sally Landry Charger
Rick Craddick
Charley Charters
Charles E. Brown
Charlie's Big Fish Charters
Charlie Pearson
Charlie's Guide Service
Charlie Keeler
Charlie's Sporting Goods
Charlie Charters-Michael Zelinski
Charlie Mac's Sport & Tackle World
Charter Boat Marlin
Capt. George Olson
Charter Boats, Inc.
Capt. Sam S. Romano, USMM
Charters Unlimited
Capt. Charles G. Swartz
Chartle Sportfishing-Joeph F. Stoops
Chatanika Outfitters-Diane E. Burgess
Chatham Strait Charters
Dickie L. Dau
Chatmon Sport Fishing Charters
Capts. Dave Chatmon & Eric Hauke
Chaudiere Lodge
Tony & Betsy Stensen
Chauffeured Fishin' Service
Ken Erb
Chaunigan Lake Lodge
Chazman Charters-Charles Glagolich
Cheat Mountain Club
Gladys Boehmer
Cheat Mountain Outfitting & Guide
Service Treve Painter
Cheeca Lodge
Cheemo Lodge Ed Granger
Chelatna Lake Lodge
Victor Andresen,Dale-Logan Raley
Chelsea Bass Masters-Wes Thomas
Cher Hooten
Bass Haven Lodge
Cherece IV Charters
Rene & Diane Rice
Cherokee Trading Post & Outfitters
David Slater
Cherry Grove Charters
Capt. Ken Metzger
Chesapeake Bay Charters
Capt. Leroy G. Carr
Chesley's Lodge & Resort
Joe Isfjord & Bryan Gafka
Chesser Enterprise-Nathan Chesser
Chicagof Charters-Paul Johnson
Chickadee Lodge
Vaughan Schriver
Chico Hot Springs Lodge-Colin Davis
Chieko Charters -John & Vivian Kito
Chihuly's Charters
Mark & Susan Chihuly
Childs Charters-John Childs
Childs Lake Lodge & Outfitters
Brian & Joan Forbes
Chilkat Charters-Norman Hughes
Chilkat Lake Lodge-William S. Samalon
Chilkoot Charters-Larry D. Pierce
Chimo Lodge & Outposts
Peter Hagedorn
Chinook Charters
Johnathan Hillstrand
Chinook Charters
Johnathan Holstrand
Chinook Charters-Tom Ramiskey
Chinook Harbor Restaurant & Marina
Chip Porter Charters -Chip Porter
Chiripa Sportfishing, Inc.
Chisholm's Kaby Kabins
Jim & Helen Chisholm
Chisholm Trail Ranch-Mickey Cusack
Chitina Bay Lodge-George Juliussen
Chock Full of Nuts
Capt. Dennis O'Braitis
Choctaw Charters-Glenn Mitchell
Choice Marine Charters
Jack J. Gilman
Chris Young Guide Service
David C. Young, Jr.
Christina Falls Outfitters, Inc.
Darwin Watson

Christine Hills-John Emory
Christine Kima-David A. Kimar
Christopher R. Ferguson
Hawk's Cay Resort & Marina
Christy's Cove Cottages Marie,
Christina & Jonathan Wiersma
Chuck's Guide Service-Chuck Uzzle
Chuck Davies Guide Service, Inc.
Mark Davies
Chuck McGuire Flyfishing
Charles D. McGuire
Chuck Porter Charters-Chuck Porter
Chuck Swartz's Angling Adventures
Chuck Swartz
Chuit River Adventures-
Clifford A. Morrison
Chuit River Lodge-Jeffrey Hauck
Chuitna River Guides-Frank Standifer
Chupu Charters
Churchill River Lodge & Outfitters
John & Barb L'Abbe
Churchill River Voyageur Lodge
Terry Helary
Churchill River Wilderness Camps
Klaas & Norman Knot
Chute Pool Lodge-Al Rothwell
Cianci's Holiday North Lodge
Frank & Lucy Cianci
Ciao Capt. Doug Mulac
Cie Jae Charters
Charles & Roberta Crabaugh
Cie Jae Ocean Charters
Charles Crabaugh
Cimarron Ridge/High Country
Outfitters Thomas L. Bailey
Cinco de Mayo Ranch/Sycamore
Ranch Michael Morris
Cinder River Lodge-Gary King, Jr.
Cinnamon Lodge-Marc Newcomb
Circle A Guide Service-Richard Archer
Circle Bar Guest Ranch
Sarah Hollatz
Circle CE Ranch-Dick & Sally Shaffer
Circle City Bass Hookers
Bill Folkening
Circle Four Hunting
Thomas I. & Thomas R. Lindley
Circle VH Outdoor Adventures
City Dock Launch Fishing
Jerry & Bonnie Stewart
CJ's Ventures-Craig A. Jackson
Clancy's Guided Sports Fishing
Rhonda Chumbley
Clarenville Aviation Ltd.-Neil Pelley
Clark's Guide Service-Edward Clark
Clarks Camp-Karla & Wayne Clark
Classic Alaska Charters
Robert Scherer
Claude's Fishing Huts
Claude J. Lambert
Clay's Joy III Charter Service
Capt. Clayton N. Baker
Clayne Baker's Stonefly Anglers
Clear Lake Cottages
Daniel & Deanne Cudmore
Clearwater Adventures
Thomas & Jody Fica
Clearwater Guides
Clearwater House on Hat Creek
Clearwater River Company
James A. Cook
Clearwater Trout Tours
Cleaver Wallis Associates
Joe & Mary W. Wallis
Cliff Park Inn-John Curtin
Clifford Cummings Outfitter
Clifford O. Cummings, Jr.
Climbing Arrow Outfitters
F. & M. Anderson
Clinch Mountain Guide Service
Mike Shaffer
Clive's Fishing Guide Service
Clive & Marilyn Talkington
Clover Bay Lodge
Stan & Bonnie Oaksmith
Clover Pass Resort
Gerald F. Engelman
Club 52 West
Coal Creek Wilderness Guided Adv.
Russel J. Lewis
Coal River Canoe Livery, LTD
John & Dorris E. Walls
Coast Mountain Wilderness Lodge
Ralph Voll
Coastal Guide Service
Capt. Vince Theriot
Coastal Hook-R's Guide Service
Paul D. Welle
Coastal Island Charters
Michael & Lori Bauer
Coastal Outfitters-CharlesHelen Keim
Coastal River Adventures
Michael E. Kasper, Jr.
Coastal Wilderness Charters
Eric R. Swanson
Cobb Bay Camp Henry Theelen
Cobham River Lodge-Richard Hebel
Coeur d'Alene Outfitters
Murray D. "Bat" Masterson
Coho Charters
Marilyn & Terrance Vraniak
Coho Guide & Air Service
Peter G. Blackmon
Cold Coast Charter Service Inc.
Eric Walline
Colimar Lodge Ltd.
Clayton Doucette & Fran Koning
Collegiate Peaks Outfitters
David Douty
Collett's Recreation Service, Inc.
Collins Guiding-Darrel A. Collins
Colorado Angler-Rhonda D. Sapp

Colorado Big Game Connections, Inc.
Robert Gee
Colorado Blue Outfitters
David G. Hargadine
Colorado Diamond D Outfitters
Thomas D. Dunn
Colorado Elite-John D. Verzuh
Colorado Fishing Adventures
Gary J. Willmart
Colorado Fishing Guides
Colorado Mule Deer Linda L. Strong
Colorado Outfitters, Inc.
Kelly Brooks
Colorado River Guides, Inc.
Brenda D. Worley
Colorado Trophies-Jay Scott
Colorado Trophy Guides
John & Jim Stehle
Colorado Wild Sports-Pat Flaherty
Colorado Wilderness Safaris, Inc. Paul
E. Mitzel, Jr.
Columbia River Guide Service
Evan Davis
Columbia River Outfitters Guide
Service
Columbine Outfitters-Greg Ward
Coman's Guide Service-Stan Coman
Comanche Wilderness Outfitters, Inc.
Scott A. Limmer
Come Away Plantation-Jodie Gunter
Come By Chance Resort Ltd.
Albert & Ilona, Joe & Mary
Come Fishing with John
John M. Lambe
Comfort Charters Philip Warren
Commercial Fisherman's Charter Co.
Steve Weissberg
Como Lake Resort Lee Burk
Compass Rose Charters
Jack & Lisa Wallis
Compensator/Western Charter
Company
Concepts in Fly Fishing
James Mershan Ferris
Conne River Outfitters
Connecticut Woods & Water
Capt. Dan Wood
Conook Charters & Hunting Guide
Serv. Gregory Harmych
Conspira Sea Charter Boat
Constable's Lakeside Lodge
E. Constable
Continental Divide Outfitters
Walter D. Easley
Cook's Camp Rene Cook
Cook Inlet Charters R. McLean
Cookie's Resort
Jack & Cookie Armstrong
Cooper's Fly Shop
Cooper's Landing-Charles Love
Cooper's Minipi Camps
Cooper Head Charters
Wayne A. Biederman
Cooper Landing Floating
Howard Mulanax
Copenhaver Outfitters, Inc.
Steven D. Copenhaver
Coppen's Resort Limited
Syd Coppen & Ed Plichta
Copper Country Outfitters
Steven C. Harvill
Copper River Fly Fishing Lodge
Jeff & Pat Vermillion
Copper River Guide Service
James & Marlene Tilly
Cordova Airboat Tours
Sharon & John Buehrle, III
Cordova Fishing Charters
Craig Lynch
Coreene-C II Sport Fishing Charters,
Inc.
Cori-Ann Charters-Joseph Roche
Cormorant Lake Lodge
Bob & Gale Extence
Cornhusker Fishing Camp
Cossette's Cove Resort
Jack & Judy Cossette
Cosy Cove Cottages-Linda & Bud Link
Cotter Trout Dock
Cotton Mesa Trophy Elk
Lester & Robert Gegenheimer
Cottonwood Anglers -Paul Jacquez
Cottonwood Lodge-William Brion
Cottonwood Meadows Guide Service
Randy P. Keys
Cottonwood Ranch & Wilderness
Exped. E. Agee Smith
Cougar Country Lodge-Jason Schultz
Cougar Mountain, Inc.-Si H. Woodruff
Coulter Creek Outfitters
Robert Johnson
Countrysport Limited-John Hergenhan
Coup Platte Hunting & Fishing
Terry Trosclair
Covered Wagon Outfitters
Edward L. Hake
Covert Alaskan Expeditions
William Covert
Cow Head Outfitters-Eileen Hynes
Cowlitz River Sportfishing
Joe Little
Cra-Zee's II Charter Dexter C. Zernia
Crackerjack Sportfishing Charters
Andrew Mezirow
Craftsbury Sports & Leaning Ctr.
John Brodhead
Craig's Guide Service
Craig A. Lawless
Craig's Guide Service
Craig L. VanHousen
Craig's Pasquia Hills Vacation Farm
Dorothy & Osborne Craig
Craig Outfitting Service
Philip S. Craig
Craig Sutton's Cast & Blast
Craig Sutton
Crain Outfitting & Guide Service
Richard A. Crain
Cranberry Wilderness Outfitters
Keith Comstock
Crane's Lochaven Wilderness Lodge
Eric Crane
Crane Meadow Lodge-Robert Butler
Crane Mountain Guide Service
Fred W. Buchanan
Crawford's Camp-Bob Rydberg
Crawford Ranch-Gayle R. Crawford
Crazy Horse- M.L. Bill Swanda
Crazy Mountain Outfitter & Guide
Phillip Ray Keefer
Crazy Mountain Raft Robert H.
Wiltshire
Creative Outdoor Sprts
Frank E. Meek
Cree Lake Lodge-Vern & Gerri Biller
Cree River Lodge Ltd.
Peter Evaschesen
Creekside Inn Bill Avarell
Crescent Beach Cottages & Motel
Kevin Harbottle
Crescent H Ranch
Crooked Creek Lodge/Delta Marsh
Canoe
John & Marlene Lavallee
Crooked Lake Lodge
Grant/Win Palmer Hugh/Della Allan
Crorkindill Steven Kreighbaum
Cross Milliron Ranch Larry Miller
Cross Mountain Adventures, LLC
Danny Moree
Cross Outfitters Larry W. Cross
Cross Pond Lodge-Neil Lucas
Cross Sound Lodge-William E. Askim
Crossed Sabres Ranch -Fred Norris
Crossroads Lake Lodge
Bruce Woolfrey
Crouchers Outfitters
Rod & Carl Croucher
Crow's Hollow-
Fred Amacher & Danny Roy
Crow Creek Sioux Tribe
Crow Rock Camp, Inc.-Wendel Dafcik
Crowduck Lake Camp
Nick & Bill Kolansky
Crowley Guide Service
Gerald Crowley
Cruiser V Charters
Stephen Novakovich
Crystal Creek Anglers
Raymond D. Rickards
Crystal Creek Lodge-Dan Michaels
Crystal Creek Outfitters
Gap Puchi
Crystal Harbour Resort
Sandy Sundmark
Crystal Lodge-John Midgett
Crystal Sea Charters Dale & Susan
Kanen
Cub II Charter Service
Capt. Larry Braun
Cudney's Guide Service
David L. Cudney
Cudrey Guide Service
Dave Cudrey
Cuelenaere Lake Lodge
Larry Cherneski
Cumberland House Outfitters Ltd.
Cup Lake Fishing Camp
Lindsay & Barry Brucks
Current Affairs Outfitting
Douglas R. Nash
Curry Comb Outfitters
William L. Knox
Curt's Guide Service-Curt Madson
Curtis' Custom Charters-Curtis Bates
Curtis Guide Service-Curtis Fletscher
Curtiss Outfitters -Ronald L. Curtiss
Cusack's Alaska Lodge-Bob Cusack
Custom Adventures-Roger Bowers
Custom Charter-Dale & June Robbins
Custom Charters-Tommy Pellegrin
Custom River Outfitters Steven
Heaverlo, J. Ellery & T. Petrick
Cygnet Lake Trailer Park
Bill & Sandi Demkier
D & D Camps Ltd.-Dick Cossette
D & D Charters Dave DeGrow
D & G Enterprises
David M. & Gail L. Floyd
D & M Charters-Debbie J. Hill
D & O Soloway Outfitters Service
Orville & Debbie Soloway
D & S Guide & Outfitter
Dennis E. Rodebaugh
D.J.'s Guide Service-Darrin Johnston
Dahl's Mini Marts-Mark Dahl
Daily Double-Ralph Botticelli
Dakota Outfitters Unlimited, Inc.
Larry Brooks
DAL Outfitters, Inc. David Lowry
Dale's Alaskan Guide Service
Dale Benson
Dale's Guide Service-Dale Hedger
Dale's Guide Service
Dale A. Piontkowski
Dale Schroeder's Charter Service
Capt. Dale J. Schroeder
Dalton Trail Lodge
Damm Drifter Guide Service
Darol L. Damm
Dan's Fly Shop-Dan Hall
Dan's Guide Service-Daniel Verkuilen
Dan's Kenai Charters-Danny L. Eades
Dan's Specialty Guide Service
Dan Ross
Dan Bailey's Fly Shop-John P. Bailey
Dan Bentsen River Trips
Dan Bentsen
Dan Mar Charters-Dan Loitz
Dana Wharf Sportfishing
Daniel's Personalized Guide Service
Daniel H. Donich
Daniel J. Humphrey Guides
Daniel J. Humphrey
Danish Charters, Inc.
Tommy M. Danish
Danny's Way Gerard Regan
Danny Haak Guide Danny Haak
Darbyshire & Associates
Ralph R. & Iele G. Darbyshire
Darcy 1 Charters
Capt. Pat Church
Darsana Lodge-Carl & Marg Boychuk
Darwin Ranch, Inc.-Loring Woodman
Dastardly Deano's Custom Flies
Deane Wheeler
Dauphin Island Marina
Mike Thierry & Terry Malone
Dave's Charter Service
Capt. Dave Sorenson
Dave Austin's Guide Service
Dave Austin
Dave Duncan & Sons Dave, John,
Clint, Todd & Brad Duncan
Dave Flitner Packing & Outfitting
David Flitner
Dave Helfrich River Outfitter, Inc.
Dave Helfrich
Dave Jauron's Guide Service
Dave Jauron
Dave Park Outfitting David R. Park
Dave Parri's Outfitting & Guide
Service David Parri
Dave Spaid Guiding-David D. Spaid
Dave Willborn Outfitter
Dave Willborn
Dave Winchester's Sporting Camps
Dave Winchester
Davey's Locker Sportfishing
David Ansel Enterprises-David Ansel
David B. Barker
David L. Wheat
Davin Lake Lodge-Wes Borowsky
Davis Point Lodge & Outfitting
Dr. Peter Kalden
Davis Whitewater Expeditions
Lyle Davis
Dawt Mill Barbara Heneger
Day-O Charters-Capt. Mike Gucinski
Day Harbor Charters
David W. & Agnes A. Miller
Daybreak Guide Service-Steve Ratey
De Warrior Sportfishing
Dead Reckon Lake Michigan Sport
Fish- Capt. John B. Zabel
Dean's Guide Service-Dean Moloney
Deap Sea Charters -David Rauwolf
DeBolt Guiding & Outfitting
Ian & Hugh Alexander
Deborah McLaughlin William
McLaughlin
Debra Jean Sport Fishing
Capt. Jim Hoffman
Deception Lake Lodge
Decker Guide Outfitters-Mark Decker
Dee Jay's Charter Fishing
Dee Norell Ranch-Franklin Dee Norell
Deep Creek Fishing Club
Steven Moe
Deep Creek Outfitters
Darla Ranwick Cluster
Deep Runner Charters
Capt. Steve Foster
Deep Sea Charters Bill Geary
Deep Sea Charters
Daniel & Jane Gorham
Deep Sea Charters
Lin L. Keightley
Deer Creek Cottage Sidney &
Kathleen Cook
Deer Horn Lodge
Norm & Cindy Tieck
Deer Horn Lodge, Inc.
Dave, Ruth, Jeff & Karen Chantler
Deer Horn Resort
Eileen S. Trandel
Deer Lake Cottages-Stan/Anita Soloy
Deer Mountain Charters, Inc.
Stephen Aldrich & Robert Simmons
Deer Trail Lodge-Marie/Ian Seymour
Deer Valley Ranch-Harold Lee DeWalt
Deery & Guides Fishing
Kenny Deery
Deets Guide Service-Dan Dieter
Del's Triangle 3 Ranch-Ray Heid
Delsbrat Charters
Robert L. Jaynes
Delta Angler Guide Service
Mike Dees
Denali Highlands Adventures, Inc. C.
Michael Yates
Denali River Guides-Joe Halladay
Dennis W. Hammond
Denny's Gone Fishin Guide Service
Dennis Wells
Denny's Guide Service-Denny Cook
Derringer Outfitters & Guides
David & Susan Derringer
Dersham's Outlook Lodge
Ed & Karan Dersham
Deschambault Lake Resort
Twylla Newton
Deschutes Canyon Fly Shop
John T. Smeraglio
Deschutes Navigation Co.
Dave Green
Deschutes Navigation Co.
William L. Miller
Deschutes River Outfitters
Greg Price
Deschutes River Outfitters
David M. Renton
Deschutes River Tours
Pete Carlson
Deschutes River Tours
David G. Randle
Deschutes Trout Tours
Paul R. Pargeter
Desert Recreation, Inc.
Fredrick A. Glaner
Deshka Silver-King Lodge
Michael, Susan & William Jarvis
Deshka Silver-King Lodge
Cathy Pearcy
Detour Marine Inc.
Devil's Thumb Fly Fishing Adv. Center
Diamond-D-Ranch & Outfitters
Obbie L. Dickey
Diamond Charters-Edwin A. Dickson
Diamond D Ranch & Outfitters
Rod Doty
Diamond D Ranch, Inc.
Thomas & Linda Demorest
Diamond Half Ranch-Hilmar Blumberg
Diamond Hitch Outfitters
Chris & Robert McNeill
Diamond J Guest Ranch
Diamond J Outfitters Joe Stuemke
Diamond Jim & Sons Mountain Rides
Jim Colosimo
Diamond K Outfitters
Charles D. Kendall
Diamond Key Resort
Dave & Maggie Powell
Diamond Lodge Guest Ranch
C. Steve Paul
Diamond M Outfitting-Terry Spriggs
Diamond N Outfitters-Brian D. Nelson
Diamond R Guest Ranch-James Slack
Diamond R. Expeditions
Peter Rothing
Diamond Willow Charters
Roger W. Fleming
Diamond Willow Inn
Leonard & Darlene Abromovich
Diamond X Bar Outfitting
Robert M. Campbell
Diana R Too-Capt. Mike Rusch
Diane Gentel James Gentel
Diane L. Smolen Charles H. Bettison
Dick Lyman Outfitters-Dick P. Lyman
Dick Pennington Guide Service, Ltd.
Alan & Dick Pennington
Dick Piffer Guide & Outfitter
Richard Piffer
Dickie's Portside Resort
Richard Gadbois
Dickson Outfitters Ltd.
David Dickson
Dillon Lake Outfitting
Arsene Nezcroche
Discount Fishing Tackle, Inc.
Michael L. Gray
Discovery Adventures, Inc.
Robert & Leslie Bell
Discovery Lake Lodge & Outpost
Paul, Nichole & Kaylee Bohnen
Discovery River Expeditions, Inc.
Lester Lowe
Discovery Voyages-Dean Rand
Dixie Outfitters, Inc.
W. Emmett & Zona Smith
DMJ Consulting Guide
Douglas M. Jones
DN & 3 Outfitters Eldon H. Snyder
Dobber IV Charters
Capt. Robert C. Dobbelaere
Dobbin Lake Lodges N. Silzer & J.
Motoshosky
Doc's Guide Service Norm Klayman
Dockside Accommodations
John & Ann Arnold
Dodge Creek Ranch-Jerry Kennedy
Dog Bay Charters of Kodiak
David Bugni
Dogskin Lake Lodge & Outposts
Dogtooth Resort
Wayne & Patty Jones
Dogwood Bass Masters-John Casper
Dogwood Valley RV/Camping Park
Hasan Choudhury
Dolphin Charters Capt. Art Viens
Dolphin Motel & Cottages
Beverley & Bayden Brownlee
Dominic's Guide Service
Don's 49er Charter Donald N. Wood
Don's Guide Service Don Kennedy
Don's Guide Service Don Sturdivan
Don Carvey Outfitting
Donald R. Carvey
Don Grieve Guide Service
Don Grieve
Don Hawkins Outfitting
Don Hawkins
Don T. S/F Charter Don Tetzlaff
Donald F. Smith Donald Smith
Donald Parady Donald E. Parady
Donkey Creek Outfitters
Steve R. Bietz
Donna Pelkey Glenn T. Pelkey
Donnelly's Minnitaki Lodge
Fran & Lil Donnelly
Donoho's Guide Service
Patrick Donoho
Donovan Lake Outfitters-
Albert Jewell
Doo Dah Charters-Laurie Flanders
Doran's Guide Service-Doran Coonse
Dorie-J John Johnson
Dos Mas Bud Aronis
Dot-E-Dee Capt. Jack Douton
Double "D" Charter Fishing
Capt. M. "Doc" Matson
Double D Guide Service
Capt. David Demeter, Sr.
Double Diamond Outfitters
Jack Wheeler
Double Diamond X Ranch
Dale Sims, Jr.
Double Dollar Cattle LLC
Wayne Iacovetto
Double H Bar Outfitting
Rick Hummel
Double H Outfitters Herb & Heather
Bailey
Double Haul Guiding
Double J Guide Service
Clifford J. Godley
Double LJ Outfitters, Inc.
Layne K. Wing
Double M Guiding & Outfitting
Mike Romaniuk
Double Mer Fishing Camps Ltd.
Howard Michelin
Double R Outfitting & Guide Service
Glen Nepil
Double Trouble Charter Boat
Doug's Guiding Service
Doug & Ellie Holler
Doug Wilhite River Guide
Doug Wilhite
Douglas Fir & Furs-Douglas H. Gauf
Douglas Roberts Outfitter
Douglas A. Roberts
Dr. Hook Charters-Leslie & Rory Vail
Dr. Steve Mack Native Guide
Dragonfly Anglers
Rod and Roger Cesario
Drawbridge Marina Karen
Druckenmiller & Ken Hershey
Dream-Fish Capt. Richard Baltzell
Dream Catcher Charters
Erwin Samuelson
Dream Charters
Chris Nelson & Jody Kruger
Dream Creek Guides
Richard Rothley, Jr.
Drift-A-Bit, Inc.-Randall Ballard
Drift-Inn Lodge-Laddy, Jeff & Morgan
Drift & Fish-John J. Lefler
Drifters Landing-John McClatchy
Drifters of the South Fork
Driftwood Enterprises
Herb Fenwick
Driftwood Lodge-Harold Schmidt
Driftwood Lodge Resort
Don & Brenda Granger
Dripping Springs Trout Dock
Drover's Labrador Adventures
Alonzo Drover
Drowsy Water Ranch-
Kenneth H. Fosha
Dry Creek Anglers-Charles Grobe
Dry Fly Outfitters
Dry Fork Outfitters-Donald Kroese, Jr.
Drybrook Environmental Adventures
Martin C. Giuliano
Duarte Outfitters Elmer Duarte
Duck Bay Lodge
Dave & Sheree Swistun
Duck Mountain Outfitters
Leslie E. Nelson
Dudman Farms-Barry Dudman
Due South III & Due South IV Charter
Boats
Duffy D-Capt. Jack Dougherty
Dufrene's Guide Service Inc.
Calvin Dufrene
Dugan Creek Outfitters
John A. Miller
Duke's Charter Fishing
Duane "Duke" Hohvart
Duke Charter-Ronald K. Anderson
Dunaway Hunting & Fishing Club
Dunc Lake Resort-Theresa Burk
Duncan Lake Camp
Ed & Faye Barnstaple
Dunckley Peak Pack Service
William L. Terrill
Dune Caper Charters-Anthony Arvay
Dunlap's Charter Service
Capt. Rick Dunlap
Dunlop Lake Lodge-Don & Pat Mackay
Durand's Fishing Guide
Duranglers Flies & Supplies
Thomas Knopick
Durango Fly Goods, LLC
Michael J. Stowers
Durango Outfitters, Inc.
Dennis Norton
Dymond Lake Outfitters Ltd.
Doug Webber
E & K's Alaskan Charters
Ernest & Kimberly Kirby
E & R Sport Fishing Charters
Capt. Rob Brileya
E & Z Inc./Whitewater Outfitters
Zeke & Erlene West
E.Fish.N.Sea Charter Service
Capt. David L. Wait
E.R.S.A. Daniel Lange
Eagle's Nest Outfitting
Kai Mark Turner
Eagle's Nest Sporting Camp
Arnold Drost
Eagle-Eye Fishing Charters
Daniel & Diane Ward
Eagle Adventures
Larry & Joanne Shaker
Eagle Cap Fishing Guides

Eagle Charters-Levi E. Hubbard
Eagle Charters-Stanley P. Mayer
Eagle Charters -Capt. Dan Nourse
Eagle Charters-Al Poskam
Eagle Charters-Harold H. Williams
Eagle Claw Charters-Michael Herold
Eagle Creek Outfitters
Charles Tuchschmidt
Eagle Crest RV-Paul Donnelly
Eagle Harbor Charters
Capt. Roy Elquist
Eagle Island Charters-Ed Leask
Eagle Lake Lodge
Orrie & Paula Colegrove
Eagle Lake Sportsmen's Lodge
Cindy & Jim Buhlman
Eagle Mountain Lodge
Eagle Nest Lodge
Keith Kelly
Eagle Nest Tours-Arthur Beck
Eagle Outdoor Sports-Rex Mumford
Eagle Outdoor Sports -Doug Smith
Eagle Point Rentals-Sally Paul
Eagle Ridge at Lusten Mountains
Kristin Althaus
Eagle Ridge Outfitter
Timothy G. Greiner
Eagle River Anglers-Robert Nock
Eagle River Guide Outfitting
Eric Havard
Eagle Song Lodge-David Jenny
Eagle Song on Trail Lake
Michael & Paula Williams
Eagle Spirit Charters
Ronald McKinstry
Eagle Spirit Outfitters-Miles Hogan
Eagle Tours-Patricia Campbell
Eaglecrest Guide Outfitters
Eagles Nest Outfitting
Billy S. Howard
Early Inn Resort & Campgrounds
Doug & Karla Dagel
Early Time Charters-Norman Rowe
Early Times Charters-Dean Bias
East Divide Outfitters-Dennis Yost
East Fork Outfitters-Mark A. McKee
East Fork Ventures-Robert J. Rehm
East Missouri Pro Guide Service
Larry Woodward
East Slope Anglers
Brad Parsch and Wayne Rooney
East Slope Outfitters -James Laughery
East Wisconsin Guide Service
David K. Eggert
Easy Charter-William J. Holman
Easy Touch Charters-Larry K. Quake
Ebben's Great Lakes Guide Service
Capt. Brian Ebben
Echo Canyon Outfitters, Ltd.
Graham Perry
Echo Canyon River Expeditions
David Burch
Eclipse Alaska
A.E. & Edith VonStauffenberg
ECOLLAMA David Harmon
Ecstasy Capt. Mike Barkely
Ed's Fly Fishing & Guide Services
Edward D. Ostapczuk
Ed Miranda's Guide Service
Ed Miranda, Sr.
Ed Venture Vacation Cruises
Edward H. Euren
Eddie Halbrook Grand Bayou
Reservoir Guide- Eddie Halbrook
Eden Camp Resort-Tom/JoyceJackson
Eden Eagle Outfitters
Gerald & Elaine Leforte
Edgecumbe Exploration
Michael Brooks
Edgewater Beach Resort
Dorothy Noffsinger
Edgewater Park Lodge
Tom Thornborrow & Bob Harris
Edgewater Resort- Tom Bosiger
Edmund Lake Lodge
Herb & Anna Dyke
Eide's Sportfishing Service
Sterling Eide
Eight Mile Fish Lodge
Larry Yahnian
Einarsson's Guide Service
Helgi Einarsson
Ejay's Portage Bay Camp
Evert & Jennie Cummer
El Venado Richard Herdell
Elbow Lake Lodge-Jack Smith
Elby Charters Robert L. Buechner
Elephant Lake Lodge
Bill & Sandy Smith
Elfin Cove Lodge Dan Baxter
Elite Charters Robert A. Carlson
Elk Cabins-Rene Pelissier/Serge Marin
Elk Country Outfitters
David Butterfield
Elk Creek Fishing Assoc., Inc.
Elk Creek Lodge-Chris Lockwood
Elk Creek Marina, Inc.-John Loken
Elk Creek Outfitters-Thomas J. Francis
Elk Creek Outfitters-Gerald K. Olson
Elk Island Lodge-Paul/Gary Zanewich
Elk Mountain Guides, Inc.
Charles & Clare McDaniel
Elk Mountain Outfitter & Guides
John Pickering
Elk Mountain Outfitters, Inc.
Gerald Seifert
Elk Mountain Outfitters, LLC
Myron J. Wakkuri
Elk Range Outfitters William J. Montanye
Elk Ridge Outfitters & Lodge
Terry Reach
Elk River Guest Ranch-William Hinder
Elk Valley Bighorn Outfitters, Ltd.
Robert Fontana
Elkhorn Adventures-Lester Connelly
Elkhorn Enterprises-Pete Clark
Elkhorn Outfitters, Inc.-Henry Barron
Elkhorn Outfitters, Inc.
Richard J. Dodds
Elkhorn Village Stables-Daniel Mulick
Elkqua Lodge-Mike & Cecilia Morris
Elkshead Guides & Outfitters
John M. Connon
Elktrout Lodge-Marty Cecil
Elliot Lake Aviation Limited/Fishland
Camp Bruno Rapp
Ellis Marine John Ellis
Ellis Professional Guide Service
Ken Ellis
Ellis, Inc. Dave Ellis
Elusive Saskatchewan Whitetail
Outfitter Harvey McDonald
Emerald Cove Lodges
Gary Pahl & Rod Hodgins
Emerald Sea Charters
Mark & Cindy Hedgecock
Emerick Alaska Enterprises
Jonathan Emerick
Emery's Bighorn Guide Service
Weston E. Emery
Ena Lake Lodge
A. Shane MacKinnon
Enchanted Circle Catskill Guide
Service Martin Redcay, Pete Zito, Cliff Schwark
Encore Charters-Gerald B. Hughes
Encounter Charters
Jerry & Barbara Burnett
End of the Rogue Guide Service
Shaun Carpenter
End of the Trail Lodge
Dave & Sandy Slanga
Endeavor Lake Michigan Fishing
Capt. Dennis Frey
Endless River Adventures
Juliet Kastorff
English River First Nations Resort
Alfred Dawatsare
English River Fishing Adventures
Enodah Wilderness Travel Ltd.
Ragnar & Doreen Wesstrom
Enterprise Sportfishing
Ephemera Guide Service
Floyd N. Franke
Epley's Whitewater Adventures
Ted Epley
Equinoxe Angling Adventures. LTD.
Pierre Morel
Eres Louis Butera
Eric Alan Mills Naomi K. Mills
Erion's Guide Service-Tim Erion
Ernie's Cottages & Campground
Ernie Martel
Ernie & Lynns Birchdale Lodge
Ernie & Lynn
Ernie Glover Ernie Glover, Inc.
Errington's Wilderness Islands
Al, Jr. & Doris Errington
Ersboat Fishing Charters
Capt. Bill Ersbo
Eruk's Wilderness Floats
Eric Williams
Escapade Charters-Willard L. Belenski
Escape Fishing Charters
Tim "Hook" Ursin, Sr.
Eskimo Fishing Adventures
Adolph, Kay, Dorothy, Albert, Valerie
Esnagami Wilderness Lodge-Eric Lund
Esnagi Lodge -Donna & Wally Leigh
Esper's Cedar Lake Camp
Terry & Kim Schale
Esper's Under Wild Skies Lodge & Outfitters
Vaughn and Judy Esper
Esposito Guide Service-Fred Esposito
Estes Angler
Estuary Anglers Mike S. McCune
Etholen Tours Forrest Dodson
Eureka Peak Lodge & Outfitters
Stuart Maitland
Eva Lake Resort Airway Ltd.
David Cunning
Evergreen Fly Fishing Co.
Franklin L. Oliverio
Evergreen Lodge Ltd.
Mal & Pat Tygesson
Evergreen Resort-Garry Morrish
Everhart's Tackle & Sporting Goods
Ken & Kathy Harrison
Ewok Cabins Harvey Barnes
Excel Adventures-Scott Childs
Excellent Adventure Outposts
Bob & Gale Extence Foron & Joyce Buckler
Excursions Unlimited-Craig Monaco
Executive Charters-Capt.RichardSleep
Executive Guide Service
Tony Allbright & Don Atchison
Executive Guide Service-Allen Tharp
Exodus Corporation
Richard A. Bradbury. Tony Bradbury
Expediter Charters-Capt. Mick Clark
Experience Montana
Allen Schallenberger
Expert Services Francis Mitchell
Explorations Northwest
Mike Halbert
Explore Alaska's Southeast
Gordon J. Williams
Expositions, Inc. Chris Fassnacht
Extreme Expeditions of WV, Inc.
Luther Toney
Eyees Right Charter Service
F.I.S.H.E.S. Floyd Peterson
F/V Eleanor S. Richard Boyce
F/V Orion Thomas W. Rockne
F/V Pamela Rae, Inc. Robert M. Thorstenson, Jr.
F/V Puffin Lady Fred Sturman
Faber Ranch-Leo M. Faber
Fair C's Charters-Darryl Cooper
Fair Valley Ranch Hunting Paradise
Travis & Dianne Hendricks
Fairchase Charters-Keith A. Kline
Fairfield Inn-Joyce Cole
Fairweather Adventures
James S. Kearns
Fairweather Charters
Kenneth K. Imamura
Fairweather Charters
Frank & Donna Libal
Fakon Charters-Tony Arsenault
Falcon's Ledge Lodge
Altamont Flyfishers
Fall Creek Outfitters
Dalbert (Del) Allmon
Fallcreek Bassmasters-Butch Isabell
Falling Spring Inn-Adin L. Frey
Falls Creek Alaskan Tours
Michael & Margie Barry
Family Charters
James & Judy Thompson
Family Charters, Inc.-Arthur Lariviere
Fantasea Charters
Keith & Janice Washburn
Fantasy Fishing Adventures
Phiip & Sharon Needham
Fantasy North Kenneth A. Cope
Fantasy Ranch Outfitters, Inc.
James R. Talbot
Far & Away Adventures
Steve Lentz
Far North Adventures, Inc.
Hal A. LaPointe
Far Out Camping
Myron Fultz,Clarke Smith
Farewell Harbour Resort
Paul Weaver
Faro Yukon Fishing Tours
Farris's Kvichak River Lodge, Inc.
Donald G. & Steve D. Farris
Farside Adventures-Glenn Clark
Fatboy Fishing-A.J. DeRosa
Father-N-Son's Sport Fishing Charters
Capt. Jeff Seefeldt
Father & Son Fishing Tours
Mark Krodel
Fawnie Mt. Outfitters & Moose Lake Lodge
John Blackwell Faye Hodges
Wallace A. Hodges
Fejes Guide Service L.T.D.
Samuel T. Fejes, Jr.
Fenton Bros. Guided-Murray Fenton
Ferro's Blue Mesa Outfitters
John Ferro
Ferrule Fly Fishing Club
Shane M. Hubbs
Fiery Fox Charters
Capts. George & Sandy Shuput
Fiesta Charters
Fin-N-Fur Charters, Inc.
Kenneth & Darlene Buttolph
Fin & Feather Fly Shop
Craig H. Campbell
Fin & Feather Resort Ron & Dee Clark
Fin Fun Charters
Capts. Gale & Mike Sells
Findlay Creek Outfitters-Eric Godlien
Fine Charter-Douglas Vincent
Finest Kind Sportfishing
Finger Lakes Outfitters-Lou Baum
Finn Fishing Team-Capt. Daniel Hill
Finn Too Charters-Capt. John Muench
Firehole Ranch
Fireside Lodge-Alan/Audrey Brandys
Fireweed Lodge-Bob Anderson
Fireweed Lodge Lake Creek
Werner & Irene Frauenfelder
First Frontier Adventures, Inc.
Gary Price & Fred Christiansen
First Island Cottages
Roly & Rhea Primeau
First Light-Capt. Bob Romeo
First Mate Charters
Capt. Dexter Nelson
First Out-Last In Charter
Craig Loomis
First Strike Sportfishing-Jeffrey Vogl
Fischer's Fishers-Dennis C. Fischer
Fish Capt. Peter Fisher
Fish-N-Chips Charters
David Ardinger
Fish 'N Hawk Charters
Capt. Ray R. Hawksby
Fish & Fowl Guide Service
Michael Herrman
Fish Alaska-Clifton Shannon
Fish Alaska Mills Enterprises
C. Larry Mills
Fish Assassin Charters
Clyde M. Campbell IV
Fish Boss Guide Service
Ronald M. Buntrock
Fish Creek Lodging-Janet Keefer
Fish Doctor-Capt. Ernie Lantiegne
Fish Doctor Guide Service
Bill Whitney
Fish Fighter Charters
Capt. Doug Pilon
Fish First! Guide Service
Fish Happens Guide Service
James Stogsdill
Fish Hawk Charters
Richard & Rita Hemmen
Fish Hawk Sea Ventures
Lon & Nancy Walters
Fish Lake Bass Club-Steve Krasowski
Fish Lipps II-Tom & Mary Lovick
Fish Man Taxidermy-Michiel L. West
Fish Montana-Leonard Moffo
Fish n' Whith Ed-Ed Pearson
Fish On Charters-Patrick Moore
Fish On Guide Service-Daniel B. Leis
Fish On with Gary Kernan
Gary Kernan and David Madden
Fish P. T. Guide Service
Pete Kelley, Jr.
Fish Pirate Charters-Ed Stahl
Fish R Plenty-Thomas Dotson
Fish Slammer Charters
Kenneth Meserve & Jeff Skaflestad
Fish Spotter III Charter
Capts. Alan & Dennis Zamecnik
Fish Tale Charters-Dale Griner
Fish Tale Lodge
Richard & Nancy Sherborn
Fish Tales Charters-Brian Abbey
Fish Tales Charters
Jerry & Leslie Gustafson
Fish Trap Charters-Capt. Tom Bohacek
Fish Wish Sportfishing & Taxidermy
Carl Rathje
Fish, Inc. -James & Stephanie Couch
Fish, Inc.- James E. Goff
Fish, P.R.N. -Larry Flynn
Fisha-Tractor Charter Boat
Fishawk River Co.-Harvey/Suzy Young
Fisheries Biologist-Paul Gerovac
Fisherman's Center, Inc.
G.L. Phillips
Fisherman's Choice Charters
Raymond & Debra Blodgett
Fisherman's Choice Charters
Capt. Brad Seymour
Fisherman's Cove-The Denzlers
Fisherman's Wharf
Fishermen's Information Services
Fishers of Men-Outfitters & Guide
Service Mark Conway
Fishfing Fantasy Charters
Capt. Steve Smith
Fishin' Again Charter Service
Capt. Ralph J. Kubsch
Fishin' Fever Charters-Capt. BobTitton
Fishin' Time Guide Service
Capt. John Knapp
Fishin Finders-Karl Finlanbinder
Fishin World-Frank Huffman
Fishing 101-Louis K. Lumsden
Fishing Alaska Style-Jeffrey Pyska
Fishing Buddies Unlimited
Albert Furey
Fishing Experience-Frank Severy
Fishing Fool Charters
Capt. John Guarney, Jr.
Fishing Guide Service
A.D. "Dee" Geoghegan
Fishing Head Quarters
Brete Thibeault
Fishing Headquarters-Dick Sharon
Fishing Lake Lodge/Bissett Outfitters
Byron Grapentine
Fishing on the Fly
Tim Dority
Fishing Pox I-Capt. Jim Belanger
Fishing Rod's Kenai Charters
Rodney W. Jones
Fishing Spirit-Jill Alford
Fishing the Cape
Fishing Unlimited
Capt. John J. Pedonie
Fishing Unlimited, Inc.
Lorane Owsichek
Fishing with Dave
David Christopherson
Fishing with Stan
Stanley W. Stanton
Fishing, Inc. Bill Herrington, Sr.
Fishtale River GuidesAndrew Couch
Fishtales-Thomas D. Stanton
Fishunter Guide Service Inc.
Nash Roberts III & Nash Roberts IV
Fishward Bound Adventures
Timothy Evers
Fishy Business Charter Boat
Five Bears Outfitters - Gary Peters
Five Mile Lake Lodge
Frank & Carol Yuhas
Five Star Expeditions, Inc.
Ed Beattie
Five Valleys Flyfishers- Chris E. Nelson
Flambeau Sports Outfitters
Flame Lake Lodge
Gary & Karen Pedersen
Flaming Gorge Flying Service, Inc.
Mark Brown
Flaming Gorge Lodge
Flaming Gorge Recreation Services
Herald Egbert
Flapper-Capt. Jeff Smith
Flasher's Canoe Camping Trips
Flat Fun Charters
Carl & Kathleen High
Flat Horn Lake Lodge-Norman Kayton
Flat Horn Lake Lodge
Chris Tonkinson and Richard Kerr
Flat Iron Outfitting-Jerry C. Shively
Flathead Trophy Fly Fishers
George D. Widener
Flatlanders- Jim Long
Flatline Outfitters
Matthew Greemore
Flayer's Lodge-Hilding/Marion Flayer
Fletcher Lake Lodge
Wayne & Jeanne Thompson
Flin Flon Outfitters - Rick Strom
Flindt Landing Camp
David & Louise Gish
Flint River Camp-The Goodman Family
Flo's Fishing Lodge-Florence Lyons
Floating-N-Fishing-Les Lloyd
Floating Lodges of Sioux Narrows
Jim & Tanis Rebbetoy
Flotten Lake Resort
Abram & Paula Rempel
Flowing Rivers Guide Service
D.L. Tennant
Fly-Fishing Montana Company
Randall J. Ziegler
Fly-In Wilderness Fishing-Bob Elliott
Fly-Inn Fishing & Safaris-Drew Dix
Fly A-Salt Service- Capt. Bob Robl
Fly Fish Alaska-Red Quill Lodge
Harold & Katharina Dungate
Fly Fish with Sandra-Sandra L. Arnold
Fly Fisher's Place-Jeff Perin
Fly Fishers' Inn
Richard W. Pasquale
Fly Fishing Outfitters
Fly Fishing Paradise
Capt. Dexter Simmons
Fly Fishing UnlimitedDonald R. Lyman
Fly Fishing with Bert Darrow
Bert Darrow
Fly Rod Shop-Summer Stowe
Fly Rodder's Heaven-Joel Malta
Flyfishing Adventures
L. Darryl Osburn
Flyfishing Durango, Inc.
Bill Leahy
Flyfishing Kodiak-Jim Lambert
Flyfishing Montana & Chile
Michael C. Mosolf
Flyfishing Outfitters, Inc.-WilliamPerry
Flyfishing Services, Inc.
Flyfishing Shop Bachmann, Stensland & Barnes
Flyfishing the Salt
Flying "J" Outfitters -Lawny Jackson
Flying "R" Charters-Capt. Roy S. Rusch
Flying B Ranch, Inc.
Robert Burlingame & Donald Wilson
Flying Bear Charters-Bruce Randall
Flying D Ranch-Rob Amaud
Flying Diamond Outfitters, LLC
John R. Adams
Flying Eagle Outfitters
Mark O. Anderson
Flying Finn Charters
Capt. Al "Willie" Williams
Flying H Ranch-John and Amee Barrus
Flying M Ranch-Johnnie W. Musgrove
Flying Raven Ranch-Matt Redd
Flymasters-Christian Pedersen
Flynn's Charter Service-Gene Flynn
Flynn & Sons Outfitters-Delnor Flynn
Foggy Mountain Guide Service
Wayne Bosowicz
Folding Mountain Outfitters, Ltd.
Dale Drinkall
Fontana Village Resort
Scott Waycaster
Fontenelle Resort Ken Reynolds
Foothills Fly Fishing Chuck Patterson
Forbe's Holiday Resort
Bill & Ellen Kloepfer
Foreget-Me-Not Charters
Tom Leslie
Forest Lawn Outfitter
Brian How
Forget-Me-Not Charters
Raymond Stein
Forget Me Not North & South
Stu Merchant
Fork Peck Outfitting, Inc.
Foscoe Fishing Co. & Outfitters, Inc.
Foster Lake Lodge-Trent Brunanski
Foster Ranch Kenels & Outfitters
Jim & Debbie Foster
Four Buck's Guide Service
Paul Buck
Four Corners Guides & Outfitters
Ted Stiffler
Four Men Lodge of the Miramichi
George Vanderbeck
Four Mile Out Camp-Allison R. Corbin
Four Rivers Fishing Co.-Jane Waldie
Four Seasons Resort
Arden & Jeanette Thompson
Fournier Brothers Outfitting
Greg Fournier
Foutz Outfitting Service
Charles F. Foutz
Fowler's Charter & Rental
Harry D. Fowler
Fowler's Kenai Charters
Robert Fowler
Fox #1 Charters-Capt. Dave "Fox" Wilz
Fox Bay Lodge
Nikolavs Steigler & Doris Ehrenstein
Fox Brothers Charter Fishing
Daniel Fox
Fox Lake Lodge
Vickie & Dave Ormerod
Foxy Lady Sport Fishing, Inc.
Frances Garncarz-Michael J. Chimelak
Frances Lee Charters
Capt. Charles Weier
Francine Melancon Milot
Francis Resort-Robert & Mildred Gay
Frank's Bait Shop
Frank Hartenstein
Fred Baraks Guide Service
Fred Bouse's Gulkana Salmon
Charters Fred Bouse
Fred Cook Guide Service-Fred Cook
Fred Lee's Fly Fishing Guide Service
Freddy J's Fish Camp

Laurie Hendershott
Henderson's Hunting Camps, Ltd.
Robert & Glenna Henderson
Henderson Springs-Mark Henderson
Henry's Fork Anglers-Mike Lawson
Henry's Fork Anglers, Inc.
Michael J. Lawson
Henry G. Bradley Robert T. Price
Hepburn Lake Lodge -Dennis
Callbeck
Herb's Sportsman's Supplies
Herring Bay Charters -Robert L. Miller
Hewitt Lake Lodge
Martin Wegscheider
Hi-Lo Charters - Bryan Lowe
Hi-Way Bait Store Don Mitchel
Hi Country Outfitters
Richard R. Cooper
Hi Valley Outfitters, Inc.
Bill Wright, Pres.
HIC Tours
James R. Ross & John Matsko
Hidden Bay Charters John Lurhs
Hidden Lake Outfitters
Henry W. Krenka
Hide-A-Way Charter Boat
Hide Away Lodge
Chuck & Danny Villeneuve
Hideaway Lodge Robert Folkes
High Adv. Air Charter, Inc.
Steve Barnum
High Adventure Air
George St. Catherine
High Adventure Air Charter
Mark, Greg & Sandra Bell, Monte
Mason,Jesse Updike,Kevin Waldrip,
Nathan Warren
High Adventure River Tours, Inc.
Randy McBride
High Cascade Descent
Todd J. Vanderzwiep
High Country Adventures
Rayland Lilley
High Country Connection
Larry C. Trimber
High Country Experience
Jeff & Kris Pralle
High Country Flies
High Country Outfitters
Chip Rizzotto
High Country Outfitters -Ray Seal
High Country Outfitters Woody,
Marlene, Matt & Marc McDowell
High Country Outfitters Fly Fishing
Lodge
High Country Outfitters, Inc.
Conrad A. Wygant
High Country Outfitters, LLC
Kathy Johnson
High Country Vacations
Bazil Leonard & Susan Feddema
High County Connections
Casey Veach
High Desert Angler
High Desert Drifters Guides &
Outfitters -Rick & Kim S. Killingsworth
High Desert Ranch, Inc.
Jay Reedy & Jeffrey Widener
High Flier Dwight & Jeff Metcalf
High Hampton Inn
High Impact Adventure Services, Inc.
High Island Ranch & Cattle Co.
Karen Robbins
High Llama Wilderness Tours, Inc.
Cutler Umbach
High Lonesome Outfitter & Guides
Thomas W. Bowers
High Lonesome Outfitters of
Colorado -Mark Lumpkins
High Lonesome Ranch -John H. Doden
High Meadows Ranch -Dennis Stamp
High Mountain Adventures
LaMont Merritt
High Mountain Drifter Guide
High Mountain Drifters, Inc.
Mike Wilson
High Mountain Hookers
High Mountain Outfitters
Pete Trujillo
High Park Outfitters Dan Aubuchon
High Peak Adventures, Inc.
Brian K. Malloy
High Plains Outfitters -Mike Bay
High Rise - Capt. Larrie Falder
High Roller Excursions -Lee Edding
High Sierra Fly Fishing - David Moss
High Spot Charters - Doug Bull
High Times Too Charter Boat
High Valley Ranch -Patrick E. McFall
Highland Marina & Resort
George Marovich
Highland Stage Company
Donald & Kristen Super
Highland to Island Guide Servide
James B. McKillip
Highlanders Outfitting & Guide, Co.
Rhonda Kellerer
Highlanding Camps -David Prevost
Highline Charters -William Webb, Jr.
Highliner Reginald Oleyer
Highwater Guide Service -Gary Walck
Hill's Charter Fishing Service
Richard Hill
Hill's Wilderness Canoe Trips
Hill Country Expeditions
Lois Hill
Hill Country Flyfishers
Hillcrest Motel & Outfitters
Kelly & Debra Morrell
Hillcrest Resort Mark & Claudia
Hilliard's Pine Island Camp
Butch & Neva Hilliard
Hills Guide Service
Clifford E. & Janice Hill
Hillside Guide Service
Hillsport Wilderness Hunting Camps
Mark & Karen Stephenson
Hillview Outfitters
Willard E. Forman
Hincks Palisades Creek Ranch
Bret Hincks
Hindman Charters
Richard S. & Terry H. Hindman
Hiwassee Scenic River Outfitters, Inc.
David Smith
Hobbs Resort Gib & Audrey Hobbs
Hobo Charters - Capt. T. Achtmann
Hoffman & Daughters
Robert B. Hoffman, Jr.
Hogancamp's Guide Service
Gregg & Paul Hogancamp
Holcomb's Guide Service
Mike Holcomb
Hole in the Wall Outfitters -Todd Earp
Holiday Glory Giffin
Holiday Charters
Ruby & Gerald Gwillim
Holiday Haven
Ernie & Sharon Kormendi
Holiday Long Range Holiday River
Expeditions of Idaho
Harold (Frogg) Stewart
Holiday Village - Doug Alexander
Holinshead Lake Resort & Outposts
Mitch Hagen
Holliday Landing - Joe Blattel
Holly Lynn Fishing Charters
Gary L. Huffman
Hollywood Charters - Ed Patzer
Holmes Lake Lodge/Recluse Lake
Camp Mike & Lavonne Dyste
Homer Baker Guide Service
Homer C. Baker
Homer Halibut Charters -Timothy Carr
Homestead Ranch-Ed F. Arnott
Hong Kong Drifter - Thomas Kilfoyle
Honokohau Boating Ltd.
Hook-Em Charters -Michael E. White
Hook-M-Up Tours, Inc.
Roy Wooderson & Jerry Peterson
Hook and Eye Charters -Sean Reilly
Hook, Line & Sinker-Jack W. Polley
Hooka-Tooka-Salmon Charters
Lyle D. Ludvick
Hooked! Charters -Capt. Jerry Bricko
Hookher Sportfishing Charters
Capt. Bill Maglione
Hooksetter's Guide Service
William Fortney
Hookup Guide Service - Jack Glass
Hooky-Lau Charters
Capt. Bruce Albright
Hoonah Charters
Gordon & Christina Pederson
Hoosier Bass 'n Gals
Hoosier Bassmasters -John Albertson
Hoosier Coho Club - Dan Messina
Hoosier Flyfishers - Al Fish
Hoosier Muskie Hunters- Jim Bagnoli
Hoover's Guide Service
Richard Hoover
Hope Fishing & Sightseeing Charters
Barbara J. Wright
Horicon Marsh Canoe Rental
Horizon River Adventures, Inc.
Vilis J. Zigurs
Horizon West Guides - Bruce Gipple
Horizons North Ltd.
Horse Creek Outfitters
Robert Bruce Malcolm
Horseshoe Charters
Capt. Robert Lechner
Horseshoe Creek Outfitters, Ltd.
Ray Jackson
Horseshoe Guide Service
Ted E. Dinsdale
Horseshoe Island Camp
Don & Marjorie Hueston
Horwood Lake Lodge
Cindy & Barry Edwards
Hot "T" Camp Jack Flowers
Hot Spot Charters -David L. Magnus
Hotline Charters - Richard W. Frost
Houston Clinton Co.
Houston Lake Camp -Ken & Iona Kronk
Howard's Guide Service
Howard's Sporting Camps
Glen Howard
Howard Charters -Christoper Howard
Howard Outfitters -Dale P. Howard
Howard Zehntner Hunting
Howard Zehntner
Howell's Timber Lodge
Howl-It Charters Steven E. Howlett
Hoyett's Grocery & Tackle
Jimmie & Jean Orr
Hua Pala Charters
Hub's Motel & Pier
Ron, Derek & Tyler Hubbard
Hubbard's Yellowstone Lodge
Hubbard's Yellowstone Outfitter
James L. Hubbard
Hubbard Creek Outfitters & Pack
Station Larry Allen
Huber's Lone Pine Camp
Walter Huber
Huck Finn Sportfishing
Huckleberry Heaven Lodge
Huddle's South Shore Resort
Roy & Kay Huddle
Huff House Joe & Joanne Forness
Hugh's Guide Service
Hugh E. Crawford
Hughes River Expeditions, Inc.
Jerry Hughes
Hula Girl Sportfishing
Humboldt Outfitters Mike K. Morrison
Humdinger Sportfishing
Hume River Enterprises
Charlie Barnaby
Hungry Fisherman Charters
Richard & Nancy Diemer
Hunky Dory Enterprises -James Kent
Hunt Alaska - Virgil L. Umphenour
Hunt River Camps- Clyde House
Hunter's Point -John & Laurie Siebolds
Hunter Banks Co.
Hunters Montana -Keith J. Atcheson
Huntress Sportfishing
Huron Charter Service -Allen Elzinga
Huron/Clinton Metrop. Auth.
Hurst Fishing Service
Husky Lake Cabin Rentals
John Roland
Huzzah Valley Camping Resort
Cottrell Family
Hyak Alaska Charters Gary McWilliams
Hyatt's Manion Lake Camp
Don & Brenda Hyatt
Hyde Outfitters
Hynes Trout Fishing & Lodging
Dan & Vera Hynesq
I & R Outfitters A. H. Knowles
Ice Water Adventures
Paul Hansen
Icelinus Charters Jeffrey Alden
Icha & Illgatcho Mountains Outfitters
Roger Williams
Icosa Village Corp.
Lina & Henri Lacroix
Icy Beaver Rentals
Don & Terry Johnson
Icy Strait Adventures
Joe & Sandra Craig
Icy Straits Charters -Robert Clark
Icy Straits Charters -Jamie F. Coby
Idaho Afloat - Bruce Howard
Idaho Angling Service
David T. Glasscock
Idaho Fishing Charters
William J. Spicklemire
Idaho Guide Service, Inc.
James L. Powell
Idlewilde Resort & Lodge
Gary & Judy Stellick
Ignace Outposts Ltd.
Brad & Karen Greaves
Ihu Nui Sportfishing, Inc.
Iilsgidaay's (Shiny Lady's) Charters
Lisa Marie Lang
Iliamna Bearfoot Adventures
Greg & Sally Hamm
Iliaska Lodge, Inc. - Ted Gerken
Ilima V Charter Fishing
Illusions, Inc.
Impulse Chartes, Inc.
IN B.A.S.S. Federation - Steve Cox
IN Bass 'n Gals - Karen Welty
Inconnu Lodge
Independent Brysan Mulkey
Independent Whitewater
William Block
Indian Bay Connections
Tony Rogers
Indian Creek Lodge
Kenneth Jonesand Valerie Abney
Indian Creek Lodge
William Dixson
Indian Creek Lodge Ken R. Jones
Indian Hills Farm, Inc.
Hersh & Karen Kendall
Indian Peak Outfitters
Ardis M. Wright
Indian River Ranch Guides &
Outfitters Jamie Schumacher
Indian Rock Camps
Indian Summer Outfitters
Rick House
Indian Trail Outfitters
Bob Cherepak
Indianapolis Bass Hawks
John Reynolds
Indianapolis Flycasters
Daniel Allen
Indiaonta Resort
Herb & Vi Humphreys
Indy Bassmasters - Dennis McGee
Indy Procasters - Tony Harlow
Ingset Guide Service
Iniakuk Lake Wilderness Lodge
Inian Island Charters Fred C. Howe
Inkrote's Guide Service
William Inkrote
Inland Charter Service
Cal Butterfield
Inland Drifters, LLC-Kimberly Moore
Inland Ocean Charters
John T. Robson
Inland River Charters Kenneth V. & L.
Colleen Conner
Inlet Charters Gary Ault
Inlet Charters Harris Miller
Inn at Narrow Passage Ed Markel
Inner Harbor Lodge
Mike & Sandy Hayes
Instinctive Outdoors - Marvin Park
Interactive Outdoors - Tim Bradley
Interior A.K. Adventures
Logan G. Ricketts
Interior Fishing Guide -Chet R.T. Higa
Intermountain Excursions
Darell Bentz
International Excursions-Pat Cooper
Intrepid, Inc.
Inverlochy Resort -Karl & Mai Saarna
Inverness Falls Resort
Stuart & Judy Cornell
Irish Lord Charters-Robert Carroll
Irish Lord Charters
Monty H. & Florita F. Richardson
Irish Rover Charters
Anastatia Gleeson & Charles Ash
Irishlord Charters Jason Sintek
Iron Head Guide Service
Jack E. Dailey
Iron Horse Outfitters-Art Griffith
Ironsides- Michael E. Caplis
Island 10 Fishing Retreat
Fred & Ruby Knecht
Island Adventures-Paul A. Chervenak
Island Adventures
Michael McVey, Gregg Parsley
Island Alaska Charters-Patrick L. Smith
Island Charters on Aukai
Island Coast Charters
Kenneth J. Rear
Island Eagle ChartersEdward C. Leask
Island Girl Charters, Inc.
Island Lake Camp
Gord & Ellie Mitchell
Island Lake Lodge
Darryl Heppner & Dennis Brears
Island Memories
Sandra L. Vinberg
Island Point Lodge, Inc.
Kevin & Frank Stelmach
Island Queen Charters
Capt. Jack Behrens
Island Rod & Flies -Stu Simpson
Island Vacation Services
Susan W. Motter
Island View Cabins-Leonard J. Ryan
Island View Lodge
Jim& Candace Bischoff
Island Wings Air Service
Michelle Masden
Islander Charters-Ole/Sandy Bartness
Islander II Charters
Iverson Sport Fishing-John Iverson
Ivory Gull Charters-Mark A. Wartes
J-Bird's Fishing Guide Service
Jay Oaks
J-Hook Fisheries - D.L. Corwelius
J-L Outfitters - Arthur J. Stevens
J-Lyn Charters-Kenneth Janice Deaton
J & B Capt.Kerry Douton
J & D Jumbo Outfitters/K. & C.
Outfitting
Jim Hoard & Kathy Hoard
J & J Charters - Jay B. Myer
J & J Charters -Capt. Jonesy Nelson
J & J Oufitters - James E. Champion
J & J Outfitters of Colorado, Inc.
Gerald L. Woolsey
J & J Smart Charters
John & Joan Smart
J & K Outfitters - P. Michael Kush
J & K Steamship Co.-John Chamberlain
J & L Guide Service
Gerald Stambaugh
J & M Charters - Jack Jaynes
J & Ray Colorado High County, Inc.
Ronald Franks
J & S Charters - John Hartrick
J & V Guides & Outfitters
Glenn Jones & Lonny Vanatta
J B Ranch Mark Balette
J Bar B Guiding & Outfitting
James D. Beall
J C Higgins Guide Service
James C. Higgins
J E Fishing Enterprises
Capt. Fritz Peterson
J R Outfitters
J&J Charters/Bottom Line Charters
James Russo
J. Fair's Hand Tied Flies
J. Lloyd Woods Game Leases
J. R.'s Outfitting John W. Rudyk
J.B.'s Guide Service - John Gilcrease
J.C. Trujillo Guide & Outfitter
J.C. Trujillo
J.R.'s Fishing Guide Service
John Riedesel
J/L Ranch Outfitter and Guides Inc.
Linda & Joe Jessup
Jack's Charter Service
Capt. Jack Remus
Jack's Fishing Resort
Jack's Kings & Silvers
Jack & Betty Petersen
Jack's Taxidermy/Guiding
Jack & Toni's Fall Lake Log Cabins
Jack & Toni Dulinsku
Jack River Outfitters- Jim Allison
Jacklin's Outfitters
Robert V. Jacklin
Jackpot Charters - Kenneth Kulm
Jackpot Charters - Linda Price
Jackson's Arctic Circle Tours
Wilfred Jackson
Jackson's Hole Adventures
Jackson Peak Outfitters
Charlie M. Petersen, Jr.
Jacobs Island Park Ranch
F. Mitch Jacobs
Jacobsen's Guide Service
Leif Jacobsen
Jacques Adventure Company
Jerry Jacques
Jake's Alaska Wilderness Outfitters
John "Jake" Caudet
Jake's Buck n Rut Hunting Camp
Jake's Horses, Inc.
Kent "Jake" Grimm
Jake's Northwest Angle
Dave Colson
Jake's Rio Grande Outfitting Service
David J. Powell
Jamal Charters, Inc.- J.S. Hanna
Jambro, Inc.- Thomas James
James & Drew Morris
James Morris
James Bay Outfitters & Air Service
Ltd. Rob Lafleur
James Outfitting & Guide Service
James & Clifford Nabess
James P. Gillam Outfitting
James P. Gillam
Jamie Prather Guide & Outfitters
Jamie Prather
Jamieson House Inn Heidi
Hutchinson
Jammin' Salmon's Guide Service
Donny Morris
Jan's Mountain Outfitters
Jan Lake Lodge Co. Ltd.
Richard & Marie-Paule Koopman
Janice Lyn Kenneth R. Deaton
Janis Robinette William H. Robinette
Jans Mountain Outfitters
Tina Quayle
Jason's Custom Charters
Jason Loren Carter
Jaws II Charters - Capt. Allen Sprang
JC Rose Guiding - James C. Rose
JD's Adventures - James D. Palin
Jeannie Sea II - Rex B. Davis
Jed's Landing Guide Service
Monte Hepper
Jeff's Fishing Charter Service
Jeff Smith
Jeff Allen Guide Service -Jeff Allen
Jeff Carr Professional Guide &
Outfitter - Jeff J. Carr
Jeff Russell Drift Boat Charter Service
Jeff Russell
Jeff Shuff'Tween Waters Inn
Jenkins Fishing Service & Motel
Eric S. & Terry G. Jenkins
Jennie Lynn Charters
Capt. Norrie Reykdal
Jennifer Smith Fly Casting
Jennifer L. Smith
Jepco Charters Jep Hansen
Jerry's Charters
Jerry S. Montgomery
Jerry's Guide Service
Gerald R. Sanderson
Jerry Clouse Guide Service-J. Clouse
Jerry Crabs Fly Fisher-Jerry Crabs
Jerry Hadden's Guide Service
Jerry Malson Outfitting
Jerry R. Malson
Jerry Metcalf Fishing Guide-J. Metcalf
Jerry Tubbs Guide Service-J. P. Tubbs
Jessica Lake Lodge-Bill & Laurie Scarfe
Jester Charter Service
Capt. Gary L. Conger
John Henry Lee Outfitters, Inc.
John Lee
Jig'm Up Guide Service-Paul Folden
Jim's Camp - Nistowiak Falls
James Daniel McKenzie
Jim's Guide Service-James McCormick
Jim's Guide Service
Jim McCormick, JamesWhetzel
Jim's Jaunts James R. Hamp
Jim's Oregon Whitewater-Jim Berl
Jim's Sport Fishing Charters
Jim Beyers
Jim's Taxidermy- Jim & Pat Wendt
Jim & Pat Lanier Weeki Wachee
Marina
Jim Borovicka Everglades Explorers
Jim Dandi Promotions Jim Hewitt
Jim Dunlevy Guide Service
James C. Dunlevy
Jim Jarvis' Guide & Outfitting Service
James Howard Jarvis
Jim Mackey's Guide Service
James T. Mackey
Jim McBee Outfitter James L. McBee
Jim Pringle's Guide Service
James B. Pringle
Jim Rivers Co. - James L. Irvin
Jim Rusk Fishing - James Rusk
Jim Schollmeyer Flyfishing Guide
James L. Schollmeyer
Jimmie D. Charters - James Decker
Jimmie Jack Charters, LLC.
James Drath & James Drath, Sr.
Jimmy Fly Charters
Capt. Jim Christman
JKB Outfitters & Guides
John K. Kajiwara
JML Outfitters
Marguerite M. & Marie Haskett
Jodan Partnership
Joann Bailey & Daniel Glaab
Joe's Alaskan Fishing Adventure
Joseph & Patti Szczesny
Joe's Guide Service - Joe Drose
Joe Bergh's River Fishing Trips
Jonas A. Bergh
Joe Cantrell Outfitting - Joe Cantrell
Joe Miller Guide Service - Joe Miller
Joe Schuster Guide/Outfitter
Joe Schuster
Joel McKellar Joel McKellar
John's Campground
John's Guide Service-John C. McMillan
John's Outfitter & Guide Service
John R. Harmon
John & Diosa's Wabaskang Camp
John & Diosa Record
John & Don's Guide Service
John Gamble & Don VanDenboss
John Brawley George Brawley
John Greene's Fly Fishing Service

John J. Greene
John H. Latham, Reg. Guide & Outfitter - Frances C. Latham
John Haney Flyfishing Services
John W. Haney
John Hanson MTI, Inc. -John Hanson
John Hazel & Company -John T. Hazel
John Huck Paul Schlafley
John Maki Outfitters - John C. Maki
John Oppelt Flyfishing Outfitter
John R. Oppelt
John Perry's West Slope Outfit
John R. Perry
John Snow's Guide Service
John S. Snow
John Theriault Air Ltd.
John Theriault
John VanDusen
Charles M. VanDusen
John W. Rokos Robert C. Rokos
Johnny's East River Lodge
Janice Lowenstein
Johnson's Pere Marquette Lodge
Johnson's Salmon Service
Brian Johnson
Johnson & Sons Enterprises
Leonard Johnson
Johnson Bros. Sportfishing Guides
James K. Johnson
Johnson Cattle Company
Johnson Outfitters -Kathryn Johnson
Johnson Outfitting- Dean Johnson
Johnson River Camp-Jean Graham
Joka's Wild Charter Boat
Jolly Rogers Charters - Dennis Rogers
Jon James Adventures - Jon James
Jones Junkets - Robert Jones
Jonny Be Good Sport Fishing Charters
Capt. Jon Verhelst
Josdal Camps - Tyrone Josdal
Joseph Fly Shoppe - Robert R. Lamb
Joseph Dubler Guiding-J. M. Dubler
Joseph R. Harris
Joseph Royzer David Royzer
Josephson Outfitting
Ed & Lisa Josephson
Journey's North Outfitting, Inc.
Nancy Kyro
Joyce Marie Charters
Thomas Mahoney
Joyce Rehr's Fly Fishing & Light Tackle
JR's Marina
JR Buffalo Creek Outfitters
John W. Robidou
Jr. Amick's Guide Service-J. R. Amick
JT Outfitters - Jeff Burtard
Judd's Resort - Ron & Sharon Hunter
Judd Cooney Outfitting & Guiding
Judd Cooney
Judith A. Rank Jerry D. Rank
Judith River Ranch - Steve Musick
Judy Ann's Alaskan - Daniel Schaff
Judy Ann AK Charters - Dan Schapt
Judy Draper William Draper
Jughead Salmon Charters
John Metcalf
Julie Buxton Stanley Buxton
Jumping Rainbow Ranch
Jun Ken Po Sportfishing
Juniper Lodge & Cottages
Frank & Eileen MacDonald
Juniper Mountain Outfitters, Inc.
Stanley & Paul Meholchick
Jupiter 12 Gilles Dumaresq
Just In Time Industries - Ron Cutler
Justus Outfitters Dan Justus
K-Bay Charters
Steve Morphis and Kenneth Copple
K-Mark Canoe Rental
K-Z Guest Ranch & Outfitters
Dave Segall
K & D Majestic Outfitters
Daniel S. Ruscetti
K & G Sportfishing Lodge
Greg & Kris Gehrig
K & K Outfitters - Marion Bricker
K & K River Drifters - Fred B. Hall
K & N Outfitting - Wade D. Nixon
K & P Outfitters
S. Van Buskirk & S. Garrett
K & S Charters - Capt. Karl Schmidt
K Lazy Three Ranch
Mary Faith Hoeffner
K R Outfitting - Kim Reyer
K. D. McKay Outfitting
Kenneth D. McKay
K. S. B. Outfitters & Guiding Service
Kenneth S. Biglow
K.E. Schultz Guide & Outfitting Service
Kurt E. Schultz & Art Gurule
KaBeeLo Lodge - Harold & Ann Lohn
Kachemack Bay Water Taxi
Michael and Diane McBride
Kachemak Marine Services-Dan Klein
Kachemak Recreational Services
Richard A. Baltzer
Kaegudeck Lake Lodge
Kahlitna Fish Camp-Roy Keen
Kahuna Kai
Kain's Fishing Adventures, Inc.
Greg Kain
Kaleidoscope Cuises -Barry E. Bracken
Kalgin Island Seaside Lodge
David Chessik
Kaliakh River Adventures
D. Scott & Candace Ranney
Kamalame Cove
Kamome Sport Fishing
Kamp Kinniwabi -Bill & Barb Beckham
Kamp Kiseralik
Kakarmiut Corp.
Kanektok River Safaris, Inc.
Qanirtuug, Inc.
Kanipahow Kamps Ltd.
Kanoe People Ltd.
Kanukawa Outfitters
Terry & Diane Carlin
Kap Outfitters -Ron & Lise Marchand
Kar-McGee's Outdoor Adventures
Karasti Trophy Lodge
James R. & Alice L. Karasti, Sr.
Karen Jones Fishing Guide Service
Karen Ann Jones
Karluk Spit Lodge
Arthur Panamaroff
Karpen's Sunset Bay Resort
Joe & Marty
Kasba Lake Lodge
Kashabowie Outposts Gerri & Dave
Sutton & Fern Duquette
Kasilof Drifters William Borgen
Kaskattama Safari Adventures
Charlie Taylor & Christine Quinlan
Katahdin View Lodge & Camps
Jack Downing
Katamiland, Inc.
Raymond F. Petersen
Katche Kamp Outfitters
Bill & Jeanne Blackmon
Katmai Fishing Adventures
Nanci A. Morris
Katmai Guide Service - Joseph Klutsch
Katmai Lodge Tony Sarp
Kaufmann's Fly Fishing Expeditions, Inc.
Randall W. Kaufmann
Kawdy Outfitters Stan Lancaster
Kawishiwi Lodge & Outfitters
Frank T. Udovich
Kayak Express - Peter B. Wright
KC's Charter Fishing
Kyle D. & Connie E. Sinclair
KCR Camp Limited
Richard & Gloria Castle
KDK Charter Service
Capt. David Koneczny
Keating Outfitters - Earl R. Keating, Jr.
Keeley Lake Lodge
Gary & Gloria Callihoo
Keetah Fish Camp
Dennis & Barbara Roper
Keeting's Sportman Hunting & Fishing - Gerald A. Keeting
Keighley's Camps - Mark Lantz
Keith Gain Eric Nordenson
Keller's Kenai Sport Fishing
Patrick Keller
Kellum Enterprises - Daryl E. Kellum
Kelly's Sporting Lodge
Carmon Kelly & Lorne MacDonald
Kelly Creek Fly Fishers
Gary D. Lang
Kelsey's Guide Service -Lanny Kelsey
Kemoo Trout Farm
Kemperman - William L.Kemperman
Ken's Charters-Kenneth/Barbara Klein
Ken Martin Professional River Guide
Ken Martin
Ken Mountain's River Guide Service
Ken Mountain
Ken Robinson River Guide
Kenneth W. Robinson
Ken Wilson Guide Service-Ken Wilson
Kenai Angler Thomas Jessing
Kenai Coast Charters -
Robert K. Reiman
Kenai Fjords Outfitters, Inc.
Terry Reece
Kenai Fjords Outfitters, Inc.
Russ Smith
Kenai Fly Fisher Stan Smith
Kenai King Drifters - David Musgrave
Kenai King Fishing Charters
Peter E. Deluca
Kenai Lake Adventures-Michael Bethe
Kenai Lake Adventures
Kevin McCarthy
Kenai Lake Adventures & Air Service
Kenneth Bethe
Kenai River Bend-Mike Kelly
Kenai River Guide Service
Raymond McGuire
Kenai River King - Daniel Paulk
Kenauk, The Seigniory at Montebello
Kenda Wilderness Lodg-The Bennetts
Kendall Point Lodge -Darren Deason
Kennebago River Kamps
Kennedy Lake
Kennisis Lake Lodge
Adelheid & Dan Buhl
Kenosew Sipi Outdoor Adventures
Ken Albert
Kent A. Walker Prince Albert
Kenyon Lake Fly-In
Kern Grieve Guide Service
Kern Grieve
Kerr's Slow Boat Charters
Clint J. & Johnny M. Kerr
Ket-Chun-Eny Lodge The St. Germain's
Ketch-All-Charters -Michael S. Krieger
Ketcham's Fishing Charter
Dennis L. Ketcham
Ketchum Air Service, Inc.
Craig Ketchum
Kettle Hills Outfitters-Victor Gervais
Kev's Fishing Charter- Kevin Pickett
Kevin's Guide Service -Kevin Hicks
Kevin's King Salmon Inc.
Kevin Zimmerman
Kevin Ender Dale W. Ender
Kevin Hackert Thomas Perilloux
Kevin Tourand Outfitting
Key-O's Guide Service
Lynn Keogh
Key Marine Resort
Gil & Val Gariup
Keystone Resorts
Barb & Lionel St. Godard
KG Guides & Outfitters
Ken D. Graber
Kidney Creek Farms & Preserve
Gary Breski
Killarney Mountain Lodge
Maurice & Annabelle East
Kilman Rental Cottages
Lorne & Myra Kilkenny
Kimball Creek Guide
Berwyn B. Bowman, Jr.
Kimberley's Eagle West Resort
Steve, Todd & Sean
King's Budget Charters - Jeffrey King
King's Guide Service Douglas R. King
King's Sportfishing - Joanne Fitzerald
King & Bartlett Fish & Game
King Bear Lodge John Bryant
King Bear Lodge
Kenneth Christoffersen, Sr. & Jr.
King Bear Lodge Danny Germany
King Bear Lodge James Ivey
King Bear Lodge
Andrew Piekaeski
King Bear Lodge
Raymond Thornton
King Buck Safaris - Larry Leschyshyn
King Catcher Charter Service
Capt. Wayne Zimmer
King Charters - Mark E. Buchner
King Creek Outfitters -Mike Rodriguez
King Fisher Charters-Terry/Kathie King
King Guiding Service - Jan King
King Halibut Charters
Lucien LaFlamme
King Ko Inn -Matt Norman & Biz Smith
King Master Charters
Helmer W. & Annette C. Olson
King of King's Guide Service
Paul Pearson
King of Kings Guide Service
Richard & Bonnie Andersen
King of Kings Guide Service
Richard Beven II
King Pint Lodge Ronald Dionne
King Point Darren Beko
King Point Lodge
Jeff Woodward & Bruno Krebs
King Point Lodge
Patrick Nelson, Jeffrey Ulsky
King Salmon Guides, Inc.
Todd Dirks
King Salmon Guides, Inc.
Aaron Ratkovich
King Size Adventures
Kenneth Bingaman
Kingfish Charter Boat
Kingfish Guide Service
Kingfisher Charter Service
Dave Benore
Kingfisher Charters
Seth Bone, Ken Heaps, Terry R. King
Kingfisher Drifting, Ltd.-Michael Truch
Kingfisher Expeditions-Steve Settles
Kings Run Charters
Lawrence B. & Suzan E. Cobb
Kingsclear Outfitters Phil Atwin
Kiniskan Outfitters Bruce Creyke
Kinn's Katch Charters
Capt. Howard Kinn
Kinogami Lodge
Robert Marilyn Plourde
Kinsley Outfitters
Kiowa Hunting Service, Inc.
Alfred H. Cata
Kirawan Custom Cruises
Frederick N. & Marti A. Anderson
Kirk Leasing Corp.
Kississing Lake Lodge Curt Enns
Kitchen Pass Charters
Steven M. & Arnel A. Whitney
Kittiwake Charters Don Ingledue
Klamath River Outfitters
Klessig's Guide Service-Jeffrey Klessig
Klick's K Bar L Ranch-Dick/Nancy Klick
Klondike Mike's Drift Fishing
Michael Johnson
Kluachesi Lake Outfitting
Kluane Outfitters Ltd. - Ross Elliott
Kluane Wilderness Lodge
Klukas Lake Ranch - Glen Kilgour
Klutina Lake Lodge
Mike & Samuel Jordan
Knee Lake Resort, Inc. Phil Reid
Knight Island Adventures
Kenneth Storlie
Knik Guide Service - John Whitlatch
Kniktuk Outfitters, Inc.-Cynthia Wener
Knobby's Fly-In Camps
Knobby & Bobbie Clark
Known World Guide Service
John Weinmeister
Knudson Charter Service
Capt. Richard Knudson
Kodiak-Katmai Outdoors, Inc.
Clint & Sharol Hlebechuk
Kodiak Adventures - Rocky Morgan
Kodiak Discoveries
Thomas H. Stick
Kodiak Island Charters
Chris & Jainan Fiala
Kodiak Kingbuster Sportsfishing
John & Joy Parker
Kodiak Lucky Hook Charters
Fred O'Hearn
Kodiak Sports & Tour-Scott R. Phelps
Kodiak Too Sport Fishing Charters
Capt. Larry Morrison
Kodiak Western Charters
David Harville & Eric Stirrup
Kodiak Wilderness Lodge
Jim Hamilton & Mitch Hull
Kohl's Clearwater Outfitter
Robin J. Kohls
Kokomo Bass Anglers - E. Prickett
Kokomo Bass Busters - Jim Wells
Koksetna Wilderness Lodge
Jonathan H. & Juliann W. Cheney
Kona Concept, Inc.
Kona Sunrise Charters
Kona Trading Co., Inc.
Kono Sport Fishing Charters
Koo-Sto Wilderness Outfitters
Phillip L. Foster
Koocanusa Resort & Outfitters
Kootenai Angler - David Blackburn
Kootenai River Outfitters
Gary McCabe
Koser's Yukon Outback
Kraft Adventures - Keith Maltison
Krause's Goose Camp/So. Whitlock
Resort Chuck Krause
Krestof Charters - David Pearson
Krog's Kamp - Mel & Bob Krogseng
Kruda Che Wilderness Guiding
KS Fisheries Geoff Widdows
Kuhele Kai
Kum-Bac-Kabins
Joyce Molyneaux
Kurtti Marine - Robert Kurtti
Kuskokwim Wilderness Adventures
Michael, Jill & Bev Hoffman
Kusstum Tours & Guide Service
John R. Bilenduke
Kutzkey's Guide Service
Albert Kutzkey
Kuu Huapala Fishing Co., Inc.
Kuuloa Kai Charters
Kuykendall Outfitters, Inc.
Leroy M. Kuykendall
KW Wapiti Outfitters, LLC
John Knoll
Kyle Wall's Trout Burn Guide Service
L'But Kick'n Charters
Dennis D. Hubble
L-B Fishing & Guide Service
Ronald W. Bloxham
L & D Fishing Tours
W. Lee Viands
L & D Fly Fishing/Three Rivers Ranch
Lonnie Lee Allen
L & K Guide Service
Lonnie Edward & Kim Peters
L & M Charters - Michael & Linda Slifer
L & M Fly-In Outpost
Larry & Mary Adams
L & M Guides & Outfitters
LeRoy Ramsay
L & M Sportfishing
Capt. Hank Searles
L & S Company
Lawrence & Shirley Rodger
L & W Enterprises
Wayne E. Lofton
L Diamond E Ranch Outfitters
Dan J. & Retta Ekstrom
L.A. Outfitting
Denesoline Corp. Ltd.
L.C. Ranch
La Ronge Eagle Point Resort
Labelle's Birch Point Camp
Dale & Linda Labelle
Labrador 2BG Adventure Inc.
Mr. F. Denis Boisvert
Labrador Interior Outfitters Ltd
Rick Adams
Labrador Salmon Lodge
Labrador Sportsfish Ltd.
Vince & Jim Burton
Lac La Peche Resort -Eloise Vigeant
Lac Seul's Scout Lake Resort
The Schreiners
Lac Seul Airways Ltd.John & Pat Renfro
Lac Seul Evergreen Lodge & Golden Eagle Resort - Gary & Pat Beardsley
Lacy's Whitewater & Wild Fish
Craig Lacy
Lady Grey Lake Outfitters
Karl Hoffman
Lady Luck Charters - Glen M. Clough
Lady Margaret -Capt. Claude Adams
Lady Van Charter - Capt. Gary Eis
Lahaina Charter Boats
Laine's Guide Service
Laine W. Lahrdt
Lakair Lodge - Kevin & Leslie Cameron
Lake Barkley State Resort Park
Lake Charters, Inc.
Robert A. Carbone
Lake Clark Air, Inc./The Farm Lodge
Glen R., Sr. & Jean P. Alsworth
Lake Co. Fish & Game Protective Assoc. - Bob Westfall
Lake Creek Lodge
Brenda & John Shrader
Lake Creek Lodge - Jeff Woodward
Lake Douglas - Albert Mitchell
Lake Erie Charter Service
Captain Dave Law
Lake Fork Outfitters & Guest Ranch
James A. Metter
Lake Hatchineha Marina
Lake Herridge Lodge
Pat & Mike Thomas
Lake Iliamna Adventures
John Baechler
Lake Kashabowie Lodge
Dan & Irene Mado & Sons
Lake Lady Charters
Capt. Lenny Westover
Lake Manitoba Narrows Ltd.
Lake Marion Guide Service
Donnie Baker, Sr.
Lake Michigan Charter Service
Mike Rusch
Lake Michigan Fishing Charter
Dave Helder
Lake Michigan Sport Fishing Charters
Capt. Eric Hauke
Lake Michigan Sport Fishing Coal.
Janet Ryan
Lake Obabika Lodge
The Herburger Family
Lake of the Woods Houseboats
Noreen Luce
Lake Placid Lodge - Charlie Levitz
Lake Retreat Outfitter & Charters
Rob Wilson
Lake Spider Charters
Capt. Pete Bragarnick
Lake Superior Excursions
Dana & ChunAe Kollars
Lake Tahoe Adventures
Lake Texoma Resort Park
Lake Tocoleen
Lake Trout with Bob - Robert Plouffe
Lakeland Express, Inc.
Capt. Dean Clemons
Lakeland Marine Rentals Ltd.
Albin Walcer
Lakeland Motel & Charter Service
Laker Charters - Capt. Craig Nolan
Lakeshore Resort-Chuck & Mary Ward
Lakeside Lodge
Norm & Brad Johnson
Lakeview Inn Wilbur- George Bauer
Lakeview Resort
John & Julie VanVeen
Lakeville Conservation Club
Ronald Yoder
LaMarche Creek Outfitting Co.
Russell B. Smith
Lambert's Ice Fishing Services
Yvon Lambert
Lamicq Guides & Outfitters, Inc.
John & Diane Lamicq
Lancaster Outfitters-Patrick Lancaster
Land O'Lakes Lodge
Christine & Robin Burke
Landing Zone Charters
Capt. Dick Dennie
Landon Ranch John i. Landon
Lang Lake Resort- Howard/Carol Acton
Lani Hendricks Thomas J. Poynter
Lannigan, Inc.
David & Vicki Lannigan
Lapham Outfitters Max C. Lapham
LaPorte Co. Bassmasters
Frank Nowak
Larry's Guide Service- Larry D. Skirvin
Larry Erickson's Alpine Outfitters
Larry Erickson
Larry Waltrip, Guide Larry Waltrip
laska Anglers Steve Voth
Lass & Ron Mills Outfitters
Lass Dudley
Last Best Place Tours
Graeme R. McDougal
Last Chance Outfitters, Inc.
Lynn Sessions
Last Frontier Adventures
Nick Pendergast
Last Frontier Charters
Ralph C. & Jacqueline J. Burnett
Last Frontier Fishing Comp.
Joe Cannava & Chris Cromer
Last Stand Outfitters August D. Egdorf
Latigo Ranch James A. Yost
LaTourell's Resort & Outfitters
The LaTourells
Laurel Highlands River Tours, Inc.
Mark McCarty
Laurel Ranch S.L. Laurel
Laurie River Lodge
Brent Fleck
Lava Creek Lodge
Lawrence's Camps -Bob Lawrence
Layla Sportfishing
Lazy-Sun Charters
Timothy Joseph Billings
Lazy 3X Ranch - David H. Farny
Lazy C2 Bar Ranch -James Kelly Sewell
Lazy Daze Charters -Capt. Jeff Baird
Lazy F Bar Outfitters- Bill Guerrieri
Lazy FF Outfitters- Kirk A. Ellison
Lazy J Outfitters, Inc.Larry - A. Jarrett
Lazy Laker Charters-Capt. Don Mitchell
Lazy TX Outfitting - Clayton W. Voss
Le Billet D'Or Ted Meskunas
Lea Guide Service - Wallace Lea
LeChasseur Sport Fishing -Joe Weiss
LeConte Outfitters
David & Wanda Helmick
Ledoux's Outfitters-Lawrence Ledoux
Lee's Ferry Lodge-Maggie Sacher
Lee Palm Sportfishers
Lee Sells Outfitter & Guide
Lee D. Sells
Lee Watson Outfitters- Lee W. Watson
Leeder Hunting Charles F. Leeder
Leelanau Yacht Charter
Lee Russell
Legal Tender III James Read
Lei Aloha Charter Fishing
Leisure Bay Holiday Resort
Karl & Klaudia Gross
Leisure Fishing Charters
George Wm. Wiese
Leisure Time Charters
Capt. Mike Pjevach
Leisure Time Charters
Albert Stuefloten

Lennie's Guided Tours
Archie Lennie
Lenny Dipaolo's Guided Fishing
Lenny Dipaolo
Lennyland Outfitters Mark J. Tierney
Leonard's Landing Lodge, Inc.
Dawn Otto
Leonard Outfitting - Randy Leonard
Lepley Creek Ranch- Matthew Halmes
Leprechaun Custom Charters
Joan L. Herbage
Leroy's Guide Service - Leroy Phillipi
Les Brandt's Trolling Service
Les Brandt
Les Enterprises du Lac Perdu, Inc.
Michel and Mary-Ann Auclair
Let's Go Fish Now -Jim H. Hindman, Jr.
Let's Go Fishing! Bluegill Page
Lew & Clark Expeditions Corp.
Michael John Geary
Lewis & Clark Trail Adventures
Wayne Fairchild
Lewis & Clark Trail Guide Service
Todd Langeliers
Lewis Charters
Nevin Dahl, Daniel Lewis
LH7 Bandera Ranch
Libby Sporting Camps
Matthew and Ellen Libby
Lick Creek Guiding Services
Michael Sexton
Lifetime Adventures-Alaska
Curtis L. Hirschkorn
Light House Harbor Co., Inc.
Bob Blake
Light Line Adventures
Steven A. Lucas
Lighthouse Charter Service
James R. Peters
Lighthouse Charters-Burgess Bauder
Lighthouse Charters
Capt. John Nolte
Lil' Hooker Sportfishing
Lil' Toledo Lodge - Ronald L. King
Lincoln's Camps - Maynard Drew
Linda-Vue Charters-Capt. Walt Boname
Linda Cain Sasser Diamond H Ranch
Linda L. Moloney
Donald G. Moloney
Lindbergh's Air Service-Brian Simms
Linden Partners, Inc. - Lee Hoyt
Lindsey's Rainbow Resort
Jared W. Lindsey
Lindwood Lodge - Gerry Lindskog
Line Stripper Fishing Adventures
Daniel E. Welch
Linehan Outfitting Co.
Timothy Linehan
Linus Charters Dennis McElroy
Lion Creek Outfitters -Cecil Noble
Lisa Mae Charters -Daniel D. Dunsing
Lisianski Charter-Denny & Paul Corbin
Lisianski Inlet Lodge -Gail D. Corbin
Lissivigeen
Little Bald Peak Lodge, Ltd.-Al King
Little Bayou Meto Duck & Bass Lodge
Jim Cunningham
Little Bear Lake Resort-Dwayne Giles
Little Big Horn Lodge
Harry L. Ergott, Jr.
Little Creek Outfitters-John Ecklund
Little Dipper Charter Service
Carl L. Hatch
Little Grand Rapids Lodge
Ernie Janzen
Little Grizzly Creek Ranch, Inc.
Leo Douglas Sysel
Little Harbour Deep Lodge
Cyril Pelley
Little Hobo Charters
Michael G. Paterson
Little John's Guide Service
John A. Kopy, Jr.
Little Man's Guide Service
Terry Blankenship
Little Pine Lodge -Wendy & Pat Tyson
Little Red River Trout Dock
Little Rockies Outfitting
David L. Rummel
Little Saint Simons Island
Little Wood River Outfitters
Robert L. Hennefer
Lloyd Lake Lodge
Richard & Mary Jean Pliska
Lobstick Lodge
Local Waters Flyfishing
Local Yocal James J. Slone
Loch Island Lodge Ltd.
Andy & Amy Wilson
Lochlomond Camp
Larry & Deb Hadenko
Lochsa River Company
Gregory Bell
Lochsa River Outfitters
Jacey Nygaard
Lockhart Guide Service
Edward D. Lockhart
Locopolis Hunting & Fishing Lodge
Lodge Across the Bay
George & Nancy Curtiss
Log Cabin Lodge George Pike
Log Cabin Resort & RV
Verne L. & Martin J. Fabry
Log Chateau Lodge
Geoff & Jenny Pinckston
Lone Cone Outfitters, Inc.
Ron M. Clements
Lone Mountain Ranch
Robert L. Schaap
Lone Tree Fly Goods -David W. Borjas
Lone Willow Creek Guide Service
Jim M. Schell
Lone Wolf Campground & Outfitting
Arnold Poirier
Lone Wolf Charters - John J. Bosarge
Lone Wolf Expeditions
Mitchell D. McDougal
Lone Wolf Guide Service
Mark A. Baumeister
Lonely Lake Outfitting
Ken Spence
Loner Guide Service, Inc.
Bradley T. Weinmeister
Lonesome Dove Charters
Patrick F. Laws
Lonesome Duck Steve Hilbert
Long's 4 Seasons Resort Ltd.
Long's Hollow Outfitting
J. Bonner Long
Long Beach Sportfishing
Long Island Charters - Jim Hanson
Long Meadow Cabins
Darren Johnston
Long Point Airways -The Wilsons
Long Point Lodge - The Bowens
Long Range Mountain Hunting &
Fishing - Sharon Biggin
Look-N-Hook Charters
Capt. Jim and Shari Nickerson
Lookout River Outfitters
Bruce & Margaret Hyer
Loomis Charters - Robert Loomis
Loon Bay Lodge
David Whittingham
Loon Haunt Outposts
Bill & Louise Coppen
Loon Lodge - Moskwa Family
Lopstick Lodge & Cabins
Lisa Hopping
Lorato Charters -Thomas/Lori Stewart
Lori's Charters Lori Blank
Lori's Pride Sport Fishing Charters
Eugene Spaeth
Los Angeles Harbor Sportfishing
Los Cuernos
Los Patos Lodge
Los Rios Anglers, Inc.
Lost Coulee Outfitters
Thomas J. Fisher
Lost Creek Guides
Lance D. Edinger
Lost Creek Lodge - Bill Sebastian
Lost Fork Ranch - Merritt G. Pride
Lost Island Lodge -Jim/Marlene Hayes
Lost Lake Wilderness Lodge
The Dunkins
Lost Marlin Charters
Kevin M. & Lynetta J. Siska
Lost Quarter Hunting Club
Ann Walton
Lost River Outfitters - Scott Schnebly
Lost Solar Outfitters, Inc.
Thoma Marucco & Gary Stoaks
Lost Solar, Inc. -Thomas J. Marucco
Lost Valley Ranch -Robert L. Foster
Lou's Charter Service
Capt. Lou Bickel
Louie's Outpost Hunting & Fishing
Service Louie Horwath
Louis Branch Argo Charter
Louis Branch
Louise Slusser
David L. MacKenzie
Louisiana Purchase Ranch Outfitters
M. Lee Tingle
Lov Ranch - James William Brennan
Love Bros. and Lee, Ltd.
Ron Fleming and Brenda Nelson
Lowe's Guide Service John Lowe
Lower Brule Wildlife, Fish &
Recreation
Lower Clark Fork River Outfitters
Donn R. Dale
Lower Cook Inlet Charters
Lower Kootenay - Don Bullock
Lower Rogue Canyon Outfitters
Randall G. Nelson
Luark Ranch & Outfitters
Pat Edward Luark
Luck of the Irish Charters
Patrick & Peggy Bookey
Luckey Strike Charters
Lucky's Dream Charter Service
Capts. Lucky & Mary Eichmann
Lucky 7 Charter - Capt. Kip Cramer
Lucky Day Outfitter - Ed Skillman
Lucky Fisherman Charters
Lucky Lady Charters
Lucky Lake Outfitters - Willard Ylioja
Lucky Lyle's Charter Fishing
Capt. Lyle Teskie
Lucky Pierre Charters -Dave Mastolier
Lucky Pierre Charters/PWS
Gary Mastolier
Lucky Strike Camp - The Bennings
Lucky Strike Charter Fishing
Capt. Doug Wills
Lucky Strike Charters - Lewis Stamm
Lucky Strike Lodge
Dennis & Lorne Normore
Lukinto Lake Lodge
Bob & Faye Harkness
Lulu Charter - Scott Hansen
Lund Outfitting - Kurt W. Lund
Lunge Lodge
Wolfgang & Barbara Strafehl
Lunney Mountain Outfitters
Brett J. Harvey
Lynell Sports Fishing, Inc.
Lynn's Charter
Capt. Lynn Frederick
Lynn-A Charter Service
Capt. Jerry Cefalu
Lynx Guide Services -Larry E. Winslow
M-Lazy-A-Ranch Outfitter/Guide
Service Robert Archibeque
M-N-L Charters Mark H. Bailleson
M & G Outfitters Mike W. Smith
M & M Guiding - Marty Myre
M & M Outfitters - Monty Hankinson
M & N Resort - Wayne Chepil
M H M Outfitters - George A. Malarsie
M&M's Whooper Hollow Lodge
Martin and Marie Budaker
Martin & Marie Budaker
M.B.K. Outfitters - Michael B. Krueger
M/V Irish Robert - Sean Martin
M/V Juno Charter - Donald D. Holmes
M/V Serrant
Mark A. & Karla Jo Clemens
Maalaea Game Fishing, Inc.
Maaluqs Lodge Lukia Lelkok, Sr.
Mac's Charters
Herman M. Meiners, Jr.
Mac-A-Tac Fishing Charters
Macannamac Camps
Jack & Sharon McPhee
Macaw Point Marine
Marvin & Suzanne Proctor
MacDougall Lodge -Joshua Tompkins
MacFarlane Sporting Camps
Dixon MacFarlane
Mache-Kino Fly-In Lodge
Denis & Val Ladouceur
Mackay Wilderness River Trips, Inc.
Brent Estep
MacKenzie Trail Lodge
Bill Warrington
Mackinaw Charters - Glen Szymoniak
Macmillan River Tours
Macoun Lake Island Lodge
Harvey Nelson & Rodgeer Herman
MacSwaney's Cabins
Mad Viking Charters
John &Marilyn Kvarford
Madd Gaffer Charters-James Bostrom
Madion Valley Ranch
Madison River Fishing Co.
Michael D. Pollack
Madson River Outfitters
Robert "Dan" Hull
Maestro's Guide Service
Michael R. Cunningham
Maestro Safaris - Maggie Joe
Magic Capt. Art Goodwin
Magic Man Charters - Stan Malcom
Magie's Guide Service
Mike Pierce
Magnum Charters
William & Sharon Kacenas
Magnum Charters - Gary/ Emily Salter
Magnum Outfitters- Roy Thompson
Magson's Camp Outfitting Services
Al & Mary Magson
Mahay's Riverboat Service
Stephen T. & Kristene O. Mahay
Maiden Bay Camp
Joan & Bill Hubbard
Main River Lodge - Gene Manion
Maine Guide Fly Shop & Guide Service
Maine Outdoors Don Kleiner
Mainely Hunting & Fishing
Captain Doug Jowett
Mainstream Outdoor Adventures, Inc.
Charles Alan Lamm
Majestic Mountain Alaskan Adv., Inc.
Jeff & Cyndi Chadd
Majestic River Charters
Michael R. & Priscilla Pate
Major Scales Charters
Dale A. Curtis
Makai Charters - Troy B. Thain
Makokibatan Lodge
Malarkey Cabin Guiding Service
Ray Dillon
Malone Guide Service
Todd B. & Travis M. Malone
Mamm Peaks Outfitters
Jeffrey George Mead
Mammoth Adventure Connection
Mamozekel Lodge & Cabins
Shirley Mahaney
Mana Kai Adventures
Manewan Enterprises Ltd.
Manfred Racine's Guiding &
Outfitting Svce. Manfred Racine
Manhattan Creek Outfitters, Inc.
Linda S. Wright-Winterfeld
Manitoba Trophy Outposts
Brett & Judy Geary
Manitouwabing Tent & Trailer Park
Harry & Sandy Vandermeer
Manotak Lodge - Rej & Linda Roy
Mansard Island Resort & Marina
J.D. Koenig
Mantagao Outfitters
Buddy or Marlene Chudy
Manx Charters - Warren Holmes
Many Rivers Alaska - Robert Maker
Many Rivers Alaska - Steven Olson
Maountain Trail Outfitters
David Gamble
Maple Grove Cottages
Reg & Lois White
Maple Grove Resort
Mar's Outfitting Service
Marcel & Nancy Seguin
Mar Nee' Rods Mark Lutsch
Maranatha Lodge
Roger & Vera Skogen
Marc's Guide ServiceMark Fenton
Margaret V Charters
Capts. Richard & Scott Anderson
Margie Two Charters
Capt. Arnold E. Franke
Marina Air, Inc. - Rick Gold
Marina Del Isle - Kathy Richmond
Marine Air Service
Joseph N. & Deborah Darminio
Mariner Charters
Capt. Paul Goodman & Paul Mariner
Marjorie F. Bowlby-Dennis M. Bowlby
Mark's Fishing - Mark Reilly
Mark's Guide Service - Master Guide
Mark Sandland
Mark & Mary Emery Wet Waders
Mark Glassmaker Fishing
Mark Glassmaker
Mark Henry's North American
Outfitters
Mark Madura Inc. - Mark Madura
Mark Miller Guide - Larry Miller
Mark Upshaw Guide Service
Mark Upshaw
Mark Van Hook Guide Service
Richard M. Van Hook
Mark Young's Hunting Services
Mark E. Young
Marlin - Capt. Alex Korenkiewicz
Marlin's Fly & Tackle Marlin Benedict
Marlin Machine Charters, Inc.
Marlin Magic Sportfishing, Inc.
Marlow's Kenai River Drifters
Neil L. Marlow
Marmot Bay Charters
Kevin W. Adkins
Marmot Bay Excursions
Andrew & Cheryl Christofferson
Marrs' Farms Gary Marrs
Marsh Bay Resort
Jim & Debbie O'Brien
Marsha Gibbs & Bob Mattson
Kesagami Wilderness Lodge
Marshall's Guide Services
Kevin Marshall
Marshland Guide Service
Capts. Vernon & Thad Robichaux
Marta R. Charters
James N. Ryman
Marten River Lodge -The Cracknell's
Martin's Cabins -Denis & Betty Martin
Martin's Camp-Bing/Dainne Hoddinott
Martin's Fishing Guide Service
Gregor P. Martin, Sr.
Marvin Deckard Professional Guide
Ser.
Mary's Blossom Shop Mary Snyder
Mary Time Charters
Doug & Mary Blossom
Masu Fishing - James Nardelli
Mataura - Capt. Tom McLoughlin
Mataura Lite - Capt. Ben McLoughlin
Matheson Island Lodge Ltd.
Marc Collette
Matheson Lake Resort Larry Olson
Matt Bridges Guide & Outfitting
Matthew Bridges, Jr.
Mattice Lake Outfitters Ltd.
Don & Annette Elliot
Maui Big Game Fishing
Maurice's Floating Lodge
Maurice Bertini
Maurice's Sportsman Outfitters
Maurice or Sandra Thibert
Maverick Charters - Paul K. Matter
Mawdsley Lake Lodge -Glen Coulter
May's Brook Camp - Wilson H. Briggs
Mayflower Outfitters
Trevor & Ross Pilgrim
Maynard's Cabins
Maynard Lake Lodge
Dale & Laura Mychalyshyn
McArdle's Resort -Craig/Paige Brown
McBride's Resort & RV Park
Dennis & Sandy Picou
McBroom & Company: Packers &
Guides
McCabe Outfitters - Gary McCabe
McClelland's Guide Service
Jack McClelland
McCombs Hunting Camp, Inc.
Susan M. Phillips
McComon's Guide Service
David McComon
McCord Lodge
Brent & Kevin Arndt
McCormick Charters Craig & Linda
McCormick
McDonald's Outfitter & Guide Service
W. Harry McDonald
McDonnell's Adirondack Challenges
Brian McDonnell
McDonough Outfitters
Robert McDonough
McDougall Lodge
Jeff Andrea, John Bitney
McFarland's Floatel
Jim & Jeannie McFarland
McFly's Trophy Guide Service
William Jordan McStay
McKenzie's Sportsmans Retreat on
Rock Creek
McKenzie River Rafting Co.
Joe & Jan Estes
McLees Guided Fishing Trips
Lawrence M. McLees
McNeely Outfitting
Shawn G. McNeely
McPuffin Charters
Fred Shultz & Dave Skidmore
McQuoid's Inn - Terry McQuoid
Mead's Spruce IslandCamp-Suzy Mead
Harv & Janna Sadlovsky
Meadowlark Ranch - Brad Custer
Meagan Sport Fishing
Mecan River Outfitters
Medano Pass Guide & Outfitter
Donny Carr
Medicine Bow Drifters
Medicine Bow Outfitters
Jared Florell
Medicine Lake Outfitters -Tom Heintz
Medicine Rapids Resort
Larry Stevenson
Megatrax Winter Snow Tours
Alex Beaulieu
Meggie Rose, Inc.
David, Megan & Cassie Carlsen
Megisan Lake Lodge George & Brenda
Nixon
Mel-Sask Outfitters
Memquisit Lodge Inc.-Jeanne Trivett
Mercer Outfitting-Ken & Pat Auckland
Meritime Heritage
Merkel's Camp-Terry & Merrill Kluke
Merritt Trading Post Resort
Jon & Marian Davenport
Meta Lake Lodge Ltd.
Joe & Marg Strangway
Meyers Chuck Lodge
Clifford E. Gardner
Michael J. Charter Boat
Michael L. Duvall Charters
Michael Duvall
Michael Perussa Enterprises
Michael Perussa
Michael Talia Guide Service
Michael P. Talia
Michel Lodge-Wayne/Kathy Berumen
Michiana Steelheaders
Michigan City Fish & Game Club
Dr. David Merrill
Mick's Adventures
Robert Allen Mick
Mickey's Big Mack Charters
Mickey E. Daniels
Mickey's Fishing Charters
Jerry Mickey
Mickey Fin Charters Lyall Hadsel
Mickey Finn Charters & Guide Service
Capt. Dominick (Mickey) Scarzafava
Mickey Finn Guide Service
Patrick L. Schatz
Mid-Columbia Guide Service
Charles Stanton
Mid Columbia Outfitters-Mike Jones
Middle Creek Ranch Company
Roy Rozell
Middle Earth Expeditions
Wayne Failing
Middle Fork Lodge, Inc.
Mary Ossenkop & Scott Farr
Middle Fork Rapid Transit #1
Greg Edson
Middle Fork River Expeditions, Inc.
Patrick Ridle
Middle Fork River Tours-Kurt Selisch
Middle Fork River Tours, Inc.
Phil B. Crabtree
Middle Fork Wilderness Outfitters, Inc.
Gary Shelton
Midnight Sun Trophy Pike Adventures
Dean Nelsen & Leon Randermann
Midwest Guiding-Richard Rightmire
Midwest Tacklesmiths
Capt. Jim Wierzbicki
MiJoy 747 Capt. Paul Brockett
Mika Ag Corp. R. Doris Karlsson
Mike's #1 Muskie Guide Service
Mike Patete
Mike's Good Time Charters
Michael Butcher
Mike's Guide ServiceMichael A.
Sexton
Mike's Salmon X-Press
Michael T. Turner
Mike Bogue's Guide Service
Mike Cochran Guide Service
Mike Cochran
Mike Cusack's King Salmon Lodge, Inc.
Mike Cusack
Mike K. Vargo Bay Breeze Yacht
Charters
Mike Lowery Guide Service
Michael E. Lowery
Mike Wilson's High Mountain Drifters
Mike Wilson
Mike Zelman & Sons Guide Service
Mike Zelman
Miles Fly Fishing Guide Service
Miles Goodman
Military Bass Angler Assoc.
Allan Needham
Mill Creek Marina
Mill Creek Outfitters
Charles E. Wisecup
Mill Pond Guide Service-Robert Whear
Miller's Guide Service
Raymond Miller III
Miller's Guide Service-Robert Miller
Miller's Motor LodgeThe Millers
Miller's Riverboat Service
Gary L. Miller
Miller's Sport Fishing- Don S. Miller
Miller Barber's Streamline Anglers
John Herzer
Miller Izaak Walton League
Miller Mountain Lemon Lake
Lawrence R. Miller
Miller Outfitters - Robert E. Miller
Millers Charters
Mark & Partheniu Miller
Millsite Trout
Milo Industries Milo R. DeVries
Mimbres Outfitters - Mark Miller
Minakwa Lodge
Etienne & Rejeanne deBlois
Mineral Mountain Lodge & Outfitters
John H. & Bobbie Martin
Ministikwan Lodge

Dave Werner
Minnehaha Camp Resort
Hartley & Sherry Moore
Minor Bay Camps Ltd.
Randy Duvell
Minowukaw Lodge and Joe's Cabins
Miramichi Fish Inn
Miramichi Gray Rapids Lodge, Inc.
Guy A. Smith
Miramichi Inn Andre Godin
Miron River Outfitters
Wayne Rodway
Mishanda Charters
Charles Pokorny
Miss Hospitality Charter Boat
Miss Joann Fishing Charters
Capt. Russ Gober
Missinaibi Outfitters Owen & Denyse
Korpela
Mission Fishing / Uptown Girl
Capt. Gary Longley
Mission Lodge at Aleknagik
Dale DePriest
Mission Mountain Outfitters
Richard R. Bishop
Missouri River Angler
Peter J. Cardinal
Missouri River Expeditions
Timothy G. Plaska
Missouri River Trout Shop
Patrick Alan Elam
Missouri Riverside, Inc.
Leonard A. Gidlow
Mista Nosayew Outfitters
Jeff Janzen
Mistik Lodge - Gary Carriere
Mistral II Charter Boat
Misty Fjords Air & Business
David P. Doyon
Mitchell's Pond Hunting & Fishing
Lodge Don MacInnis
Mitchell & Roane's Alaska Fly-Outs,
Inc.
Steve A. Mitchell & D.C. Roane
Mitchell Ledge Pool Camps
Roger & Cynthia Mitchell
Mitchells' Camp
Don & Mary Mitchell
Mitkof Island Charters, Inc.
Gregg Magistrale
Miwapanee Lodge Resort
MJ Outfitting Services
Moak Lodge
Glen & Len Heroux & Les Greig
Moby King Charters Robert R. Estes
Modeste Outfitters - Morris Modeste
Moe-Z Charters -Michael Comstock
Moe Fishin - Larry L. Moe
Moegy's Guide Service
Lee & Mary Moeglein
Mojo Guides - Moe Neale
Monarch Guides - Ken Kays Kupilik
Monashee Outfitting-Volker Scherm
Monkman Outfitting-Bob Monkman
Monod Sports
Monroe Cattle Co.- Mike Monroe
Montana's Master Angler Fly Service
Thomas M. Travis
Montana Adventures In Angling
James McFadyean
Montana Bird Hunts-Dennis Kavanagh
Montana Blue Ribbon Outfitters Big
Sky -Edward G. Renaud
Montana Casting Co. - William Joyner
Montana Experience Outfitter
Carl A. Mann
Montana Fly Fishing-Michael Mouat
Montana Fly Fishing Adventures
Patrick J. Bannon
Montana Flycast
Dennis Kavanagh
Montana Flyfishing Co.-Kirk Johnston
Montana Guide Service
Edwin L. Johnson
Montana High Country Tours, Inc.
Russell D. Kipp
Montana Outdoor Adventures, Inc.
Randy J. Cain
Montana Outdoor Expeditions
Robert James Griffith
Montana River Guides
Gregory G. Mentzer
Montana River Outfitters
R. Craig Madsen
Montana River Trips-Daniel Groshens
Montana Riverbend Outfitters
Robert J. Zikan, Sr.
Montana Rivers to Ridges
Daniel J. Pluth
Montana Safaris - Rocky J. Heckman
Montana Trout Club
Montana Trout Lodge -David Couch
Montana Trout Trappers - Jim Cox
Montana Troutfitters Orvis Shop
David L. Kumlien
Montana Wilderness Outfitters
David & Tena Kozub
Montauk IV Capt. Steven May
Monte's Guiding & Mtn. Outfitters
LaMonte J. Schnur
Montella From Montana
Richard Montella
Monterey Sport Fishing
Monture Face Outfitters - Tom Ide
Monture Outfitters -James Anderson
Monument Hill Outfitters
Don Polzin
Moody Blue Charters
Capt. Judith Feuerstein
Mooncrest Outfitters, Inc.
Robert Model
Moore's Lodge Al & Babs Debes
Moose Creek Ranch, Inc.
Kelly Van Orden
Moose Horn Lodge - Ron Helliwell
Roxann Lynn Marvin Peterson
Jeff & Heather Schuab
Moose John Outfitters
Moose Lake Lodge
Moose Point Camps
Moose Range Lodge
Moose River Company
Mark H. Eddy
Moose River Landing
Moosehill Cabins Ltd.
Michael & Margaret Gillam
Moosehorn Lodge Eric Napflin
Moosehorn Resort
Alan & Miriam Burchell
Moosehorn Roadhouse
James Butts
Moosewa Outpost
Ivor & Brenda Horncastle
Moquin Marine Charters
Eugene Louis Moquin
Morang's Guide Service
Michael S. Morang
Moreno Valley Outfitters
Robert Reese & Mike Bucks
Morest Camp Joan & Glen Currie
Morice River Outfitting
John Shepert
Morin's All Seasons Resort Ltd.
The Morins
Morning Glory Ked Schoming
Morning Mist Charters
Wayne & Barbara Fleek
Morning Peace River Guides
Pete Brown
Morning Star Ben Griffith
Morning Star Fishing Charters
Capt. Larry Griffith
Morrison's Rogue River Lodge
Morrison Guide Service
Michael E. Morrison
Mosby Charters Lewis Mosby
Moser's Idaho Adventures
Gary L. Moser
Mossbak Guide Service
Gary D. Enoch
Motel Bienvenue
Ray & Pauline Dubreuil
Mother Goose Lodge- Vernon Logan
Mother Goose Lodge-Donald Wallis
Motlong's Rod & Reel
Dick & Alice Motlong
Motor Vessel Explorer
Richard N. Friedman
Mount Peyton Outfitters
Don Tremblett
Mountain Air Services
Mountain Angler, Ltd.
Mountain Cove Lodge
Grace & Michael Piano
Mountain Enterprises
Gary & Robin Edwards
Mountain Fly Fishing
Mountain Home Lodge
Warren Shewfelt & Julie Dale
Mountain Lakes Vacation Center
Joan & John Carter
Mountain Leisure Trading Co.
Sherman Brown
Mountain Man Guide Service
Joe Eggleston & Tim Breen
Mountain Man Tours -Greg J. Coln
Mountain Monarchs of Alaska
David J. Leonard
Mountain Point Bed & Breakfast
Jeffrey & Marilyn Meucci
Mountain Point Charter & Boat Rental
Stella Callentine
Mountain River Tours, Inc.
Paul W. Breuer
Mountain Sky Guest Ranch
Shirley Arnesault
Mountain State Outfitters-Bill Murray
Mountain Top Ranches
Mary & Bob Roesler
Mountain Trails Outfitters
A. Lee Bridges
Mountain Trails Outfitters
Butch Rawls
Mountain View Camp
Bill & Terry Buckley
Mountain View Cottages
Clayton "Cy" Eastlack
Mountain View Guide Service
Jack T. Rose
Mountain View Resort
Michael & Yvonne Schut
Mountain West Outfitters
Shane Dykster
Mountain West Outfitting, Inc.
Aaron R. Neilson
Mountain Wilderness Outfitters
Jim Garmon
Mountainaire Adventures, Inc.
Douglas Cole
Moyie River Outfitters
Stanley A. Sweet
Mr. B's Richard S. Bartolowits
Mr. C's Chuck Martin
Mr. Champ Charter Boat
Mr. O's Sporting Goods
Michael Olden
Mr. Walleye Taxidermy & Outfitter
Robert R. Check
Mt. Blanca Game Bird & Trout
Bill Binnian
Mt. Kineo Cabins
Dick & Elaine Wallingford
Mt. Lassen Trout
Mt. Shasta Fly Fishing Guide Service
Muddy River Boat Works
Thomas E. Jackson
Muddy River Guides & Outfitters
Robert Hoenike
Muddy Water Anglers
Andrew Von Antz
Muleshoe Outfitters & Guide Service
Jack Howser
Multiple Use Managers, Inc.
Gordon Long
Muncho Lake Outfitters
Arnold Henhapl
Munro Park May Munro
Munroe's Wilderness Outpost Camp
Brian Dick
Munroe Lake Lodge Jack Stoneman
Munsey's Bear Camp
Mike & Robin Munsey
Muskeg Excursions
Johnnie R. & Fran C. Laird
Muskego Point Resort
Grant, Judy & Jennifer Hughes
Muskie Daze Guide Service
John Brylinski
Muskrat Run
Muskwa Outfitters - Ralph Merasty
Muskwa Safaris - Garry & Sandra Vince
Mustang Outfitters & Big Game
Hounds James S. Stahl
My-Time Cruises - G.L. Gucker
My Bonnie - Capt. Sal Tardella
My Mistress Sportfishing
Myers Hunting Services, Inc.
Donald G. Myers
Mystic Angel Charter Boat
Mystic Magic Wilderness Lodge
Mystic Saddle Ranch-Jeff & Deb Bitton
Mystic Sea Charters
Mystic Warrior Charters
Michael J. Musewski
Mythos Expeditions Kodiak
David & Janice Kubiak
N-Bar Land & Cattle Company
Thomas E. Elliott
Nagagami Lodge
Nagle Lake Outfitters
Bob & Stella Rodwin
Naiscoot Lodge - The Lutschers
Nakina Outpost Camps & Air Service
Don & Millie Bourdignon
Naknek River Angling - James Young
Nakwasina Charters - Mark T. Johnson
Namekagon Outfitters
Nan-Mar-Lin Charter Service
Nancy B - Capt. Howard J. Beers
Nancy Guide Service
Nancy Jean Charter Service
Capt. Clete Challe
Nancy Rusch - David E. Rusch
Nanika Guiding Jim Tourond
Nanmark Cottages
Terry & Liz Hyatt
Narrow's Edge
Robert & Beth Oyler
Nash Bar Lodge
Lorne & Kathleen Hawkins
Natalia Charters Bruce Schactler
Natron Air Virgil Mosiman
Natron Air Chuck Osmond
Natron Air -Edward & Marion Osmond
Natural Adventures, Inc.
Thomas E. Tietz
Natural Anglers - Capt. Barry Kanavy
Natural High Rafting-James C. Mabry
Naturalistic Taxidermy Outfitters
David Clark
Naughty Lady Charters-Bill Carlozzi
Nauti-Gal Charters
Eileen & Patrick Kolehouse
Nautical Charters of Alaska
Jerry W. McCowin II & Julie VonRuden
Neal Outfitters Lloyd Neal
Nedrow Enterprises
Monte "Wes" & Sandra Kay Nedrow
Nejalini Lodge Al & Phil Reid
Nekton Charters
Nelson's Gods Lake Lodge
Nelson Tomalty
Nelson River Outfitters
Bill Cordell
Nemecek Insurance Rick Nemecek
Nepisiguit River Camps
Kenneth Gray
Nerepis Lodge
Reginald & Cecily Fredericks
Neshobe Creekside Innovations
Ronald Lewis
Neshoto Guide Service
Chris Weier
Nestor Falls Fly-In Outpost
Dave & Michelle Beaushene
Nestucca Valley Sporting Goods
Ray S. Hammer
Nevada Guide Service
James R. Puryear
Nevada Trophy Hunts -Tony Diebold
New & Gauley River Adventures, Inc.
Skip Heater
New Buffalo Steelheaders
New Easy Rider Sportfishing
New Englander on the Kenai, Guide
Svc -Ronald & Deborah Kim Verney
New Highrock Lodge Ltd.
Randy & Jill Darnold
NewLo-An
Nick Cates & Buzz Brizendine
New Mystery Charter
Capt. Brian Eggert
New River Scenic Whitewater Tours
Richard Smith
New River Small Mouth, Inc.
Dave Kees
New West Outfitters-David B. Moore
Newfoundland & Labrador Hunting
Ltd. Roland Reid
Newfoundland Adventures Ltd.
Todd Wiseman
Newfoundland Adventures Ltd.
Todd Wiseman
Newhalen Lodge, Inc. - Bill Sims
Newmart Fishing Resort
Humen & Mauthe
Newport Landing Sportfishing
Niangua River Oasis
Bob & Barbara Burns
Nick's Guide Service-Dominic Hallford
Nicky Boy Charter Fishing
Capt. Nick Waranka
Nielsen's Fly-In Lodge
Don & Lynn Pursch
Night Lake Lodge-D.L. (Dave) Hollett
Nikiski Boat Wor - Bill Boutilier
Nimmo Bay Resort - Craig Murray
Nine Lives Charters - Michael Dobson
Nine Sixteen Ranch Guide/Outfitter
Terrell Shelley
Ninilchik Charters - Michael R. Flores
Ninilchik General Store
Duane Giarratana
Ninilchik Saltwater Steven Smith
Ninilchik Saltwater Charters
Peter & Susan Ardison
Ninilchik Village Charters
Stephen Vanek, Jr.
Nipigon River Bear Hunts
Bob Bearman
Nipissing Lodge
The Conrads & The Craftchicks
Niska Hunting & Fishing Camp
Nisutlin Bay Outfitters
Philip Smith
Niut Trails Outfitting Eric Hatch
No Cut Throats Outfitting
Craig A. Clevidence
No Mercy Sportfishing
No See Um Lodge, Inc.
John W. Holman
No Strings Sportfishing, Inc.
Noah's Guide Service-Jeremy Baum
Noah's World of Water - Noah Hague
Noatak Canyon Outfitters
David M. Aldridge
Noble - Capt. Dale Florek
Noland Point Fishing Resort
Nomad Fishing Charters
Arthur Martin
Nopiming Lodge
Marge & Blaine Guenther
Nor'wester Lodge & Outfitter
Carl & Luana Brandt
Norbert's Wagger Sport
Norbert Chaudhary
Nordic Lodge - Donna Carlson
Nordic North
Charles Hostetler & Phillip Weidner
Nordic Raven Charters
James L. Dybdahl
Norfork Trout Dock
Norjernan Ronald Halus
Norm's Just Fishin' Norm Brady
Norm Harder Outfitter
Norm Harder
Norman H. Guth, Inc.
Norman Guth & Mel Reingold
Normandy Lodge
Klaus & Wilma Brauer
Norse Lodge Bob Comton
North-East Flyfishing
North-Wright Air. Ltd.
North Alaska Expeditions-Justin Johns
North Alberta Outfitters
Troy & Lisa Foster
North Alta Ventures
Dollard & Shelly Dallaire
North American Adventures
Everett Clifford
North American Outfitters
North American River Runners, Inc.
Frank Lukacs
North American Wilderness
Adventures - C.E. "Woody" Main
North Arm Adventures
North Bay Adventures
Michael R. Addiego
North Camps on Rangeley Lake
North Coast Adventures, Inc.
Wayne Price
North Coast Charter Assoc.
Dale Robert
North Coast Marine Services
Rick Brown
North Country Guiding - Al Morelli
North Country Jet Boat Charters
North Country Lodge - Don Beland
Jack & Georgia Clarkson
North Country Lodge
Dale & Doreen Leutschaft
North Country River Charters
William C. O'Halloran
North Delta Guide Service
North Fork Fishing Service-Glen Gross
North Fork Guides - Kenneth R. Hill
North Fork Store & Cafe
North Haven Lodge - Jim Marple
North Idaho Llama Outfitters
Thomas P. Taylor
North Knife Lake Lodge
Stewart & Barbara Webber
North Lake Alaskan - Michael Parker
North Lake Guiding Service
Mrs. Edward Fredericks
North of 49 Guide Service - im Hyslop
North of 49 Outfitters - Lorne Weir
North of 54 Outfitters
Glen & Kelly Whitbread
North Pacific Business
Kaylen, Leonard & Michaela Kelley
North Pacific Charters - Dan Leathers
North Pacific Marine Services
Patrick A. Day
North Point Charter Boat Assoc.
North Pole Wilderness Guide
Outfitters Darrell Needham
North Ridge Guide Service
Richard Higgins
North River Guide Service
William L. Conner
North River Guides
William E. Anker & Darrell Needham
North Shore Lodge & Airstrip
Tom & Chris Guercio
North Spirit Lake Lodge Ltd.
Bill & Valerie Nelson
North Star Charters - David L. Lucher
North Star Charters - Herman Nelsen
North Star Guiding Service, Inc.
Michael F. Newell
North Star Outfitters, Inc.
Robert F. Moreland
North tar Sailing Adventures
Mark Canil & Mark Vevera
North View Hunting & Fishing Lodge
Wayne DeLeavey
North West River Outfitters
Craig Hughson
North Woods Lodge - Wade McVicar
Northeast Alberta Wilderness
Outfitters, Inc. - Charles Graves
Northeast Kingdom Guide Service
Harry Burnham
Northeast Kingdom Llama
Expeditions - John & Gail Birutta
Northeastern IN Trout Assoc.
Northern Angler Fly Fishing
Adventures John & Tracy Yury
Northern Comfort Wilderness
Adventures - The Coscos
Northern Comfort, Inc.
William Walker, Edgar & Stephen Pyle
Northern Cross Resort Ltd.
Jeff Jesske & Co.
Northern Drift Exposure
Robert Peacock
Northern Echo Lodge
Jim Carol Eberle
Northern Exposure
Jacquie and Marcus Gaskins
Northern Exposure Guide Service
Pete & Dick Rodin
Northern Flight Guide Service
Mike A. Schell
Northern Forest Guide Service
Roland Vosine
Northern High Plains Outfitters
Edwin R. Anderson
Northern Land Services, Inc.
Northern Lights Charters
Ken & Dawn Teune
Northern Lights Fishing Lodge
Yves Ste. Marie
Northern Lights Haven Lodge
Vernon H. Schumacher
Northern Lights Lodge Ltd.
Ted & Diana Ohlsen
Northern Lights Resort - The Millers
Northern Lights Resort
Hermann & Lise Stroeher
Northern Lights Sportfishing
Northern Llight Charters
Capt. Larry D. Mortimer
Northern Magic Charters
Dave Tousignant
Northern Manitoba Outfitters
Jack & Georgia Clarkson
Northern Marine Charters
Northern Outdoors, Inc.
Suzanne Hockmeyer
Northern Pack & Paddle
Ekiah Pickett
Northern Reflection Lodge
Eddy Jones
Northern Spirit Lodge
Greg & Michelle Petryk
Northern Sports Fishing
Aster Caines
Northern Star Charters
Stewart W. Willis
Northern Trading Voyages
Dick & Betty Feenstra
Northern Ventures Chad Smith
Northern Waterhen Outfitters
Arnold Nepinak
Northern Wilderness Adventures, Inc.
Nick Pierskalla
Northern Wilderness Outfitters
Weldon & Peter Prosser
Northern Woodsman Outfitting
Les Allen
Northernaire Lodge - Jane Burgess
Northland Charter - Larry E. Freed
Northland Outfitters Northland
Wilderness Expeditions -A. Robertson
Northstar Adventures Inc.
Bix Bonney
Northstar Charters- Richard R. Straty
Northstar Fishing Adventures
Michael L. Chaussee
Northward Bound- James Harrower
Northway Adirondack Guides
Michael diPalma
Northwest Adventures Guide Service
Joe Paul
Northwest Angle Resort
Bob Nunn & Gary Dietzler
Northwest Catskill Mountaineering
Thomas J. Owens

Northwest Charters -Scott Anderson
Northwest Charters
Stanley K. Divine
Northwest Colorado Scenic Tours
Charles L. Mead
Northwest Drifters
Dave Andreatta & Dan Stumpf
Northwest Drifters
Daniel C. Stumpff
Northwest Eco-Ventures
Christopher D. Culver
Northwest Fly Fishing Outfitters
John M. Hagan, II
Northwest Flying Ltd. Jack Pope
Northwest Indiana Steelheaders
Mike Ryan
Northwest Outfitters
Jens & Leslie Klaar
Northwest Ranching & Outfitting
Heidi Gutfrucht
Northwest River Company
Douglas A. Tims
Northwest Traditions
Adam F. Payne
Northwest Voyageurs
Jeff W. Peavey
Northwest Waters Outfitters
Northwest Whitewater Excursions
Dennis R. Brandsma
Northwest Wilderness Adventures
Brad Stoneman
Northwind Charters-Capt. J Kudlacik
Northwinds/Pine Grove
Rod & Gail Munford
Northwood's Guide Service
Northwoods Adventures
Gary D. Strasser
Northwoods Lodge - Robert Clark
Northwoods Ventures Outfitting
Cyril Smith
Northwoods Wilderness Guide
Service John Huston
Norton Bay Charters Abraham
Anasogak, Sr.
Norton Sound Guide Service
Nourse's Sport Fishing
Capt. Ken Nourse
NOVA Chuck Spaulding
Nova Guides, Inc.-Steven J. Pittels
Nu-Cho Expeditions - Tom Ellis
Nueltin Fly-In Lodges - The Gurkes
Nugent's Chamberlain Lake Camp
Nungesser Lake Lodge
Bob & Rosie Kohlnhofer
Nutimik Lodge - Janet Wilson
NW River Guides - Dave McCann
Nyliaq Alaska Charters
Richard M. Tate
O'Brien's Guide Service - Dick O'Brien
O'Brien Enterprises -Stephen O'Brien
O'Donnell's Cottages & Canoeing
Valerie O'Donnell
O'Malley's Fishing Charters
Leonard E. O'Malley
O'Sullivan's Rainbow Al & Donna Reid
O-Pee-Chee Lake Lodge
Siobhan & Rolland Nipshagen
O J's Northport Charters
Richard Seiferlein
O.A.R.S., Inc. - George Wendt
Oachs Bros. Fishing Guide Service
George A. Oachs
Oak Lake Lodge
Jerry & Wanetah Helgason
Oak Leaf Game Calls & Guide Service
Roger A. Sannwald
Oak Mountain Lodge
Clarence LeBlanc
Oakridge Inn - Vijay Patel
Oars + Dories, Inc.
Curtis M. Chang
Oasis Du Gouin - Jackie Leblanc
Ocean Activities Center
Ocean Cape Charters
Lars E. Johnson
Ocean Charterboat
Joseph Rohleder
Ocean Side Country Lodge
Chris Rowsell
Odeeo Charters Randall Odens
OFC Outfitting
Michel C. Maurello
Offshore Adventures Charter Service
Offshore Adventures - Pete Kelly
Offshore Hunters, Inc.
Offshore Salmon Charters
Phil Klobertanz
Ohio Division of Wildlife
Vicki Snyder
Okimot Lodge -Wayne & Rona Currie
Okra Charters
Capt. Mike Wilchenski
Olan Yokum Guide Service
Old Glendevey Ranch, Ltd.
Garth Peterson
Old Moe Guide Service
Terry Collier & Timm Mertens
Old Riverton Inn
Mark & Pauline Telford
Old Slovacek Home Place
Clyde M. Shaver
Old Town Float Base Yvonne Quick
Old West Angler & Outfitters
Jim Yeager & Ernie Strum
Oldland & Uphoff
Reuben G. Oldland
Oldsquaw Lodge
Ole Creek Lodge
Don & Marjorie Hangen
Olga Bay Lodge, Inc. -James D. Jones
Oliver Lake Wilderness Camp
Michel Dube
Olivier's Fly-In Camps/Horne Air Ltd.
Maurice & Ruby Olivier
Olson Bay Resort
Gary & Barbara Detoffol
Olson Yukon River Tours
Marvin James McGuffey
Olympic Peninsula Sportfishing
Ted A. McManus
Omeco III Charter Boat
Omega II Charter Service
Capt. Jay Levy
On A Fly SportfishingOn The Fly
One Eye Outfit - Mike McDonough
One That Got Away- Cliff Tinsman
Ontario North Outpost Barz & Clark
Ontario Wilderness Houseboat
Rentals Stewart & Yvonne Gill
Opatcho Lake Guide & Outfitters
Ralph Maida
Open Bay Lodge Ltd.
Basil & Pam Lemieux
Open Season Sometimes Sno'd Inn
Sheila Bliesath
Opeongo Mountain Resort
Bob & Chris Peltzer
Orange Torpedo Trips of Idaho
Scott Debo
Orban's Outfitting- Darrell Orban
Orca Charters
Maurice W. Widdows
Orca II Fish Guides- Jonathan Wackler
Oregon-Alaskan Outfitters/River
Guides Don A. Lee
Oregon Alaska Sportfishing
Tim Marshall
Oregon Blacktails Guide Service
Perry Allen
Oregon Fishing Adventures
Gary F. Krum
Oregon Outdoors - Dennis Dobson
Oregon River Outfitters
Dan E. Simmons
Orion River Specialists-James Coyle
Orion River Specialists
Matthew Holsinger
Orion River Specialists
James Coyle & Russel E. Stec
Orland Outfitters - Jeff Gonzales
Orvis New York
Orvis Roanoke
Osborn River Service - John G. Osborn
Oskondaga River Outfitters
Allan & Mary Ward
Oso Ranch & Lodge
John & Pamela Adamson
Osprey Capt. Joseph A. Wysocki
Osprey Alaska Richard Fowler
Osprey Alaska, Inc.
Charles & Irene M.Lukey
Osprey Enterprises-Kenneth Herrick
Osprey Expeditions Ospry Adv./
Meadow Creek Outfitters
Cheryl Bransford
Ossa-Win-Tha Resort Ostrov
Wygodnny Enterprises
Albert Wilson & Kim Elliott
Oswald Cattle Company
Stephen Oswald
Oswold Pack Camp Ralph Oswold
Ottawa County Visitors Bureau
Malinda Huntley
Otter Cove Bed & Breakfast
Ginnie S. Porter
Otter Creek Campground
George Araskiewicz
Otter Creek Outfitters-James Wilkins
Otter Falls Resort
Gordon & Jackie Zechel
Otter Falls Wilderness Adventure
Otter Guide Services-James Hall
Ouktok Outfitters
James M. Knopke
Ouray Livery Barn
Howard Lewis Linscott
Out of the Blue Charter & Guide
Service - Bruce Tompkins
Outdoor Activities - John C. Couser
Outdoor Adventure Program
Outdoor Adventures Plus
Larry Kirkpatrick
Outdoor Adventures, Inc.
Robert J. Volpert
Outdoor Alaska Don Goffinet
Outdoor Connections
Nicholas J. Kamzalow
Outdoor Enterprises
Gerald Thompson
Outdoor Source - John Campbell
Outdoors Unlimited - Glen J. Gulay
Outer Limits Charters - J.M. Gilman
Outercoast Charters -Larry Trani
Outland Outfitting
Jerry & Geraldine Cook
Outlaw Charters & Ultimate Predator
R. Stephen Yaw
Outlaw River Runners/Great Bear
Greg Nelson
Outlook Enterprises -Jerry L. Smith
Outlook Lodge - Robert Dersham
Outrageous Charter Boat
Outwest Anglers - Brian Klein
Ouzel Expeditions - Bill Stoabs
Herb Wottlin, Jr. - Rob Wottlin
Ouzel Expeditions, Inc.
Randall Knauff
Over The Hill Outfitters-John Neely
Overland Cross Country Lodge
Wayne & Diane Elliott
Overland Express - Johann Overland
Owl's Nest Lodge
Betty Ann & Wayne Hawthorn
Owl's Nest Lodge Inc. - Ron Parsons
Owyhee Guide & Outfitters
Clinton L. Fillmore
Oxbow Outfitters - Bubba Cole
Oxbow Outfitting Co.- Donald DeLise
Oxbow Outfitting Co.
Jonathan J. Feinberg
Ozark Sunrise Expeditions
Ralph Flippo
Ozzie's Charter Service
Capt. Ozzie Streblow
P&D Riverboat Services
Paul & Diana Pfeiffer
P.J.'s Fly Fishing & Resort Lodge
P.O. Pluggers Bass Club
Michael Price
P.T. Outfitters
Paul E. Menhennett
Pace & Harkins Fishing Service
Pacific Blue Sport Fishing
Pacific Blue Water Venture, Inc.
Pacific Blue, Inc.
Pacific Charters
Joe & Diane Svymbersky
Pacific Gold Charters-James Harrigan
Pacifica - Guy Ashley
Pack Bridge Outfitters
Robert Hamilton
Pack Saddle Trips
Pack Trails North Adventures
Packs Jodie & Tracy Pack
Pacmar Corp. - Ted Pratt
Pacomia Northstar Guide Service
James M. Harrigan
Pagosa Rafting Outfitters
Wayne Walls
Painkiller Offshore Fishing Team
Karl T. Cerullo
Paint Lake Resort
Bill & Barb Traviss
Paintbrush Trails, Inc.
Wanda Wilcox
Painter's Lodge - Harley Elias
Painter Creek Lodge, Inc.
Joe Maxey & Jon Kent
Paintrock Adventures-Outfitters
Unlimited Todd Jones
Pala II Charters - Claude Henning
Palco Enterprises
Richard L. Teague
Palfrey Lake Lodge
Mrs. Larry G. Day
Palliser River Outfitters
Gordon Burns
Palmquist's "The Farm"
Pamela Big Game Fishing, Inc.
Panasea IV Charter Boat
Panorama Camp
Denis & Ginette Rainville
Pantera Charters-Capt. Edward Bullen
Panther Tract, Inc.- Howard Brent
Para-Sail Beachwatch, Inc.
Para-Sail, Inc. - Jeffrey Porter
Paradise Adventure
Kurtis A. Nunnenkamp
Paradise Adventures
Ned S. Chadbourn
Paradise Bar Lodge- Court Boice
Paradise Cove Lodge- Dick Carlson
Paradise Fishing Excursions
James R. French
Paradise Guest Ranch- Jim Anderson
Paradise Lodge
Ken & Terry Korball & Gene Korthals
Paradise Lodge - John Lewis
Paradise Outfitters- Stephen R. Ayers
Paradise Valley- David R. Handl
Pardoe Lake Lodge - Vern Hunt
Pari of Dice Charters
Capt. Howard Petroski
Parker Recreational Services
Ken Parker
Parker/Boyce Guide Service
James M. Boyce & Bruce E. Parker
Parkland Outfitters- Georg Voelkel
Parks' Fly Shop - Richard C. Parks
Parry South Air Service
Dietmar Zschunke
Parsley's Charter - John Parsley
Parson's Pond & Triple K Outfitters
Roger Keogh
Pasayten Llama Packing
Lanette E. Smith
Pasco's Inlet Charters-Jeffrey Pasco
Pass Creek Outfitters
Lee Sinclair
Passage to Utah
Pat Bowen The Rod & Gun Club
Pathfinder Guide Service
Robert Foshay
Patricia Ikens Floyd G. Ikens
Patricia M. Ray Roger D. Ray
Patrick's AK Fishing - Patrick Johnson
Pau's Deep Creek Charters
Paul Goedert II
Paul's Fishing Tours - North of 60
Paul's Sport Fishing Guide Service
Paul F. Asicksik, Sr.
Paul H. Gabbert Gary Sevesind
Paull River Wilderness Camp
Wayne Galloway
Pawistik Lodge - Scott Jeffrey
Pawling Mountain Club
Paxson Alpine Tours
Kris & Murray Howk
Payne River /Tunulik River Fishing
Camps Steve Ashton
Peace of Selby, Inc.
Art & Dee Mortvedt & Be Sheldan
Peacock's Yukon Camps Ltd.
Peacock Ranch Outfitters
Darren Peacock
Peak River Expeditions
Peal's Resort
Peanuts IV Charter Service
Gene Stauber
Pearl Guide Service-Capt. Mark Lyons
Pecan Creek/Dutch Mountain
Gene Hall Reagor
Peer's Snake River Rafting
Darryl Peer
Pehrson Lodge Resort
Steve & Cathy Raps
Pelahatchie Lake
Pelican ChartersNorm Carson
Pelican Narrows U-Fly-In Ltd.
Ray Fournier
Pelly Lake Wilderness Outfitters
Dennis LeVeque
Pend Oreille Charters Ltd. Co.
Dan Jacobson & Keith Snyder
Peninsula Adventures
John & Dawn Lesterson
Peninsula Charters Bob Pennini
Peninsula River Charters
Ron Latschaw
Pennock Island Charters
Vic Utterback
Penquin Resort
Judy & Bob Partridge
Perch America, Inc. Joe Bala
Peregrine Charters
Robert Gibson & Jackie Feigon
Peregrine Guides & Outfitters, Inc.
John Todoverto
Peregrine River Outfitters
Thomas Klema
Perfect Charters - Steve Carlson
Perrin's Hunting & Fishing
Blake Perrin Jerry Arnett
Pete's Guide Service Peter W. Evans
Peter Rose Corp.
Peter Wiebe Outfitting/Grand Slam
Outfitter
Peter Wiebe & Barbara Wiebe
Peter Zito Guide Service
Peter Zito
Peters Hunting Service
Harley Peters
Petersen Outfitting - Greg Petersen
Peterson's Adventures
Jeff Peterson
Peterson's Fairmont Corral, Inc.
William H. Peterson
Peterson's Guide & Charter Service
William W. Peterson
Peterson's Point Lake Camp
Jim, Margaret, Amanda & Chad
Peterson
Petersons' Reed Lake Lodge
Kathy & Corky Peterson
Petre's Fishing Charters
Dennis & Chris Petre
Phantom Charters George Kirk
Phantom Mtn. Adventures
William L. & Shelley A. Stewart
Pheasant Haven Farms
Dennis & Jerry Kuhlman
Pheasant Ridge, Inc. Peter K.
Rittenour
Phil's Smiling Salmon Guide
Philip Desautels
Philip Olson Rodney Rogus
Phoenix Adventures -John P. Diskin
Phoenix Charters
Capt. Steven-John Bignell
Phoenix Fishing
Pickerel Arm Camp-The Edwardson's
Pickerel Bay Cabins-Ray or Gail Twedt
Pickerel Point Concessions
Picnic Cove Charters -John Timmer
Piedra Enterprises-Charles Piedra
Pier One Sportfishing & Lodges
Capts. Frank & Charles DeNoto
Pier Plaza Charter Service
Pierce Brothers Outfitting
William Leon & Howard Pierce
Pierce Lake Lodge
Pike Haven Resort
John & Nancy Hoffman
Pike Island Lodge & Outposts
Ron McKenzie
Pikes Peak Outfitters Gary Jordan
Pilgrim's Retreat
Joe Page & Kathy J. McKelvey
Pillar Creek Guide & Outfitter
Joseph Katancik
Pine Acres Resort & Outfitters
Rene & Joyce Lavoie
Pine Beach Lodge - H.C. Johnson
Pine Cliff Lodge
Richard & Kaylene Foley
Pine Cove Lodge - Minnie Massicotte
Pine Cove Resort
Pine Grove Cabins
Eileen & Gary Hobbs
Pine Grove Resort
Margaret Lucyshyn
Pine Grove Resort Cottages
Bill & Carol Chambers
Pine Island Lodge -Brian Burgess
Pine Point Resort Ltd.
William & Arlene Haney
Pine Portage Lodge-The Watson's
Pine Ridge Lodge & Wilderness Tours
David & Wayne Holloway
Pine Ridge/Bartlett Creek Outfitter
Robert M. Labert
Pinebrook Custom Flies- John Conrad
Pines Ranch Partnership
Dean Rusk & Richard Steamer
Pinewood Lodge
Raquel & Jeff Lincoln
Piney River Ranch- Kara Heide
Pinkham's Fishing Lodge
Donald Gardner & Virginia Pinkham
Pinta IV Charters-Capt. Gerald Pienta
Pinware River Lodge
W. Arthur Fowler
Pioneer Charters David G. Logan
Pioneer Lodge, Inc.
Steven H. & Gwendolyn A. White
Pioneer Lodge/Dog Lake
Mike & Claude Gratton
Pioneer Mountain Outfitters
Tom & Deb Proctor
Pioneer Outfitter
Charles A. & Cliff Page
Piper Enterprises - Charles Piper
Pipestone Fly-In Outposts
Mike & Patti Henry
Pipestone Lake Lodge Ltd.
Marvin Bather
Pipestone Point Resort
Peter & Shirley Haugen
Pippin Plantation
Pirate Charters - Capt. Gary Frazier
Pisces Charter Service
Lynn N. Ray
Pit River Guide Service
Robert H. Akins
Pitka Mountain Outfitters, Ltd.
Colonel R. Anderson
PJ Charter Boat
PK Outfitters/Missoulian Angler
Paul W. Koller
Placid Bay Lodge
Dennie & Bev Shillinglaw
Plaisted's Camp
Plateau Creek Outfitters
Joe E. Garcia
Platt's Guides & Outfitters
Ronald R. Platt
Play Pretty Charter Boat
Playin' Hooky
Capt. Robert DeMagistris
Playin' Hooky - Capt. Chuck Nelson
Playin Hooky Charters
Capt. John Troen
Pleasant Cove Fishing Resort
The Bishops
Pleasant Hill Canoe Livery
Plum Bluff Charters - Gary R. Buzunis
Plummer's Lodges - Cameron Baty
Pocket Change - William C. Lyle
Point's North Alaska Wild. Outfitters
Mike McDaneld
Point Adventure Lodge, Inc.
Mark Kneen
Point Loma Sportfishing
Pointer Lake Fishing Lodge
Bryce Liddell
Points Unknown
Poisne Sam Hryhorysak
Poitry In Motion Steven Poitry
Polar Bear Camp & Fly-In Outfitter
Billy Konopelky
Polar Star Lodge- Norah & Ross Finch
Polaskan Charters - Ray Majeski
Pollards Ute Lodge- Troy R. Pollard
Pond's Resort - Keith & Linda Pond
Pond's...on the Miramichi
Ponderosa Outfitters
Norman Bruce Ayers
Ponds Porter Kove Kamps
Doreen L. Pond
Pontiac Cove Marina Tim Morgan
Popeye Charters, Inc.
Vincent & Jean Mitchell
Poplar Bay Park & Tourist Camp
Barry & Linda Crawford
Poplar Ridge Outfitters, Inc.
Harvey McNalley
Port Fly Shop Jim Dionne
Port Lions Lodge
Steve & Peggy Andresen
Port Pacer II Charters
Capt. Jerry Myers
Portage Ch. General Store & Lodge
Chris & Leona Carr
Portage Lake Charter Service
James Bennett
Portland River Company
John W. Tilles
Poseidon Services
Joan W. Gottfried
Possible Tours Charters
Lou Kircher
Potomac Highland Outfitters
Michael Messenger & Keith Busmente
Potter's Services- Gerald O. Potter
Poudre River Outfitters
Rex L. Schmidt
Pourvoire Lac du Blanc- Linda Poitras
Powder River Outfitters
Kenneth F. Greslin
Powderhorn Outfitters
Vincent Woodrow Tanko
Powderhorn Primitive Outfitters
Cameron Lewis
Powell's Outfitters - Tony Powell
Pozniak's Lodge
Robert & Cecile Fielding
Prairie Bee Camp- Steve & Mary Rupp
Prairie Outfitters
Potter & Westin & Slabik
Prather Outfitters- Ned & Lyle Prather
Predator Charter Service
Capt. Ron Kline
Presa Vieja Ranch- Jesus M. Garcia
Press Stephens-Outfitter
Prestages Sportfishing Lodge
John & Betsy Prestage
Priest Lake Guide Service
Gary Brookshire
Priest Lake Outdoor Adventures
Priewe Air Service

Richard Trzesniowski
Prime Time Charters-David Pinquoch
Prime Time Charters
Capt. Gregory W. Switzer
Prime Time Charters-Peter C. Unger
Primland
Prince of Wales Lodge- Will Jones, Sr.
Prince William Sound Adventrues
Gary & Libbie Graham
Pringle's Guide Service
Gerald A. Pringle
Private Land Outfitters- Travis Rowley
Prof. Big Game Guide & Outfitters
Jack Cassidy
Professional Big Game Outfitters
Bud Nelson
Professional Chartering
Robert Tait
Professional Guide Service
Bruce R. Coate
Professional Guide Service
Randy Dorman
Professional Marine Services
Harold D. DeHart
Profish-N-Sea Charters
Steven R. Zernia
Profitt's Farm & Ranch
Kenneth Profitt
Prompt Delivery Capt. Dale Ahlvin
Pronto Alan Fay
Propp's Rod & Fly, Inc.
Proud Lion - Richard Praklet
Proud Mary Charters
Capt. Bill Garceau
Providence Bay Tent & Trailer Park
Chick & Irene Cornish
Provider - Capt. Rick Anderson
Pruden's Point Resort
Pruett's Fish Camp
Ptarmigan Air Steven Williams
Puffin Charters, Inc.
James L. & Barbara M. Cheatham
Puffin Family Charters
Leslie A. Pemberton
Pukisimoon Outfitters - Fred Hobbs
Pulchritude Mike Hampel
Pullin Ventures - Denver & Tom Pullin
Purcell Wilderness Guiding &
Outfitting - Gary Hansen
Purgatoire Outfitters - Jay Waring
Purnell's Rainbow Inn -David Purnell
Purple Sage Outfitters
Linda A. & Wesley W. DuBose
Putnam's Landing-Bill & Sherri Shipley
Putney, McNeal Enterprise, Inc.
Pybus Point Lodge- Alan Veys
Pyramid Llama Ranch
Ann Patricia & Kevin Copeland
Pyramid Outfitters - Steve Whiteside
Qatuk's Kobut River Charters
Virgil F. Coffin
Quaking Aspen Guides & Outfitters,
Inc. Dave Mapes
Quality Adventures, Inc.
Cort, VanAlstyne & Van Nostrand
QUAPAW Penelope Gregory
Quarter-Circle Circle Ranch
Quarter Circle "E" Outfitters & Guest
Gail Eldridge
Quarter Circle Circle Ranch
John Judson
Quarter Circle E Guest Ranch
Quarter Circle E.M. Outfitters
Ernest E. McCollum
Quarterback Charters
Karl & Robyn Amundsen
Quarterdeck and Mercer's
Roger Mercer
Quarterdeck on Gull Lake
Alan & Jane Gunsbury
Quesnel Lake Wilderness Adventures
Ken Davis
Quick Creek Bassmasters
Dave Brumett
Quick Silver Guide Service
Richard J. Andrest
Quicksilver Charter Boat
Quiet Cove Charters
Thomas R. Kinberg
Quiet Trails Canoe Outfitters
Pat Stern
Quill Gordon Fly Fishers
Gordon S. Rose
Quinnat Landing Resort
David McGuire & Joe Chandler
Quinns Caravan Charters
Michael & Jill Quinn
Qwik Fish Guide Service
Jerry E. Hartman
R-Fly Charters
Randall Mark Phillips
R-N-A Charters
Ron & Cindy Matteson
R-W's Fishing - Ken Weilbaches
R & B Guide Service
Ronald W. Howland
R & D Charters - Dan Murphy
R & H Enterprises - N.G. Hollo
R & J Outfitters - Robert Parker
R & R Charters- Ray Jackson
R & R Guiding - Ryan Rogowski
R & R Hunting - Gary J. Rowley
R & R Ranch - Ralph R. Royster
R & R Wilderness Lodge
R. Jenson & R. Reylonds
R R Charters - Guy J. Bonhrand
R&R Outdoors, Inc.- Robert D. Black
R.a.M. Outfitters- The Despres
R.J.'s Greystone Guide & Outfitting
Ronald Tull Jones
R.J. Cain & Company Outfitters
R.J. Cain
R.J. Charters - Rick Wood
R.O.W. /River Odysseys West
Peter Grubb & Betsy Bowen
R.W. Outfitters - Robert W. Wetzel
R.Z. Guide Service
Rick Zugschwerdt
Rach Outfitters/Flathead Charters
Jeff E. Rach
Rader Lodge - Jeffrey A. Rader
Raft, Inc. - Michael L. Huddleston
Raft, Inc. - Don W. Strasser
Rafter S Ranch - John M. Sirman
Raftopoulos Ranches
John & Steve Raftopoulos
Rain-Bou Outfitters & Guide
Glenn M. Oliver
Rainbird Charters - Dwight N. Bloom
Rainbow Airways
Rainbow Bay Resort Jerry S. Pippen
Rainbow Charter Capt. Gary Gros
Rainbow Connection Charters
Capt. Steve LeRoy
Rainbow Cottages Resort
Tony & Heather Kenny
Rainbow Expeditions-John Nicholson
Rainbow Guide Service
Joseph Daniel Biner
Rainbow King Lodge
Thomas V. Robinson
Rainbow Lodge-Rick/Ricky Lawrence
Rainbow Outfitters - Jim L. Becker
Rainbow Point Lodge
Bob & Gale Extence
Rainbow River Lodge - Chris Goll
Rainbow Tours Jack Montgomery
Rainbow Trout Ranch
Rainbow Trout Resort
Raindancer Sport Fishing Charters
John M. Brooks
Raindog Charters - Scott W. Raneg
Rainier Charters - Thomas Rightmier
Rainmaker Charters- Richard Pegau
Rainy's Flies & Supplies
Rainy Hollow Wilderness Adventures
Ltd.
Raleigh's Guide Service
Raleigh Stone
Rally Killer Charters- Capt. C.J. Crisp
Ralph Flippo's Guide Service
Ralph Flippo
Ralphy Boy II Charter Sportfishing
Capt. Dave Goethals
Ram Creek Outfitters
Steven Leuenberger
Ramble House
Ramrod Charters
Wayne Musilek & Richard W. Deaver
Rams Head Outfitters- Stan Simpson
Ranch Country Outfitters
Perry McCormick
Ranching for Wildlife -Jarrell Massey
Randa's Guide Service-Denis Randa
Randall's Resort
Scott & Peggy O'Brien
Randolph's Landing
Nate & Lynn Bristow
Randy's Fishing Trips
Randy's Guide Service-Randy Horne
Randy Brown's Madison Flyfisher
Randall W. Brown
Randy Petrich Big Game Hunts
Randy Petrich
Randy Rathie Outfitter
Rapid River Outfitters
Kerry Neal Brennan
Rapids Camp Lodge
Jerry Shults & Richard VanDruten
Rascal Charters
Rather Rough-It Adventures
Carl A. Bowman, Jr.
Rathsack Charter Service
Capt. Mike Rathsack
Raven's Fire, Inc.
Barbara Bingham
Raven Adventure Trips, Inc.
Art Krizman
Raven Charters - Scott P. McLeod
Raven Fishin' Physician
Joseph Turcotte
Rawhide Adventures
Fred & Rod Ellis
Ray's Guide Service - Ray Slusser
Ray's Hunting & Fishing Lodge
Raymond & Daphne Broughton
Ray & Shirley Courson
Jigg's Landing
Ray Atkins Guiding & Flying Service
Ray Atkins
Razor Creek Outfitters
Ron K. Brink
Real Alaska - Agnes Alexie
Real Alaska Adventures, Ltd.
Stephen Conner
Red's Camps - Ron MacKay
Red's Kern Valley Marina
Red Buck Sporting Camps
Sandra & Thomas Doughty
Red Cedar Outfitters
Red Dog Charters
Mert Stromire & T. Fitzgerald
Red Dog Outdoors- Kelly R. Short
Red Dog Sports- Mert Stromire
Red Feather Guides & Outfitters
John Todd Peterson
Red Indian Lodge
Herb & Mary Anne Hoffman
Red Mountain Guest Ranch
William Ridgeway
Red Mountain Outfitters- Jim Flynn
Red Mountain Outfitters
Les G. Nader
Red Pine Lodge- Garry & Cathy Litt
Red Pine Wilderness Lodge
James & Janice Bowden
Red River Adventures & Outfitters
Kim Meger
Red River Corrals - Archie H. George
Red River Outfitters
Lawrence W. Smith
Red Rock Outfitters
Red Rock River Co., Inc.
Steven Summers
Red Rockn' Llamas- Bevin E. McCabe
Red Wilderness Adventures, Inc.
David Taylor
Red Wing Charters- Harold Corson
Red Woods Outfitters
Nolan F. Woods
Redd Ranches - David Redd
Redd Ranches Guide & Outfitter
Paul David Redd
Redside River Guide Service
Robert C. Bryant
Redstone Trophy Hunts
David & Carol Dutchik
Redwing Outfitters - Bob Daugherty
Redwood Empire Outdoor Adventure
Reel Action Guide Service-Don Wood
Reel Adventures - Gary Fuller
Reel Adventures- Donald Schneider
Reel Affair Charters
Timothy Twaddle
Reel Alaska Ryon & Angela Morin
Reel Charters - Patrick J. Lorentz
Reel Class Sportfishig
Reel Easy Sportfishing
Capt. Paul A. Orzolek
Reel Krazy - Capt. Steve Gober
Reel Magic Charters - Mark Hammer
Reel Odyssey Charters, Inc.
Capt. Paul Marchand
Reel Pleasure Charters - Wally Turner
Reel Pleasure Sportfishing
Reel Vermont Fishing/Canoe Rentals
Don Heise
Reel Women Fly Fishing Adv.
Reelclass Charters, Inc.
Derek W. Floyd
Reeliable Fishing Charters
Daniel B. Nore
Reelin' - Capt. Ernest Celotto
Reindeer Lake Trout Camp
Ron & Cindi Holmes
Remember Alaska
David & Nadine Hillstrand
Remote Sportsmans Rentals
Willy Keppel
Rendezvous Lake Outpost Camp
Billy Jacobson
Rendezvous Outfitters
Herbert A. Moore
Rendezvous Outfitters & Guides, LTD
William R. Eby
Renegade Sport Fishing
Renegade Sport Fishing Charters
Capt. Tim Mueller
Reno Fly Shop, Inc.-John D. Stanley, Jr.
Renshaw Outfitting, Inc.
Jim & Lynda Renshaw
Repair Altenatives Co.
Donald, Connie & Kreg Polzin
Repak's Backpak & Bushwak
Paul Repak
Reputation Guide & Kennel
Gay Lynn Lang
Restoration Through Recreation
Rocky & Sharon McElvea
Resurrection Bay Charters
Darrell T. Robinson
Revilla Fishing Charters
Dewie & Debra Hamilton
Rhythm & Blues Sportfishing, Inc.
Rich's Fishing Guide Service
Rich Bogle
Rich's Guide Service- Rich Wade
Rich's Last Resort- Rich Sphar
Rich Brown Guide Service
Richard's Canoe Rental
Jerry & Karen Richard
Richard Haslett Wayne Smith
Richard P. Helfrich Dick P. Helfrich
Richard Rang Lake & Stream Charters
Richard Rang
Richards Kenai River Charters
David Richards
Richmond's Alaskan Guide
Phillip Richmond
Richmond's Alaskan Guide Service
Phillip Michael Richmond
Rick's Guide Service- Rick Smith
Rick's Lodge
Rick Edinger & Sons -Rick D. Edinger
Rick Mah Charters - Rick Mah
Rick Miller Fly Fishing - Rick Miller
Rick Rule Sportfishing
Rick Warren Guide & Outfitting
Ricky Warren
Rick Wren's Fishing on the Fly
Evelyn Wren
Rickard's Bait & Tackle-Sherry Catley
Riddle's Custom Service
Jack Riddle
Riddle's Guide Service
Stephen S. & Donna L.Riddle
Ridge Country Outfitters
Dean Randell
Ridge Runner Outfitters
Chad Christopherson
Ridge Runners & River Runners
William E. Davis, Jr.
Ridgetrack Guide & Outfitting
Craig & Cathy Krumwiede
Ridgewood Resort- Ginny Matyska
Rifflin' Hitch Lodge-Gudrid Hutchings
Rim Rock Outfitters- Monty G. Elder
Rimrock Guides & Outfitters
Bryan K. Adair
Rimrock Hunts - Dan Artery
Rimrock/Little Creek - Alan Baier
Ring's Fishing Guide Service
Floyd Ring
Ring Dang Doo Charter Boat
Ringo's Guide Service
Brian Ringeisen & Karrie Burns
Rio Paisano Ranch - Casey Taub
Rippling Brook Flyfishing Outfitters
Rich Youngers
Riptide Outfitters - R. Steve Scheldt
Rising Trout Guides & Outfitters
Daniel J. Bastian
Rising Wind Dojo - Philip Fyfe
Risky Business Charters
Capt. John Hoffert
RiteOFF Michael D. Justice, President
Ritz Sporting Goods
River's Bend Outfitters
Glenn D. Summers
River "1" Inc. - Dannie A. Strand
River & Sea Outfitters- Dave Forsted
River & Trail Outfitters
W. Lee Baihly
River Adventure Float Trips
Mel & Dianne Norrick
River Adventures, Ltd.
Sam Whitten
River Bend Flyfishing
Charles Miles Stranahan
River Bend Resort
Glenn & Pam Voytilla
River Bend Sportsman's Resort
Ralph Brendle
River Drifters Whitewater Tours
Ann & Bill Kemnitzer
River Excitement- John Marshall
River Fox Charters - Robert Herz
River Odyssey's West, Inc.
Peter H. Grubb
River Point Resorot & Outfitting Co.
Steve & Jane Doschak
River Queen of Oscoda, Inc.
River Quest Excursions
Alan W. Odegaard
River Resource Enterprises
Mark Jones
River Road Outfitters- Herbert Weiss
River Run Guide Service
Wesley Carkin
River Song Lodge - Philip Tremrco
River Trips Unlimited, Inc. - Irv Urie
River View Cabins -Colin/Jean McKay
River Wrangellers
Kevin & Suzanne McCarthy
Rivercliff Trout Dock
Riverdale Tourist Camp
Gerry & Georgette Roziere
Riverfront Hunting Club
Raymond Olson
Riveride Motel & Outfitters
Robert Hines
Riverkeep Camp
Riverlake Cottages & Campground
Ed & Helen Larson
Riverland Camp & Outfitters
Jay & Maryann McRae
Rivers Bend Outfitting- Kip Gates
Rivers Edge Outfitters
Vernon L. Patterson
Rivers Edge Trading Co
Rivers II - Karen Calvert & Eddie Lilly
Rivers Path Outfitters
Frank & Tami Armendariz
Rivers Path Outfitters -Don Hill
Rivers Path Outfitters - Bill K. Kremers
Riverside Anglers
Peter McNeil & Dave Ziegler
Riverside Campground & Motel
Riverside Canoes & Kayaks
Riverside Guides & Outfitters
Jeff Bevans
Riverside Lodge
Kenneth Hayes, Ed Matwick
Riversong Adventures - Carl L. Dixon
Riversong Lodge - Daniel Brown
Robert Carey, Mitchell Coe
Riversong Lodge
Gordon Descutner, Tim Lynes
Riverview Lodge- Irene & Pat Blaney
Riverview of Frankenmuth
Jerry Kabat
Riverview Plantation- Cader B. Cox, III
Rizuto's San Juan River Lodge
Peggy Harrell
RJ's Guide Service
Capt. Randy VerDow
RL Outfitters - Dwain Rennaker
Road Creek Ranch
Roaring Fork Anglers Roaring Fork
Guide Service- John R. Gross
Rob's Canadian Wilderness Resort
Rob & Sandy Brodhagen
Robert Dupea Outfitters- Rob Dupea
Robert J. Juba Robert Juba
Robert McReynolds Fishing Charters
Robert Semanski John Emch
Roberta's Charters- Capt. Tony Ripple
Roberts River Rafting Adventures
Monte Roberts
Robertson's Guiding Service
John Robertson
Robertson Enterprises
Ken Robertson
Robichaud Outfitters
Bernard Robichaud
Robson Outfitters
Dale R. & Janette Robson
Rock Bottom Fishing Hole Outfitters
Larry Bosiak
Rock Creek Fishing Co. - John Erp
Rock Creek Guest Ranch- Gayle Gibbs
Rock Creek Outfitters
Robert Eugene Thompson
Rock Creek Ranch
Rock Creek Ranch, Corp.
Rockview Camp
Susanne & Andre Rieser
Rockwood Lodge Tim Austin
Rocky Fork Guide Service
Ernest C. Strum
Rocky Lake Cabins
Duane & Glenda Bohlken
Rocky Meadow Adventures
Rocky Mountain Adventures, Inc.
G. David Costlow
Rocky Mountain Adventures, Inc.
Dan Shoemaker
Rocky Mountain Fisherman
Monte G. Andres
Rocky Mountain Horseback Vacations
Rocky Mountain Lodge, Ltd.
Henry Fercho
Rocky Mountain Outfitter, Ltd.
Rocky Mountain Outfitters
Gary W. Bohochik
Rocky Mountain Ranches
Lawrence J. Bishop
Rocky Mountain Rides-Dave Hemauer
Rocky Mountain River Tours, Inc.
David F. Mills
Rocky Mountain Whitewater
Patrick W. Doty
Rocky Outfitters Rocky L. Niles
Rocky Point Charters Walt Payne
Rocky Point Outfitters
Orvall Kuester
Rocky Point Resort
Jerry J. Felciello
Rocky Point Resort
Jim & Kathy Schueller
Rocky Point Resort
Clarence F. Whittle
Rocky Reef Resort
John & Patti Odle
Rocky Shore Lodge
Norm & Sue Cook
Rocky Top Outfitters Steve Packer &
Jimmy Buck Ward
Rod 'n Real Charters
Rod & Randy Berg
Rod & Gun Resources, Inc.
J.W. Smith & David K. Gregory
Rod & Real Fishing Adventures
Robert Stock
Rod & Reel Fly Shop
Edward L. Wagner
Rod and Real Charters/BC Charters
Joseph Conkright
Rod Bender's Lance Domonoske
Rod Bender Charters Capt. Charlie
Portes, Jr.
Rod Wintz Guide Service/Wason
Ranch Rod Wintz
Rodger's Guide Service
Rodger Affeldt
Rodger Carbone's Fly Fishing Guides
Rodger R. Carbone
Roe's Charter Service
Richard M. Roe
Roebling Inn on the Delaware
Don & JoAnn Jahn
Rogue Excursions Unlimited, Inc.
Terry O'Connors
Rogue Rafting Company
Devon M. Stephenson
Rogue River Guide Service
Paul Lopes
Rogue River Outfitters
Dennis R. Hughson
Rogue River Raft Trips
Michelle Hanten
Rogue Sport Fishing Unlimited
Michael A. Hoefer
Rogue Whitewater Co.
Mike & Shawn Ayers
Rogue Wilderness, Inc.
Robert R. Rafalovich
Rohr's Wilderness Tours
Rohrer Bear Camp, Inc.
Richard A. Rohrer
Rolly Outfitters
Ron & Kelly Shykitka
Ron's Alaska Lodge George Wing
Ron's Guide Service
Ronald W. Van Iderstine
Ron's Guide Service Ronald E. Jones
Ron's Guide Service Ron Rogers
Ron's Riverboat Service
Ronald & Marilyn Wilson
Ron-D-View Ranch & Outfitting
Ron Pfeffer
Ron Adkins Guide Service
Ronald G. Adkins
Ron Dungey & Sons Ronald F.
Dungey
Ron Jones Guide Service
Ron Jones
Ron Laubon Ross Wellman
Ron Loucks Outfitting Ron Loucks
Ron Mills Outfitting Ronald E. Mills
Ronald Stewart Ronald L. Stewart
Rosalyn's Fishy Business
Rosalyn Stowell
Rose Fishing Service
Rose Hill Plantation
Rose Marie Charter
Cat. Paul Lohman
Rosebob Salmon Charters
Bob Holzer

Ross' Camp Pat & Wayne Howard
Ross & Nelson Outfitters & Guides
Jim Ross & Joe Nelson
Ross Fishing Charters
Jerry R. Ross
Ross Johnson Pro. Big Game Outfitter
Ross Johnson
Ross Marine Recreations
C. Alan Ross
Ross Marine Tours
Timothy J. Ross
Rouser Capt. Larry G. Simpson
Route Lake Lodge
Hermann & Claudia Vogel
Route to Trout
Anthony Joseph Colaizzi, Jr.
Roy Savage Ranches Roy E. Savage
Royal Charters & Tours
Royal Tauno Hill, Sr.
Royal Gorge Outfitters
Bill Edrington & Bill Carson
Royal Outfitters Tyrone L. Throop
Royal River Outfitters
Jonathan Royal Magee
Royal Sea Charter
Donald Bentley
Royal Windsor Lodge
Art & Olga Jalkanen
RR Charters Richard "Rick" Richardson
Ruby Ranch
Ruby Range Wilderness Lodge
Ruby Springs Lodge Paul & Jeanne Moseley
Rudy Steele Guides & Outfitters, Inc.
Rudy Steele
Rue's Charters David Rue
Rugg's Outfitting Raymond Rugg
Rum Runner Charters
Chris & Teri Conder
Runnin Bear ChartersRance J. Dailey
Running Creek Ranch
Edward E. Houghton
Running M Outfitters- Monte McLane
Running River Fly Guide
Stuart W. Howard
Rupertsland Guiding & Outfitting Services - Werner Batke
Rush's Lake View Ranch -Keith S. Rush
Russ Willis Outfitting-Richard K. Willis
Russell's Churchill River Camps
Jim Russell
Rust's Flying Service-Todd/Hank Rust
Rustic Fly & Spin Helen Kurtz
Rustic Resort Marina
Ruth Ann's All-Brite Charters
Don & Ruth Ann Albright
RW's Fishing William
Davis and Ron Weilbacher
RW's Guide Service - Gary Byerly
RW Guides Service- Garry Keller
Ryan's Campsite -Robert/Jean Lucier
Ryan's Resort - Ken Williams
S & H Bait & Tackle Inc.
Mike Holcomb
S & K Outfitting & Guide Service
Paul E. Gingery & K. Kyle Revell
S & S Outfitters David J. Bream
S.E. Salmon Excursions-Steven K. Scott
S.S.S. Chartes-Michael/Susan Boarland
S.W. Montana Fishing Co.
David V. Marsh
S.W.A.T. Charter Service-Jerry Rankey
Sable Mountain Guides-John D. Ayers
Sac Bay Lodge Camp
Fred & Heidi Wittwer
Saddle Springs Trophy Outfitters
Bruce Cole
Saddle Tramp Outfitters
Thomas Bullock
Safari River Outdoors - Barry Samson
Saganash Outpost Camp
Richard Landriault
Sage-N-Pine, Outfitters
Paul L. Strasdin
Sage & Spirit Karen Frost
Sage and Spirit
William & Karen Frost
Sage Charters Dan P. Bilderback
Sailcone Wilderness Fishing
Sailfish - Biloxi Shrimping Trip
Sally Mountain Cabins
Corey & Sally Hegarty
Salmon & Magruder Mountain Outfitters Don Habel
Salmon & Sons River Guide Service
Kevin Hall
Salmon Deport, Inc.
Capt. Bill Silbernagel
Salmon Falls Resort
Alvin & Shirley White
Salmon Forks Outfitters
William H. Tidwell
Salmon Grabber Charters
Capt. Ed Maxon
Salmon Hole Lodge - Scott Smith
Salmon King Lodge - Lucie Drovin
Salmon River Challenge, Inc.
Patrick L. Marek
Salmon River Experience
Charles C. Boyd
Salmon River Lodge -Janice Balluta
Salmon River Outfitters
Steven W. Shephard
Salmon River Tours Co.
Michael D. McLain
Salmon Run Charters
Capt. O. Fred Miller
Salmon Run Charters- Dale Mulford
Salmon Seeker Charters
Capt. Dan McNamara
Salmon Stone- Lawrence F. Heilman
Salmon Unlimited of Indiana
Jessie Childress
Salmon Unlimited of Indiana
Bob Vanberg
Salmon Valley Guide Service
Kathleen Rae Gliksman
Saltery Lake Lodge
Bill Franklin & Doyle Hatfield
Saltwater Adventures
Greg Krenpasky
Saltwater Sportsman Charter Service
Timothy Schwartz
Salty's Touring & Guiding Service
Clyde Saltz
Salty Dog Charters - Tim Rebischke
Sam's Hunting & Fishing Camps
Sam Caines
Samantha B Charters -Tom Young
Samoset Lodge - Ruth Hauta
San-Pahgre Outdoor Adven./ Outfitting - Stuart D. Chappell
San Juan Back Country
Delbert & Laura Smith
San Juan Ranch Outfitters
Scott MacTiernan
San Juan Troutfitters - Harry Lane
Sanctuary Charters
Capt. Doug Carlstrom
Sand Bay Resort
Bill & Barb Davis
Sand n' Surf Charters
Scott & John Wood
Sanderson's Guide Service
Bill Sanderson
Sandi-Kay Charters Ray J. Zernia
Sandjpiper Sportfishing Charters
Capt. Robert Vicek
Sandpiper Charters Paul Kropp
Sandpiper Sport Fishing
Capt. Tom Morrell
Sandpiper Trophy & Sport Fishing Serv. Capt. Larry Boraas
Sandusky Charter Boat Assn.
Sandy Beach Lodge
Roger, Wade & Tom Mitchell
Sandy Haven Camp
Annette & Howie Thomas
Sandy Point Camp
Bill & Penny Higgins
Sandy Point Lodge - Bruno Jaurnell
Sanfort & Sun Outfitting
Gregory F. Sanford
Sanity Charters - Ken L. Larson
Santa Rita Ranch - Ruben Garza
Santee Guide Service
Santee State Park
Santilli Enterprises -Stephen L. Santilli
Sappa Creek Hunt Preserve
Sappah & Son Guide Service
Terry Sappah
Sappah & Son Guide Service
Terry L. Sappah
Sarah Lake Outfitters -Mr. Senchuk
Sasa-Ginni-Gak Lodge -The Johnsons
Sasagiu Rapids Lodge
Dorothy & Steve Samu
Saskoba Outfitters
B. Murray & G. Kostuchuk
Saucy Tomato - Capt. Leroy Wenger
Saunatuk Fishing Lodge
James & Sharon Gruben
Saunders Camps - Calvin Saunders
Saunders Floating- WilliamSaunders
Savanne River Resort & Campground
David & Patricia Coates
Sawtooth Guide Service, Inc.
Robert L. Cole
Sawtooth Mountain Guides
Kirk D. Bachman
Sawtooth Wilderness Outfitters
Darl & Kari Allred
Sawyer's Deschutes Guide Service
Lynn A. Sawyer
SBL Company
Scales 'N Tales Charters, Inc.
Eddy L. Sison
Scana Fish Guides- Bret Herrick
Scenic Bays Charters- Bruce Bays
Scenic Day Charters- Mike Cottrell
Scenic Lake Tours- Hank Byrd
Scenic Rim Trail Rides
Scenic River Charters -Timothy Jewett
Schaefers Guide Service #1
Steven D. Schaefers
Schaefers Guide Service #2
Schaefers & Damon
Schell's Camp & Park
Don & Carolyn Hoshel
Schirmer's Fly Shop- Edward Schirmer
Schlegel Ranch Co.- Wesley Schlegel
Schmidt Enterprises
Linda Bergdoll-Schmidt
Schneider's Guide Service
Kenneth LeRoy Schneider
Schrader's Eastern Shore Shooting
Scoffield Ranch Outfitters
George B. Scoffield
Scoop Lake Outfitters, Ltd.
Darwin Cary
Scoot's Guide Service
Donald & Diana Weigand
Scott Lake Lodge
Blaine & Susan Anderson
Scott Stewart Fishing Service
Scott A. Stewart
Screaming Reel Charters
Thomas O. Drennan
Screwy Louie's Sport Shop
Capt. Louie Parseault
SE Alaska Outfitters- Thomas T. Zwick
Sea-AK Charters - Bruce A. Smith
Sea-Nic Fishing & Wildlife
Darrell Riggs
Sea-Run Outfishing Adventures
Scott Chafe
Sea-Trek Charters- Darwin E. Jones
Sea Bear Charters - John B. Phillips
Sea Breeze Charters- Dennis Lanham
Sea Crest Charters- Rocky Ertzberger
Sea Cruise Alaska- George Eliason
Sea Dancer Sportfishing, Inc.
Sea Dawn - Donald T. McCarthy
Sea Dog Sport Fishing Charters
Capt. James Schlegel
Sea Fever Charters -L.A./ Joann Wilson
Sea Fish Alaska - Joe R. Garrison
Sea Flight Charters- Leah W. Jenkin
Sea Genie, Inc.
Sea Gull Charters- Dick Overfield
Sea Hag Fishing Charters
Capt. Sue Kalk
Sea Haven Beachcombers
Alan Andersen
Sea Hawk
Sea King Charters
Gary S. Bernhardt
Sea Lure Fishing Charters
Sea Otter Lodge
Tim & Lynne Graves
Sea Otter Sound Fish Camp
Allen & Barbara Richter
Sea Pass Charters
Capt. Jim Tsepas
Sea Pool Cabins Hugh Wentzell
Sea Quest Charters
Samuel & Marvol Barnard
Sea Quest Charters George Huntington
Sea Reaper Capt. Jeff Hardy
Sea Scape Adventures
Richard E. VanMeter
Sea Sound Charters
William C. Steffen
Sea Sprite - Capt. Peter Wheeler
Sea Star Charters
Sea Star Charters - Erin / Kelly Railing
Sea Strike, Inc.
Sea Trek Charters - Ken Nelson
Sea Venture Charters
Gary Plumb
Sea Verse Charters
Sea Wife Charters
Seadog Charters- Capt. Paul Pinan
Seafood Safaris- Jon Todd Weck
Seagull Charters- Capt. Ted Hatter
Seagull Charters - James H. Meneely
Seagull Lodge -Ed & Kevin Blondin
Seagull Marina & Campground
Seaguy's Leroy Edenshaw
Seahawk Charters - Capt. Ken Klas
Seahawk III - Capt. Judd Barnes
Seahorse Charters- Capt. John Brisson
Seal River Wilderness Adventures
Mike & Jeanne Reimer
Sealand Charters - Rick Hinson
Sealaska Cruises, Inc.
Richard F. Billings
Seamans Alaskan Fishing Adventure
Joseph & Lora Seaman
Seamist Charter & Guide Service
Malcolm Doiron
Seaview Charters - James M. Heston
Seaweaver Charters- James S. Franzel
Seawind Cruises -Ken & Barb Gehring
Sebago Lake Cottages
Ray & Fran Nelson
Seboomook Wilderness Campground
Secret Bait Charters
Capt. Robert J. Dumovich
Secret Cove Charters -Dan Oneil
Secret Pass Outfitters -Steven Wines
Secret Pond Camps & Guide Service
Mark Carver
See Alaska Charters- Anthony Leichty
See Alaska Tours & Charters
Randy & Judy Henderson
See Alaska with Jim H. Keeline, Inc.
Jim H. Keeline
See Fish Ventures Inc.-Tabor Ashment
See Fish Ventures, Inc. -Tom Ellefson
See Fish Ventures, Inc.
Sharm Setterquist
See Shore Charters
Capt. Steve Propsom
Seethe North Tour Service
Sok Chang
Seldovia Fishing Adventures
David & Peggy Choninger
Seldovia Sports Charters & Ecotours
William N. & Shirley H. Spencer
Selway-Magruder Outfitters, Inc.
Kendall Lee Wells
Selway Lodge, Inc. Rick Hussey & Patricia G. Millington
Selwyn Lake Lodge
Gord/Mary Daigneault-Wallace
Semmer Charters
William J. Semmer
Sentinel Rock Outfitters - Ray Kagel
Serendipity Boat Charters- Jim Catlin
Serendipity Farm
Forrest & Suzanne Garret
Serene Fly-Fishing Adventures
Pete Serene
Serenity Charters
James Whigman
Service Transfer -Michael K. Snowden
Seseganaga Lodge
Darrill "Butch" & Tom
Seven Lakes Lodge
Steve Cobb Jack & Tom Kissock
Seven Lazy P Guest Ranch
Charles C. Blixrud
Seventh Heaven Charter Services
Capt. Bob Barlow
Sevogle Salmon Club-Michael French
Sevy Guide Service, Inc.
Robert J. Sevy
Shadd Lake Cabins- Nancy McKay
Shadow- Kenneth L. Malay
Shadow Lake Ranch- Shadow Oaks
John D. & Pauline L. Doty
Shadow Wood, Inc.- Robert I. Zagorin
Shadowland Charters- Edward Svec
Shady Lady
Capts. John & Julie Gadzinski
Shamanz Charters
Robert & Rose Shymanski
Shamrock Ranch Outfitters
Bruce Wilson
Shandy & Sons Charters
Anthony Shandy
Shandy & Sons Charters
David Shandy
Share Alaska Charters
Harry A. Sevirina & Larry A. Cutbirth
Sharron's Outfitting Service
Debi Hatch
Shasta Tackle & Sportfishing
Shattuck Creek Ranch & Outfitters
Andre Molsee
Shavano Outfitters - Jim E. James
Shawner Charters - Richard Nitz
Shearwater Charter Boat
Shearwater Lodge & Charters
Steven F. Hemenway
Sheep Mountain Outfitters
Tim Haberberger
Sheer Pleasure Sportfishing
Sheerwater Guide Sevice
Barry T. Jones
Shelikof Expedition Company
David J. Krause
Shella's Fishing Charters
Shella R. Maddox
Shelter Bay Charters
Mitch Mattson
Shelter Cove Lodge
John Patterson & Larry Christian
Sheltowee Trace Outfitters
Rick Egedi
Shenandoah Lodge Charlie Walsh
Shepp Ranch Idaho
Virginia Hopfenbeck
Sherrod Ranch -Donald Lee Sherrod
Sherwood Outfitting-John Sherwood
Shesley River Outfitters- Rudy Day
Shgen-Doo Charters- Gabriel George
Shihan Pete Traina Special Protection
Shining Falls Camps
Ralph & Ruth Rutledge
Shining Tree Tourist Camp
Bob & Sue Evans
Ship Island Excursions
Shiplet Ranch Outfitters- Bob Shiplet
Shippa Hoy Charter Fishing
Capt. Warren Nelson
Shoestring Charters
Don L. & Lisa M. Butler
Shogomoc Sporting Camps
Muriel Way
Shon-A-Lei Sports & Marine
Shooter Charters- Capt. Mike Harrison
Shooting Star Camp
Shane & Betty Looby
Shore Nuf Charters
Shores Charters, Inc. - John Yoe
Show Me Safaris - Mark Hampton
Showalters Fly-In Camps
The Showalters
Shuregood Adventures
Donald W. & Christine M. Graves
Shuswap Camp
Heinz & Gerda Loewenberg
Sid's Guide Service-Sidney M. Wolford
Sierra Club Outings
Sierra Grande Outfitters, Inc.
Leslie D. Ezell
Sifton Wilderness Adventures
Sights Southeast Stephen Berry
Sikanni River Outfitters
Doug Percival
Silence of the North
H. Kirtzinger & M. Schlosser
Silsby Lake Lodge
Kip & Mickey Thompson
Silver Bear Creek Outfitters
Bruce Crossley
Silver Birch Resort & Outfitters
John Friesen
Silver Bullet Outfitters, Inc.
Robert W. May
Silver Cloud Expeditions, Inc.
Jerry Myers
Silver Creek Outfitters, Inc.
Terry W. Ring & Roger Schwartz
Silver Dollar Charter Boat
Silver Fox Charters - Wayne E. Conley
Silver Fox Charters
Peter D. & Linda L. Udelhoven
Silver Fox Outfitters
Kevin Martin & Ronald Roll
Silver Goose Lodge John F. Hatley
Silver King Charters- Leo E. Evans
Silver King Charters
Bob & Joanne Saxton
Silver King Charters
Donald E. Westlund
Silver King III Charter Boat
Silver King Marine
Mike & Astrid Bethers
Silver KingLodge Robert Saxton
Silver Lining Charters- Earl D. Cagle
Silver Nailor Charters
Capt. James J. Silbernagel
Silver Peaks Outfitters
Scott E. Williams
Silver Poplar Grove Camps
Bill & Gail Paul
Silver Salmon Creek Lodge
David Coray
Silver Springs Outfitters
Brian R. Tartar, Lynn Dalton Tomlison
Trent Snyder
Silver Tip Outfitting
Garry & Zay Debienne
Silver Wind Charters
Steve & Helen Keller
Silverado Outfitters, Inc.
Larry Kibel
Silversides - Dennis S. Becklin
Silversides Sportfishing
Eli R. Ribich
Silvertip Fishing Service
Ronald Lundamo
Silverwater Lodge
Mike & Heather Jeschonnek
Silverwolf Chalet Resort
James & Bonnie Kennedy
Silverwood Fishing Lodge
The Holl's
Silvey's Flyfishing Guide Service
Brian D. Silvey
Simoneau's Outfitting
Simpson's Sportsman's Lodge
Simpson Charters Joe Simpson
Simpson Outfitters, Inc.
Mike W. Simpson
Singletree Outfitting
Fain D. Richardson
Sisip (Duck) Outfitting Camp
Robert McKay
Siskiyou Adventures, Inc.
Eric Peterson
Sitka's Secrets
Kent Hall & Bev Minn
Sitka Alaska Fish Buster Charters
James L. Lecrone
Sitka Sea Charters
Charles E. Wilbur
Sitka Sea Roamer- Mike Reif
Sitka Sound Charters -ohn B. Morrell
Sitka Sport Fishing Charters
John C. Yerkes
Sitka Super 8 Ronald Rivett
Siwash Safaris, Inc.- Paul Ellis
Skagway Sport Fishing
Skinner Brothers Outfitters
Robert Skinner
Skip Dove - Kenai River Guide
Skip & John Dove
Skipper's 22nd Street Landing
Skipper Charter Boat
Skipper Charter Service-Dave Ristow
Skookum Charters Kent John
Skunk Hill Guide Service
John Robinson
Skwentna Goods-Kevin & Susan Boyce
Skwentna Landing Corp.
Skwentna River Fishing- Roy Mackie
Skwentna Roadhouse
Raymond Doyle
Skwentna Roadhouse & Lodge
J.W. Cox
Sky's the Limit Adventures
Michael Sizelove
Sky Hi Outfitters
Sammy Frazier & Robert Homsher
Skyline Guide Service, Inc.
Victor J. Jackson
Skyline Lodge Jim & Pat Hron
Skyline Park
Skytop Lodge
Slam Dunkin Guide Service
Jason Dunkin & Bret Gesh
Slammin' Sam's Charters
Samuel & Lesly Peters
Slammin Salmon
Gary E. & Sussanne Hull
Slammin Salmon Charters & Excursions
James & Jacque Vaughan
Slammin Salmon Guide Service
Terrence F. Luckett
Slate Falls Outposts & Redpine Lodge
Verne & Andrea Hollett
Slate Falls Vindar Outfitters
Marjorie Chyk
Slater Creek Cattle Company, Inc.
Larry L. Lyster
Sleeping Lady Charters
Roy Chambers
Sleeping Lady Charters
John Phelps & Bill Masker
Sleeping Lady Charters
Bill Masker & John Phelps
Sleeping Lady Charters
John Phelps
Sleepy Hollow Lodge
Larry P. Miller
Slim's Cabins- Jim & Veronica Woods
Slip & Slide Guide Service
Franklin J. Rigler
Slipp Brothers, Ltd.
Ronald & Duane Slipp
Slipper Skipper Charters
Harold Bailey
Slippery Winds Wilderness Lodge
Doug & Georgie Knipe
Small Fry Charters- Tim Fulton
Smith Enterprises - Robert C. Smith
Smith Pheasant Hunting
Lyle & Dan Smith
Smith River Outfitters, Inc.
Gary D. Lindstrom
Smitty's Salmon Safari - Larry Snyder
Smokey's Alaskan Fishing Adventures
Ron, Anne & Jason Scribner

Smokin Joe's/Norrie Johnson Guide
Svc Norton Johnson
Smoky Lake Reserve
Smoky Mountain Outdoors, Unltd.
Jeff Reed
Smoky Mountain Outfitters
Bruce T. Butler
Smola Flyfishing
SMS Guide Service
Steven M. Scrimsher
Snake Dancer Excursions
Gregory C. Albouco
Snake Mountain Guide Service
Harvey Pete
Snake River Adventures
Michael L. Luther
Snake River Outfitters-NormanRiddle
Snake River Pack Goats-Steven A. Silva
Snap-It Charters
Capt. Snap D. J. Peterson
Snoopy' Adventures
Keith & Debbie Stephens
Snoopy III Charters
Norman & Mildred Lang
Snow's Cove, Inc.
Michael W. Holman
Snowline Marine Adventures
Edward G. Klinkhart
Snowmass Anglers- Ivan L. Perrin
Snowmass Falls Outfitters, LTD
Thomas M. Turnbull
Snowmass Oxbow Outfitting
Bill Lund
Snowmass Whaitewater, Inc.
Bob Harris
Snowshoe Lake Hunting & Fishing Inc.
John & Ron Hicks
Snowy Mountain Safaris
Snowy Range Ranch Outfitters
Patrick R. Landers
Snowy Springs Outfitters
Shawn Little
Snug Haven Resort
Donna & Brian Graziotto
Snug Outfitters, Inc./B. Mason
Outfitters William W. Mason, Jr.
Snyder's Idlewild Resort
Jerry & Judy Snyder
Soaring Eagle Outfitters
Sockeye Charters
Thomas H. Hagberg
Sodus Point Charters
James & Pat Abel
Solitary Angler Van Beacham
Solitude River Trips
Al and Jeanna Bukowsky
Sombrero Ranches, Inc.
Rex Ross Walker
Somerset Charters - Troy Curtiss
Son-Of-A-Gun Charters/Alaskan
Ocean Kemper
L. Sackman & Doug Morgan
Sonny-Bob Lodge
Bob & Pat Curtis
Sonny "D" Charters
Capt. Anthony C. DiCola
Sonora Resort Alan Moss
Sorensen's Resort
Sorry Charlie Charters
Michael & Laurle Coates
Sou'wester Outfitting
Dean & Bonnie Wheeler
Sound Adventure Charters
John & Anne Herschleb
Sound Experience
Roger & Marilyn Stowell
Sound Sailing - Rick Fleischman
Sourdough Charters
Ron Somerville, Vincent Strahmann
South Bay Cabins & Services
Percy Depper
South Bay Lodge - Bob Lammers
South Bay on Gull Rock
Mary & Harry Spenceley
South Ford Expeditions, Ltd.
John Hill, Jr.
South Fork Lodge- Spence Warner
South Forty Enterprises Richard D.
Hofmann, Jr & Paula Terrel
South Ram Outfitters -Lorne Hindbo
South Ridge Sporting Camp Ltd.
William Prosser
South Shore Charters
South Shore Lodge
Jim & Gail Weinkauf
South Side Outfitters
Rudy & Marion Usick
Southeast Alaska Adventures
A. Clark & Josephine M. Emery
Southeast Alaska Guiding
Hans Baertle & Mike Sofoulis
Southeast Alaska Ocean Adventures
Noel Johnson
Southeast Alaska Outdoor
Adventures Mike & Paul A. Yanak
Southeast Alaska Sports Fishing
Larry McQuannie
Southeast Coastal Charters
Domenick Monaco
Southeast Excursions Alaska
James E. Elstad
Southeast Guide Service
Scott Newman
Southern Belle Charter Boat
Southern Latitudes Fly Fishing Chile
Southern Maine Guide Service
Ronald St. Saviour
Southern Oregon River Trips
Brian J. Wager
Southern Outdoor Center, LLC
Thomas Sherburne
Southern Seaplane Inc.
Lyle Panepinto
Southern Vermont Guide Service
Michael Schnaderbeck
Southpark Outfitters - Max Oertle
Southside Wilderness Lodge
Mike & Jean Young
Southwest Adventures
Corey Veach
Southwest Indiana Bass Club
Jeff Norris
Southwest Montana Flies
Sparrowhawk Outpost Camp
Brett & Barry Arnason
Specialized Guide Service
Gerald Willard
Specialty Adventures - Greg Hublou
Specialty Tackle & Guide Service
Curt Thompson
Speer's Guide Service
Deen, Manuel, Rob & Gary Speer
Speerfish Charters - Capt. Jim Speer
Spellbound Sportfishing
Spence's Mantario Outfitters
Steve Spence
Spencer's Fishing & Hunting Lodge
Dell Spencer
Sphinx Mountain Outfitting
Gregory J. Doud
Spinner Fall Guide Service
Spinning Dolphin Charters of Lanai
Spirit Lake Lodge
George & Connie Coonradt
Spirit of Alaska Wilderness
Adventures G. Steele Davis
Spirit of AuSable - James E. Moon
Spirit Walker Expeditions
Split Shot Guide Service
Harry E. VanGelder
Spoonfeeder II Charters
Capt. Brian Saari
Sport Fishing Enterprises
Howard Kinn
Sport Fishing Guide Service
Allan L. Howard
Sport Fishing Kauai
Sportfishing Charters
Ed Murphy & Fred Brown
Sportfishing Kona, Inc.
Sporting Classics @ the Broadmoor
Resort
Colleen Betzing
Sporting Country Guide Service
John A. McRoy
Sports Den Fishing Team
James Golden
Sports Fishing Specialties
Sports Lure
Sportsman's Fishing & Hunting Lodge
D & J Goran
Sportsman's Inn/Baranof Expeditions
James M. Boyce
Sportsman's Lodge- Ruffo Schindler
Sportsman's Paradise- Ed Horner
Sportsman Charter Service
Sportsman Inn Guide Service
Sportsman of Lake City, Inc.
Paul Hudgeons
Sportsmen of Northern Indiana
Spotted Horse Ranch Dick Bess
Spring Brook Camps- Eugene O'Neill
Spring Creek Guide Service
Don Schnable & Sons
Spring Creek Resort
John Brakss & Rick Ray
Spring Creek Specialist- James Marc
Spring King Charters, Ltd.
Ray & Ellen Hepting
Spring River Ranch Fishing Club
Springcreek Anglers Ltd.
Springfield Trout Farm
Springhaven Lodge -The Scales
Spruce Island Charters
Herman L. Squartsoff
Spruce Shilling Camp
Chris & Verva Gaebel
St. Bernards Aviation Ltd.
Kevin J. Hackett
St. Joe Hunting & Fishing Camp, Inc.
Will & Barbara Judge
St. Paul's Salmon Fishing Club
Jules Goodman
St. Peter's Fly Shop Frank Praznik
St. Vrain Angler Stores, Inc.
Dale Darling
Stajduhar Ranches & Outfitting
John & Steven Stajduhar
Stan's Guide Service-Stanley Sumner
Stan Fisher Outfitter & Guide
Stanley Fisher
Stanley's West Arm Resort
Marvin & Carol Wisneski
Stanley Potts Outfitters
Stan & Joy Potts
Stanton Airways-John/Helen Stanton
Star Charter H. Giese
Star Dust Charters- Floyd Raduege
Star Kissed Charters
Capt. Charlie Maslanka
Star Outfitters
Jeffry J. Corriveau & Dennis R. Craig
Starfish Jere & Karen Christner
Starfish Charters - John Joyner
Starlight Lodge - Patrick Schuler
Stars N Strikes Sportfishing
Starter Charter 1 - Capt. Dave Burt
Starved Rock Lodge
Charlotte Wiesbrock
Stead Leasing, Inc.-Vladimer Ponican
Steam Boat Mountain Outfitters
Steamboat Inn - Jim VanLoon
Steamboat Lake Fishing Co., Inc.
Hans Berend
Steamboat Lake Outfitters, Inc.
Donald Wayne Markley
Steckel's Sportfishing - John Steckel
Steelblue Chameleon Lodge
Mark E. Kimball
Steelhead Lodge, Inc. - D. Bihlman
Steen's Wilderness Adventures
Jim, Connie & Shawn Steen
Steiner Bros. Guide & Outfitting
Ray Steiner
Steller Charters- William Foster
Stetson Ranches, LLC
Franklin Stetson
Steve Beyerlin Guide Service
Robert S. Beyerlin
Steve Blake Hunting & Fishing Guide
Steve Blake
Steve Fillinger Outfitters, Inc.
Steve Fillinger
Steve Tooker Guide Service
Steven Morrill, Ralph Morrill
Steward Ranch Outfitters
Laverne Gwaltney
Stewart Lake Airways Ltd.
William & Lynn Krolyk
Stikine Straits Sport Charters
Alan J. Sorum
Stillwater Gun Club, Inc. -Mark Beam
Stillwater Trailer Park-Bill/Gina Barnes
Stillwaters Outfitting-Lee R. Scherer
Stingray Charters -Capt. Ken DeVey
Stocker's Guide Jim Stocker
Stockton Outfitters- Billy D. Stockton
Stockton State Park Marina
Doug Hufferd
Stoddard Hunting & Fishing Camp
Clinton Norrad
Stone Creek Outfitters
Bob Helmer & Clay Bassett
Stone Wing Charters Capt. S. Terhorst
Stoney Ridge Outfitters
Leo MacCumber
Story Creek Outfitters
Frank Menegatti
Stoutsville Resort & RV Park
Don & Nancy
Stovall Ranch Linda - Joy Stovall
Straightline Products, Inc.
Larry Mann
Straightline Sports
Strawberry Hill Resort Ltd.
Andrew McCarthy
Streak'n Charters - Danny Kern
Stream Fever - Bob Linsenman
Streamline Peter Cammann
Streamside Guide Service
Wayne Martka
Streamside Outfitters
Strictly Trout David L. Deen
Strieby's Guide Service
Jerry Strieby
Strike Zone 1 - Capt. Ron Clark
Striker Charters - Capt. Tom Keefe
Stubbs Guide Service
Richard L. Bench II
Stukel's Birds & Bucks
Frank, Ray & Cal Stukel
Stump Jumper Charter
John Pangborn
Sturgeon Bay Outfitting Service
Leonard & Terry Stagg
Sturgeon Landing Outfitters
Stylin Darrell M. Stahoviak
Sucharda Charters
Capt. John W. Sucharda
Sudbury Aviation Ltd/No.Trails
Outpost Camps-Marg. Watson-Hyland
Sudden Impact Guide Srvice
Patrick D. Kelley
Sudsy Charters - Stephen J. Hauth
Sugar Bear Charter Boat
Sugar Point Resort- Steve & Bunny Fox
Sugarbear
Sullivan's Fishing Camps
Warren Sullivan
Sulphur Creek Ranch
Tom T. Allegrezza
Summer Breeze -John & Pam Jensen
Summer Hawk Sportfishing
Summer Rain Sportfishing
Summerberry Outfitting Services
Peter & Doug McAree
Summit Guides Dale K. Fields
Summit Station Lodge
Sun Canyon Lodge Lee Carlbom
Sun Dog Outfitters- Daniel L. Lahren
Sun Raven Guide Service
Katherine Howe
Sun Seeker Corp.
Sun Valley Outfitters, Inc.
Todd Van Bramer
Sun Valley Rivers Company, Inc.
Jon Charles McGregor
Sunbeam Bungalows Ltd.- David Bain
Sunbeam Fleet
Capt. John Wadsworth
Sundance Expeditions, Inc.
Sunday Silence
Sundown Jack Smith
Sundown Outfitters
David N. Cordray, Paul D. Griffith
Lyle G. Reynolds
Sundowner Sport Fishing Charters
Sunnahae Lodge, Jerald R. Mackie
Sunny Hill Resort - The Allinghams
Sunnybrook Farms
Sunrise Outfitters Mark Daly
Sunrise Outfitters, Inc.
Leroy F. Schroeder
Sunset Charters - Capt. Chris DiDio
Sunset Cove Camp
John & Louise Unsworth
Sunset Cove Lodge
Doris & Franz Rittscher
Sunset Guest Ranch
Mike C. McCormick
Sunset Guiding & Outfitting
Duane D. Papke
Sunset Lodge - John Gilkerson
Sunset Ranch, Inc. -Patsy Wilhelm
Sunset Shangrila Fishing & Hunting
Lodge -Donald & Joan Lyons
Sunset View Lodge - Bob Parker
Super Pro Guide Service
Superior Charter Fishing Service
Capt. Alex Kotter
Sure Strike Charters- Kirk Agnitsch
Sure Strike Charters
Capt. Rich Greenough
Susan Charters - Joe McClure
Susitna Basin Airboat - Richard Ames
Susitna River Guides - Wetzel Betts
Susitna River Safaris -Thomas Kean
Susitna Riverover Charters
Daniel Tucker & Frank Prat
Susitna Riverover Charters
Frank Pratt, III
Susitna Safaris - Douglas/Conrad
Sutherland & A. J. Sutherland
Sutton's Place Lyle Sutton
Sven-Erik Jansson Associates
Sven-Erik Jansson
Sweetcast Angler - Steve Pauli
Sweet Old Boys
Marsden P. (Tiny) Case
Sweetwater Guide Service
Michael Padua
Swelltime Charters - James R. Lee
Swifter Drifter - Tyland Vanlier
Swiftwater Lodge - Greg W. Turner
Swiftwater Steelhead Trips
Roger J. Monger
Swiss Colony Cottages
Ernie & Regina Allen
SWS Charters Steve Terrell
Sydney Lake Lodge
John & Ute Fahlgren
Sylvan Dale Ranch Susan & David
T's Charter Boat Service
Trish Leverenz
T-Bone's Dive Shop - Chris Wooten
T-N-T Adventures
Joe M. Torrez, Jr.
T & A Johnston Outfitting
T. Johnston
T & D Amisk Cabins
T & J Outfitters
Sue Jameson & Walter Tycksen
T & R Guide Service
T K Fishing Adventures
Terry & Kelly Lawson
T Lazy B Ranch - Robert L. Walker
T Lazy T Outfitters - Tom Toolson
T. Mike Murphy & Sons
T. Mike Murphy
T.C. Lewis Lodge Paul Peck
T.M.B. Charter Service- Steve Paslaski
Table Rock Fishing Guide Service
Jim Neeley
Tackle & Bait Shop - Jerry Nauss
Tackle Box Adventures
Wayne Nugent
Tackle Buster Halibut Charters
Weldon S. Chivers
Tackle Shack -Donald & Rose McNellis
Tacklebuster Halibut-Michael Johnson
Tacom Alaskan Adventures
Tony Monzingo
Taddingers
Tads Alaskan Trophy Fishing
Tad Waldrip
Tahawus Guide Service, Ltd.
Joseph Hackett
Tahltan Outfitters Fletcher Day
Tahoe Sportfishing Co.
Dean Lockwood
Tail Out Guide Services
Andrew J. Carmichael
Take-A-Chance Charters
Simeon Dushkin
Take 5 Charters -Capt. Kenneth Jeske
Takedown Alaskan Guide Service
Charles & Sandra Hoskins
Takhini River Guiding
Tal Camp/Alaska Flyfishing-Tom Lerot
Talaheim Lodge- Mark & Judi Miller
Talaheim Lodge - Tobin Osteen
Talaview Resorts - John Barichello
Rjay Lloyd & Rex Maughan
Talaview Resorts - Roger Orben
Talisman Charters - Robert S. Johnson
Talkeetna Rafting - Murray Nash
Talkeetna River Guides -Gerald Sousa
Talkeetna Riverboat
Mac Stevens, Jr. Kelly Ernst
Tall Tales Charters
Charles E. & Joanne Collins
Tall Timber Lodge Cindy Sullivan
Tall Timber Lodge & Marine
Kathy & Wayne Smith
Talla Bend Wildlife
Talmadge Marchbanks
James P. Whaley
Talofa Associate Joe C. Ashcraft
Talon Air Service, Inc.
Alan C. Helfer
Talstar Lodge-Claire Dubin
Talstar Lodge/Self Wylie Betts
Tama Kwa Vacationland
Isolde & Herbert Krob
Tamarac Sportfishing Dock
John Chippi
Tamarack Lodge - William A. McAfee
Tamarack Preserve, Ltd.
Tammy Too Charters Milo
DeVries & Kenneth Melvin
Tan Lake Outfitters- Jim Knowles
Tanaku Lodge
Dennis Meier & Jim Benton
Tanana River Charters
Kenneth E. Edwards
Tangent Charters
Greg & Deborah Scheff
Taquan Air Service, Inc.
Jerry A. Scudero
Tartan Charters- William L. Urquhart
Tasiujatsoak Wilderness Camp
Chesley & Cathy Andersen
Tata-Chika-Pika Lodge -The Neils
Tate Island Fishing Lodge
Richard Chrysler
Tatnall Camp - Rolly & Linda Lebrun
Tatonduk Flying Service-Robert Everts
Tawanta Ranch Monte Farnsworth
Tawaw Cabins
Emil & Merrel Berg & K. Wolffe
Tawow Lodge - Jim & Hazel Corman
Taylor's Place Fishing Camp
Taylor Creek Ranch - Vic Taylor
Taylor Streit Fly Fishing- Taylor Streit
Taylormade River Treks
Chris & Shawn Taylor
Tayor Creek, Inc.-William Fitzsimmons
Tazin Lake Lodge- Gordon Wilson
Tchaika Fishing Guide Services
James E. Bullock, Jr.
Team Navy Charters
Daniel W. Knight & Richard M. Collins
Team Turtle Charters
Capt. Van R. DeZwarte
Tecolote Charter Services
R.R. Rouquette
Ted's Charter Fishing Service
Goutos, Russell & Borgh
Ted's Trophy Fishing - Ted Forgi
Ted Fay Fly Shop
Ted Jowett Outfitting Service
Ted Jowett
Ted McLeod's Sunset Country
Outfitters Inc.
Ted McLeod & Lana Hurd
Tee's Bait & Guide Service
Tee Kitchens
Tee-Pee Outfitters
Donna & Letitia Hohle
Teller Wildlife Refuge - Mary Stone
Telluride Anglers
Telluride Whitewater, Inc./Telluride
Outside - William C. White
Temagami Lodge -Julia & Paul Forsyth
Temagami Riverside Lodge
Roger Watson & Linda Dorr
Temagami Shores Inn & Resort
The Bickells
Temple Bay Lodge -Bob/Peg Paluch
Ten Mile Boat Rental & Guide Service
Bill J. Stubblefield
Ten Mile Lake Camp
Richard & Michelle Carpenter
Tenacious Charters
Michael T. Lockabey
Tenakee Hot Springs Lodge
Samuel & Juan McBeen
Tenderfoot Outfitter & Guide
Paul, Steve & Jim Pike
Tent Town Outfitters-M. Mahlberg
Terrapins Ronald E. Dick
Terry's Boat Harbor
Terry & Vicky Thurmer
Terry's Guide Service - Terry Focke
Terry's Unforgettable Charters &
Expd. Terry Durkin
Teton Ridge Guest Ranch
Albert Tilt, III
Teton Valley Lodge, Inc.
Randy Berry
Tetsa River Outfitters- Cliff Andrews
Texas Creek Outfitters
David M. Butcher
The Adventure Center-Jack Schmidt
The Trout Fitter - Harley S. Kennedy
The AuSable River's Original Guide
Service
The Back Forty Bed & Breakfast Ranch
The Balsams - Jerry Owen
The Bass Man - Joseph Burke
The Battenkill Anglers
Tom Goodman
The Bawana Group- Ernie Norton, Jr.
The Big K Guest Ranch
Kathie Williamson
The Birches on Moosehead Lake
The Black Water Company
Ron Thompson
The Blackwater Bass-Guide Service
Monte J. Tabor
The Boulders - Kees Adema
The Bow River Company- Don Pike
The Bunny Clark- Capt. Tim Tower
The Bwana Group- Phil Weber
The Canal Lakes Resort
Ray Sedgwick
The Clearwater Crossing Lodge
Todd Earp
The Clevelander
The Complete Fly Fisher
David W. & Stuart Decker
The Cove Lodge
John Thomas & Gordon Wrobel
The Craig Wild Bunch, Inc.
Many Funkhouser
The Dolphins Resort- Clint Cameron
The Executive Angler
Kevin Leigh Derks
The Feathered Hook Fly Shop & Guide
Service

The Fishhook »Dominic "Dee" Carestia
The Fishin' Hole - Jack D. Jermain
The Fly Fishing Shop
The Fly Shop
The Flyfishers Den
The Fraley Ranch- Tom & Barb Fraley
The Gambler - Capt. Ron Maglio
The Glorie B II Charter Boat
The Gone Fishing Company
Chad Butler
The Guide Shop - Charles E. Peterson
The Gunnison Country Guide Service
John C. Nelson
The Hideout, Flitner Ranch
Kathryn Flitner
The Hoaky - Capt. Neil Hoak
The Hobbie Hut - Vince Smith
The Homestead
The Hungry Trout Motor Inn
Jerry and Linda Bottcher
The Inn at Manchester
Stan Rosenberg
The Island House - Kim Sedlack
The Island Lodge - Bob & Chris Phillips
The John B. Gulley Flyfishing Guide Service - John B. Gulley, II
The King and I - Michael L. Ashton
The Last Resort - Jimmie Dwayne Blair
The Lodge - John Talia
The Lodge at Cabin Bluff
The Lodge at Chama - Frank Simms
The Lodge at Hidden Basin
Theresa J. Brigman
The Lodge at Palisades Creek
Chip Kearns
The Lodges of East Yellowstone Valley
The Lucky Strike - Capt. Ken Turco
The Lyons Den - Calvin & Mary Lyons
The Mary E. Charter Svc. - Emil Dean
The Missouri River Trout Shop & Lodge
The Montana Trout Club - Greg Lilly
The Mountain AnglerJackson Streit/ John P. Streit
The Nets End - Josh Rago
The New Canoe West Resort
Harold Breault
The New Vickery Lodge
Rick & Fran Hubbs
The O'Fishial Charters of Alaska
William A. & Kathy A. Coe
The Ocoee Adventure Company
Larry Mashburn
The Ogoki Frontier, Inc. -Paul Boucher
The Old Kirby Place
The Old River Lodge Vicki & Alex Mills
The Outfitter Sporting Goods, Inc.
Larry Seaman
The Outpost Lodge
Jim& Ann Kehoe,Tom & Jill Olson
The Ozark Angler
The Peak Fly Shop
The Pines Steve & Nancy Norris
The Reel Life
Manuel J. Monasterio
The Reflective Angler
Eric W. Troth
The River's Edge - David W. Corcoran
The River Company
Olivia Falconer James
The Rivermen
Steve & Howard Campbell
The Rose - Capt. Bruce Haws
The Santa Fe Flyfishing School & Guide Ser.
The Sea Ranch Lodge
Rosemary McGinnis
The Spruce Fly - John Martin
The Stevensons' - Harold R. Stevenson
The Tackle Shop - Tim Combs
The Takle Shop, Inc.
The Terraces Cottages
The Timberdoodle Club
The Troutfitter - Dominique Eymere and Bradley Sorock
The Vermont Sportsman-Bob Beaupre
The Walking River Guide
Warren P. Huff
The Whales Eye Lodge & Charter
Rick & Karen Bierman
The Wild River Inn
Todd & Ann Marie Sheltra
The Williamson Inn-Govane Lohbauer
The Yankee Fleet
The Yellow Breeches Huse- Matt Zito
The Yellowstone Fisherman
Kent B. Lombard
Theodosia Marina-Resort, Inc.
Bret & Melonie Cook
Think Wild Enterprises - Eugene Clark
Thistlethwaite Outfitting
Thomas Bay Lodges
Frank H. & Ruth A. Kerr
Thomas Fishing Lodge
Dennis & Evelyn Thomas
Thomas Laffan - Janette Velting
Thompson's Angling Adventures
Howard A. Thompson
Thompson's Camps, Inc.
Garry Thompson
Thompson's Guiding & Outfitting
Glen Thompson
Thompson's Halibut Charters
Billy E. & Billy Jo Thompson
Thompson Charters Jim Thompson
Thompson Lake Lodge/Triple Lake Camps Mike Chursinoff
Thompson Outfitters, Inc.
Teddy Thompson
Thor's Trophy Outdoor Guide Service
Thor S. Yarabek
Thorburn Aviation Ltd.
Gene Ploughman
Thousand Islands Inn
Allen & Susan Benas
Thousand Lakes Resort
George & Jenny Brown
Thousand Springs Tours
J. Russell LeMoyne
Three Eagle Charters
Thomas J. Dawson
Three Eagles Enterprises
Donald J. Henry, Jr.
Three Lakes Camp
George & Donna Hawes
Three Queens Outfitting D.L. "Cougar" & Janice Osmonovich
Three Rivers Outfitters
James B. Maxwell
Three Rivers Resort & Outfitting
Mark A. Schumacher
Three Sons Charter Boat
Three Sons Charters
Michael F. Amberg
Thubun Lake Lodge
Thunder Bay Resort
Thunder Bow Outfitters
Mike Robinson
Thunder Buck Charter Service
Capt. Butch Wisnefske
Thunder Mountain Outfitters
Larry Bartlett
Thunder Mountain Outfitters
Cameron Garnick
Thunder Prairie Guide Service
Timothy R. Larson
Thunder River Guides
James K. Boyles, Jr.
Thunderbird Camps
Thunderbird Lodge
Mike & Mary Williams
Thunderbird Resort
Paul & Nancy Vollmar
Thy Rod & Staff
Tibbels Charter Service
Tide Change - Gary Adams
Tide Runners - Jay & Jane Griffel
Tides-In Charters - Glenn Melvin
Tidewater Charter- Reginald Krkovich
Tight Lines Fishing Trips
Jeff & Laura Helfrich
Tightline Charters
David & Marilyn Denney
Tightlines Ronald Diltz
Tigra II Capt. Peter Kriewald
Tikchik Narrows Lodge, Inc.
Tim's Charters Timothy J. Carsini
Tim's Guide Service Tim Charron
Tim Berg's Alaskan Fishing Adventures Timothy & Carol Berg
Tim Bergs Alaskan Fishing- Guy Cox
Tim Hills Enterprises - Tim Hills
Tim Bermingham's Drift Boat Guide Service - Tim Bermingham
Tim Pond Wilderness Camps
Harvey & Betty Calden
Timber Creek Guide Service
Mike Kilcher
Timber Edge Camps-Ron/Marg Lodge
Timber Point Camp
Mike & Marlene Johnson
Timber Trail Guide Service
Bill & Marge Forsberg
Timberdoodle Lodge
Neil & Brenda Smith
Timberidge Air & Outposts
Corky Sischo
Timberlane Lodge Manitoulin
The Mackan Family
Timberline Guide Service
Gregory A. Andersen
Timberline Outfitters - Perry Abbott
Timberline Outfitters - Jerry Cazares
Timberline Outfitters - Stanley Galvin
Timberline Outfitters- Willis Newman
Timberline Outfitters- Craig Oceanak
Timberline Outfitters
Nicholas G. Perchetti
Timberline Outfitters
Derald Wlasichuk
Timberline Outfitters & Guide Service
Douglass C. Frank, Jr.
Timberwolf Whitewater Expeditions
Larry Meek
Time Flies
Time Out Charters
Capt. David Mulligan
Tincup Wilderness Lodge- Larry Nagy
Tip of the Cape Angling Adv.
Tippecanoe
Raymond B. & Heather L. Kelley
Tite Line Fishing
John Seidel
TJR Corp.
TN Bar Cattle Co., Inc. - Curtis Kuester
TNT Alaskan Adventures
Tamara Pellegrom
Tobin Lake Resort- Connie Anklovitch
Tobique & Serpentine Camps, Ltd.
Donald McAskill
Toby's Trophy Treks - Toby Coleman
Tod River Outfitters
Joyce & John Erickson
Todd's Guide Service -R. Todd Puett
Todd's Igiugig Lodge
Larry & Elizabeth Todd
Togiak River Fishing Adventures
Bud Hodson & Ron McMillan
Tok Guide Service- Jeffrey Van Zandt
Tom's Alaskan Outdoor
Thomas Robertson
Tom's Guide Service - Tom A. Bugni
Tom's Guide Service - Tom McKinven
Tom's Outdoor- Thomas Castillo, Jr.
Tom & Kathy's Bed & Breakfast
Tom Cat Charters Tom Klemz
Tom Fritzlan & Family- Tom Fritzlan
Tom Jasper River Guide Service
Thomas E. Jasper
Tom Loder's Panhandle Outfitters
Tom Loder
Tom Payne Outfitting - Tom Payne
Tom Richardson's Rogue Guide Service - Thomas P. Richardson
Tom Sawyer River - Tom Joseph
Tomilson Unicorp./Miss Holly
Russ Tomilson
Tommy's Guide Service
Tommy W. Countz
Tommy Rietow
Tonapah Lodge & Outfitters
Frank, George & Jean Murnick
Toneda Outfitters
Ed R. Wiseman
Tonga's Launch Service
Darcy & Dan Tonga
Tongass Adventures Mark S. Guillory
Tongass Maritime Excursions
Michael & Claudia Herrick
Toni Lake Don Mobley
Tony Hoza Guide & Outfitter
Anthony Hoza
Top Gun Charter Boat
Top of Texas Hunting Dick Cook
Top of the World Sportfishing
Greg A. Jerich
Topsail VIII Charters, Inc.
Tornado's Canadian Resorts Inc.
Rogerson's Lodges
Tory Mountain Outfitters
JPaul S. Fowler
Totem Bay Outfitters
Debbie White & Ronnie Jackson
Totem Lodge - The Browns
Totem Point Lodge
Sylvia & Joe An Bill & Cathy Fliris
TR Fly Fishers Newsletter
Tracy Lee Charters-Capt. Kelly Thurow
Tracy Vrem's Blue Mountain Lodge
Tracy Vrem
TradeWinds Charter Service
Bill Currie
Trail's End Lodge - The Williams
Trail Creek Outfitters, Inc.-Layne Davis
Trail End Camp & Outfitters
The Hrechkosys
Trail Ridge Air - Geoff Armstrong
Trail Ridge Air, Inc. Glenn Curtiss
Trail Ridge Air, Inc. James Jensen
Trail Ridge Outdoors Thomas Clinkenbeard
Trail Skills, Inc. Robert Getz
Trailhead Adventure Treks
John & Michael Washburn
Trails End Outfitters Rolie Morris
Trangle T Outfitters Ed James Tibljas
Trans-Michigan Scuba Charter, Inc.
Trapper Creek Outfitters
John A. Metz
Trapper Don's Lodge & Outfitting
Don & Lynn McCrea
Trapper Jim's Lodge
James & Jolatne Soplanda
Trapper Mike's Outfitting Service
Mike Snihor
Trappers Lake Lodge - Ross Wheeler
Treasure Island Charters
Ronald & Janice Phillips
Trees Resort
Deb Johnson & Bruce Hanrahan
Trek Trail/Panangling
Trembling Pines Outfitter
Roy Mulvahill
Tri-Lakes Guide Service
Snider, Chafin & Kendall
Tri-River Charters
Robert Meals, Richard Petrini
Tri Lakes Bait & Tackle
Charlie Davis & Sam Krumrey
Tri Mountain Outfitters
Andy Celander
Tri River Charters
Bob & Maxine Stickles
Triangle C Ranches - Ron Gillett
Trinity Canyon Lodge
Triple Creek Outfitters - Roy G. Ereaux
Triple Creek/Thunder Bow
Charlotte A. Zikan
Triple G, Inc. - Paul Alan Echtler
Triple H. Lodge - Thomas L. Hoseth
Triple M Outfitters - Mark J. Faroni
Triple O Outfitters, Inc.
Harlan, D.A. & Barbara Opdahl
Triple Play Charters
Capt. Hanford "Skip" Davis
Triple Tree Ranch - Margaret Deutsch
Triton Charters - Hans von Rekowski
Triveet Lake Fly-In- Stuart Warrener
Trophies Only
Richard & Lorraine King
Trophy Blacktail's - Bill Danielson
Trophy Case Guides
Trophy Charters Glenn Keller
Trophy Charters II - Capt. Mike Stowe
Trophy Charters III - Skip Stafford
Trophy Class Outfitters - Mike Lawson
Trophy Connection
Trophy Guide Service - Ken Orrell
Trophy Hunter - Capt. Ron Helbig
Trophy Hunter Charter Service
Capt. Gary Hopp
Trophy Hunters Charters -Scott Tuthill
Trophy King Lodge-Michael Boettcher
Trophy King Lodge
Jeffrey Christensen
Trophy King Lodge - David Cozzini
Sandy Kellin, Mark Kimball
Trophy Mountain Outfitters
Dean F. Silva
Trophy Quest Outfitters-Dean Regehr
Trophy Seeker Charters
Capt. Bruce Schaller
Trophy Stone Safaris, Ltd.
Curt Thompson
Trophy Time Outfitters - Sean Pond
Trophy Trout Outfitters & Guides Service Richard R. Reinwald
Tropical Sun Sportfishing
Troublesome Creek Fish Co.
Joe & Chris Crum
Trout & Shad Chasers
Edward Carbonneau
Trout Creek Flies Dennis Breer
Trout Creek Outfitters, Inc.
Ray & BarBetta Cox
Trout Fishing Only - William M. Abbot
Trout Lake Dene Lodge
Trout Magic - Raven Wing
Trout Tracker Charters
Capt. Paul Lyman
Troutback Flyfishing Guide Service
Troutfitters - Frank M. Stanchfield
Troutfitters of Aspen/Guides West
Gary Hubbell
Trouthawk Outfitters
Randolph R. Scott
Troutwest Thomas J. Laviolette
True Blue Charters & Ocean Sports
True North Adventures
Tim & Val Matheson
True North Charters - Carl W. Mielke
Donald E. & Sandra Terrell
True North Lodge
True North Outfitting Co.
Jim Hudson
True North Safaris Ltd. - Gary Jaeb
Tsimshian Halibut Charters - John Hill
Tsuniah Lake Lodge - Eric Brebner
Tsylos Park Lodge & Adventures
Lloyd McLean
Tuckamore Wilderness Ldoge
Barb Genge
Tuckaway Lodge - Vincent Swazey
Tuckaway Shores
Phil & Paulette Thomas
Tuff Trout Ranch, LLC -David A. Gitlitz
Tumblehome Lodge
Ed & Shirley Giffin
Tuna Sea Charter Boat
Turn-Again Sports- Kenneth Manning
Turnagain River Outfitters
Eugene Egeler
Turner's Guide Service - Scott Turner
Turtle Lake Lodge
Maurice & Jeanette Blais
Tuuqak Charters
Steven R. & Linda S. Carpenter
Tweedsmuir Park Guides & Outfitters Bob Nielsen
Twelve Acre Lodge
Douglas Enterprises Ltd.
Twin Bay Resort Ltd.
Ken & Naomie Selb
Twin Bridges Campground & Canoe
John & Frankie Stogsdill
Twin Buttes Ranch Outfitters
Steve Titus
Twin Charters Sportfishing
Twin Forks Resort
Twin J Hide-A-Way-Jim & Judy Taziar
Twin Lakes Outfitters - Don Pelley
Twin Lakes Outfitters -Bill Pocock
Twin Marine - Curtis Lockwood
Twin Mountain - W.A. Roesch
Twin Oaks Resort - Mel Forester
Twin River Outfitters
Basil C. Neely, Jr.
Two Fingers Fishing Camp
Two Leggins Outfitters
David C. Schaff
Two M River Outfitters, Inc.
Michael W. Murphy
Two Rivers Charters
John W. Kalmbacher
Two Rivers Sport Fishing Charters
Two Spirit Guest Ranch & Retreat
Lee Cryer & Denise Needham
Tyee Charter Service - Jay Lloyd
Tyee Outfitters - Jay Skordahl
U-Bar Wilderness Ranch
U Charters - Capt. Randy Even
Uchi Lake Lodge - Judy Henrickson
Ugashik Lake Lodge
Gus Lamoureux
Ugashik River Lodge, Inc.
Ultima Thule Outfitters
Ultimate Charters- Roy & Millie Self
Ultimate Rivers
Umiakovik Fishing & Hunting Ltd.
Harvey Calden
Umpqua River Adventures
Douglas M. Brown
Umpqua River Guide- Terry Jarmain
Unalakleet Lodge- Mary A. Brown
Uncle Noel's Bait & Tackle
Todd Sudol & Randy Savage
Uncle Noel's Guided Fishing Tours
Noel Sudol
Uncompahgre Guide Service
Larry Lorenz & Clark Adkins
Uncompahgre Outfitters, Inc.
Chris Hutchison
Under Sail Adventures
William B. & Kathleen Fliger Bailey
Ungava Adventures
Sammy Cantafio
Unicoi Outfitters
Unique Wilderness Adventure
United States Outfitters of Arizona
Van Hale
United States Outfitters, Inc.
George Taulman
Unreel Guide Service - John Iverson
Unuk River Post Willialm Neumann & Charlie Pinkepank
Up the Creek/Talketna
William Bentley
Uppa Charlie's Up River Adventures
Evan & Annie B. Chocknok
Upper-Edge Outfitters
Rick Borysiuk
Upper Delaware Outfitters
Bill Fraser
Upper Missouri Pro Guide Service
Ralph Gravos
Upper Oxbow Adventures
Debbie Norton
Upper Stikine River Adventures, Ltd.
Jerry Geraci
Upriver Richard Beedy
USAF Academy Outdoor Adventure
Mike Bosso
Ute Indian Tribe Fish & Game/Outfoor Rec. Program
Utik lake Lodge
Roger Whittington & George Dram
Uyak Air Service
Oliver "Butch" Tovsen
V2 Expeditions
Leonard D. & Deborah K. Verrelli
Vail Fishing Guides - Mark C. Lokay
Vail Rod & Gun Club
Michael James Jouflas
Valarie's Fishing Guide Service
Valarie L. Early
Valdez Sea Adventures
Wallace A. Evans
Valentine -Chad & Miriam Valentine
Valerie Shilakes Russell Holland
Valhalla Charters- Bruce L. Blandford
Valley Hunting Service
Cliff Bankston
Valley King Charter - Charles Lee
Valley River Charters
Mathew Peterson/Jonathan Lindsey
Valley Rod Shop/Valley
Rene Roberts
Valley View Ranch
James Peterson
Van Doren's Orvis Shoppe, Ltd.
Van Saun Charters
Rod Van Saun
Vaseux Lake Lodge
Peter & Denise Axhorn
Vector Guide ServiceJohn Gumpert
Ventna Adventure Charters
Bobby Padie
Venture Northwest Guide Service
Dean R. Swerin
Ventures North
Chris & Linda Erickson
Venwood Lake Hunting & Fishing
Vermilion Bay Lodge
Gord & Susanne Bastable
Vermillion Lake Camp
Vermont Bound Outfitters
Jack Sapia
Vermont Fly Fishing Specialist
Vern's Venture - Vern Feltham
Vestby Angling Adventures
Mark Vestby
Viapan Camp - John Brothers
Edwin Taylor & Tamara Smid
Vickers Enterprises, Inc
Larry Vickers
Vickers Lake Outfitters
Martin McLaughlin
Victor Colvard Guided Fly Fishing
Victor H. Colvard
Victoria Outfitters - Dave Evans
Victorian Inn - Ann & Wayne Duez
Viking Charters - Norm Tikkanen
Viking Lodge - Ted Smith
Viking Outpost Cabins, Ltd.
Hugh & Craig Carlson
Viking Trail Outfitters - Martin House
Viking Trail Outfitters
Wallace Maynard
Village Charters-Capt.Clyde Neumann
Violator Charters- Capt. Jim Theyerl
Virg's Landing
Vision Quest - Guided Hunts
Chris Furia
Visions - Capt. Bob Worth
Vista Lake Outfitters
Dennis & Evelyn Mousseau
Vista Verde Guest Ranch - John Munn
Vixon Corp.
Vogels Homestead Resort
Tim & Jennifer Long
W 3 Outfitters - Dale R. Hopwood
Wabash Valley Flyfishers
Chris Thomas
Wade's Fishing Lodge
Joyce Holmes & William Bacso
Wade River Guide Service
Fred H. Wade
Wadin Bay Resort
Wayne Buckle & Audrey Miller
Wagners Guide Service
Vince & Leslie Wagner
Wahoos Adventures TN, Inc.

Melissa France
Waikiki Marine Sales
Wakami Outfitters - Marty & Ina Elliott
Wakomata Shores Resort Ltd.
James Burns & Norma Johnson
Walker Guide Service/Carl's Bait Shop
Ron Walker
Wallace Guides & Outfitters
Bill & Fred Wallace
Walleye Guides Unlimited
Daryl Kerzman
Wallona Transport - Leroy Wallona
Wallowa Llamas
Laurence "Raz" Rasmussen
Wally's Charter Service
Wally Friedman
Wally's Guide Service -Walter L.Martin
Wally's Place
Gen Assailly & Wally Nicklin
Wally Ramsay Guide Service
Wally D. Ramsay
Wally York & Son, Inc.
W. Travis York
Walser's McGregor Bay Camp
Mary & Gary Walser
Walsten Outpost Camps
Neil & Kevin Walsten
Walt's Guiding & Outfitting
Walter & Betty Mallery
Walt Morris Walter Morris
Walt Reynolds Fishing
Captain's Cove Motel and Marina
Walter Mrotz III Richard L. Close
Walton's Kay Vee Lodge
The Waltons
Waltonian Inn Lodge & Cottages
Frank & Thea Marusich, Nadia Day
Wamair Service
William & Kathy Mowat
Wanderer - Capt. Claude Adams III
Wanderin' Star Charters, Inc.
Gary & Kayron McCoy
Wapiti Company - Mark Malesic
Wapiti Fine Flies & Outfitting
Jack Mauer
Wapiti Outfitter & Guides, Inc.
Jon Garfall
Wapiti River Guides Gary Lane
Wapitti Valley Guide & Outfitting
Jonathan D. Baysinger
Wappapello Guide Service
Jeff Fansler
War Eagle Outfitters & Guides
Ken & Dolly Jafek
Ward Brothers Charters
Bernie Ward
Wardell's Guide Service
Layne Wardell
Warrens' Bunky Ranch
DeVon E. Warren
Warrens Guide Service - Tom Rogers
Washahigan Lake Lodge
Jean Johnson & Dave Fisher
Washow Bay Lodge - Ron Chekosky
Wason Ranch
Water Dog Fishing CHarters
Mark Stubbefield
Water Ouzel Express - Jerry G. Barber
Waterfall Ranch Outfitter- Edwin Zink
Waterfall Resort
Waterfalls Lodge
Bob & Marilou Rogers
Waterhen Band Outfitting
Chief Harvey
Waterhen Lake Resort- Skownan Black
Bear Ruth & Thomas Pfister
Waterhen Lake Store & Resort
Waterhen River Lodge
Clarence & Della Popowich
Watermark Adventures- Pat Harper
Waters Charter Service- Bud Waters
Waterwitch Charters
Capt. Wayne Voigt
Waterwolf Guide Service
Stephen Ramsay
Watson's Harmony Beach Resort
Tim & Char Watson
Watson Ranches - James Lee Watson
Watta Lake Lodge
Robin Wotherspoon
Waukegan Charter Boat Assoc.
Wauklehegan Outfitter
Ronald J. Painter
Wave Dance Charters
Wayne & Marla Sanger
Wavedancer - Capt. John Stolte
Waverly Waters
Wawanaisa Resort
Peter & Dorte Wiltmann
Wayne's Guide Service
Webster's Outdoor Adventures
Jeff & Cathy Webster
Wedge Hills Lodge - Diane Fortier
Weeping Trout Sports Resort
Roger & Debra Schnabel
Weight-N-Sea Charters - Sean Mitchel
Weigner's Backcountry Guiding
W. Mark Weigner
Weimer Hunting Camp
Jody C. Weimer
Weise Adventures - James R. Weise
Weiss Lake Landing
Weitas Creek Outfitters -Steve Jones
Wekusko Falls Lodge
Dwayne, Tony & Susan Brew
Welch Guide Service Dale Welch
Welcome Lodge Nipissing
Gary & Angela Martin
Wellborn Bros. - David A. Wellborn
Wellborn Bros. - Joseph R. Wellborn
Wellington Maritime

John P. Wellington
Wellman Lake Lodge & Outfitters
Linda & Alvin Wiebe
Wellsweep Ranches - David R. Seely
Welovet Lodge Shawn Bowes
Wes' Guide Service
Wesley T. Yamaoka
West Arm Lodge-Ray & Ron Pedneault
West Branch Angler
Harry Batschehet and Ray Finney
West Coast Outfitting - Bob Welsh
West Fjord Charters
Gary & Neoma Scheff
West Fork Outfitters -Ronald M. Corr
West Fork Outfitters- G. Eugene Story
West Harbor Towing - Art Richter
West Hawk Lake Resort
John & Carol Surowich
West Kettle Outfitters, Ltd.
Peter Grosch
West Laramie Fly Store
West to North Tours - Patty West
West Virginia Lakes Fishing & Tours
Robt. A. Wiseman, II/H. T.Salmon
West Wind III -Capt. Cecil V. Brooks, Jr.
West Woods Outfitters
Neil Sweetapple & Neil MacArthur
Westbank Anglers
Western AK Sport Fishing
August & Kim Egdorf
Western Colorado Outfitters
Gordon Blay
Western Fishing Adventures
Brad Staples & Denny Haak
Western Guide Services
Randy L. Walker
Western Mountain Outfitters, Inc.
Dudley Henderson
Western River Expedition
Western Rivers - Fred J. Tedesco
Western Rivers Flyfisher
Western States Ranches
Western Timberline Outfitters
Jammin D. Krebs
Western Waters - Edward J. Lawn
Western Waters -Gerald R. Nichols
Western Wilderness Outdoor Adv.
Judy Kay Stewart
Western Wildlife Services
Westfork Guide Service
Westwood Lodge - Tim & Emilie Lies
Wet & Wild Kenai Fishing
Jeff Moore
Wetherill Ranch George Hughes
Whale of a Tale Charters
Marcellus Fegley
Whale Pass Lodge
Robert & Denise May
Whaler's Cove Lodge
Richard L. Powers
Whales Resort, Inc.
William R. Fannemel
Whales Tale Marine Service &
Charters Albert R. Manchester
Whalesong Charters
Garry & Kim Brand
Whatshan Guides & Outfitters
Ken Robins
Whetstone Creek Lodge
Gerald & Marg Hallihan
Whip-Poor-Will Lodge
Bruce & Jan Jameyson
Whiskey-Jack Lodge Ron & Kim
Fowler
Whiskeyjack's Outfitting Service
Jim Dudgeon
Whisper Marine Charters
Douglas R. Ogilvy
Whispering Hill Trophy Hunters &
Outfitters - Jay Stewart
Whispering Pine Outfitters
Gordon & Lynn Utri
Whistling Elk Outfitters, Inc.
John C. Ziegman
White Birch Guide Service
Capt. Paul R. Bois
White Birch Lodge - Bob Walsh
White Buffalo Ranch Retreat
White Cloud Charters
Al C. & Vickie F. Levine
White Cloud Outfitters
Mike Scott & Louise Stark
White Dog Trail Company
Jeff Whittemore & John Wainwright
White Fox Hotel Outfitting
Robert Shatula
White Iron Beach Resort
Kerry & Sandy Davis
White Lake Resort Ltd.
Hans & Hannelore Wutschke
White Lightning - Capt. Ted Harris
White Oak Plantation
White Otter Outdoor Adventures
Randy P. Hess
White Outfitters - Bill G. White
White Pine Lodge
Joseph & Mary Ellen Schaut
White River Air/Mar Mac Lodge
Don MacLachlan
White River Ranch- David J. Prather
White Savage/Joyce Marie Charters
Ricky Thompson
White Swan Lake Resort
Gerry Wenschlag
White Water Fishing Trips
Carl R. (Skip) Zapffe
White Water West - Stan Watt
Whiteface Guide Service
G. L. Scott
Whitefish Bay Camp-Bob/Peg Hunger
Whitefish Lake Fishing
Jim Crumal

Whitefish Lodge-John/ Lorna Chiupka
Whitehaven Cottages
Bill & Linda Strain
Whiteley's New Frontier
Scott Whiteley
Whiteshell Lake Resort
Liberty & David DesRoches-Dueck
Whitewater Adventures Idaho
Kenneth C. Masoner
Whitewater Information & Rafting
Tom Louisos
Whitewater Shop River Tours
Stephen J. Guinn
Whitewater Travel, Inc. - Kyle Coon
Whitewater Warehouse/Wilderness
Whitewing Resort & Floating Lodges
Dave & Bobbie McDonald
Whitmore Enterprises
Shawn M. Whitmore
Whitten's Outfitters & Guide Service
Lewis Arnold Whitten
Whiz's Sport Fishing Charters
Capt. Jim Wisnicky
Widrig Outfitters, Ltd. - Chris Widrig
Wigwam Lodge-Kent & Shelley Spears
Wild Bill's Guide Service
William C. Burnett
Wild Child Family Sailing Charters
Wild Country Outfitters
Clinton, Lloyd & Michael Madden
Wild Country Outfitters, Inc.
Jerry E. Strong
Wild Creek Lodge, Inc.
Wild Horse Creek Ranch
William R. Shields & Rick Hankins
Wild Idaho Outfitters, Inc.
Frank Giles
Wild Man Outfitters/Poplar Point
Resort
Wild River Adventures - Bob Jordan
Wild River Adventures
Robert Y. Jordan
Wild River Outfitting- Harold Westdal
Wild Sport Services
Randolph B. Rigdon
Wild Trout Outfitters
Jeffery D. Bingman
Wild Trout Outfitters - John F. Herzer
Wild West Adventures - Gary Robbins
Wild West Charters
Wild Wings Outfitters
R. Button, R. Ross & B. Carter
Wild Wings Sporting Club
Wild Wings, Inc. - Walter Harris
Wildass Outfitters
Robert Henry & Chester W. Mayer
Wilderness Air Limited
Bob Huitikka
Wilderness Aware Rafting-Joe Greiner
Wilderness Bear Guides
Art & Craig Henry
Wilderness Bound Outing Service
Jack Demers
Wilderness Charters
Christopher White
Wilderness Connection, Inc.
Charles G. Duffy
Wilderness Enterprises
Joe & Vici Letarte
Wilderness Expeditions, Inc.
Wilderness Experiences
Lamont E. Albertson
Wilderness Fishing Adventures
Russ Rose & Sheri Lockwood
Wilderness Gardens Outfitters
Fred Salter
Wilderness Horizons
Howard Hewitt & Lester Goobie
Wilderness Inquiry - Greg Lais
Wilderness Lodge-Judy & Eric Wismer
Wilderness Lodge & Skyline Outfit,
Inc. Greg Deimler
Wilderness Lodge & Skyline Outfitters
Cameron E. Lee
Wilderness Lodge Ltd.
Gregory C. Grabacki
Wilderness North
Wilderness Outfitters - Arnold D. Elser
Wilderness Outfitters - Gene Mercer
Wilderness Outfitters
Scott, Shelda, Justin & Jarrod Farr
Wilderness Outfitters
John Everett Stoltz
Wilderness Outfitters
Clark & Sandra Vanbuskirk
Wilderness Outfitters, Inc./Baril Bay
Camp Gary & Marcy Gotchnik
Wilderness Outfitters/Burntwood
Lake Lodge Larry Gogal
Wilderness Place Lodge
Brant Bounous,Kyle Bowerman
Wilderness Riders Outfitting
Bruce J. Duffalo
Wilderness Ridge Resort - Jack Crider
Wilderness River Outfitters
Bruce Greene
Wilderness Trails Ranch-Gene Roberts
Wilderness Trails, Inc. - Martin Banak
Wilderness Trout
Wilderness Ways Kenneth Bailey
Wildewood Fly In Lodge & Outpost
Richard Kungle
Wildlife Adventures, Inc.
Jack E. Wemple
Wildlife Outfitters - Richard Wemple
Wildman Lake Lodge - Master Guide
Keith N. Johnson
Wildwater Excursions Unlimited
Jon Dragan
Wildwater Expeditions Unlimited, Inc.
Chris Dragan
Wiley Point Lodge - Eric Brown

Will's Copper King Charters
William Bailey
William's Canoe Fishing
William Richard Knight
William's Outdoor Adventures
William C. Sheppard
Williams Guide Service
Don A. Williams
Williams Guide Service
Patrick C. Williams
Williams Lake Lodge
Peter & Kathy Stieglitz
Williams Narrows Resort
Jerry & Joyce Karau
Williams Peak Ranch Co.
Michael Miniat
Williams Ranch Co. - Rowdy McBride
Williamson River Club
Willie "D" & Me Charter Service
Jacqueline & Wilfred Dentz
Willie Bee Charters - Capt. Gary Lodel
Willie Jo Guide Service
Billy F. Smith, Sr.
Willimans Wildlife Lodge & Guiding
Williwaw River Tours David Dowling
Wilson's Guide Service
Wilson's Guided Sportfishing
James E. Wilson
Wilson's Lodge
Wilson's Sporting Camps, Ltd.
Keith Wilson
Wilsons Shane,
Wayne & Scott Snell
Wilton Earle & Sons - Leon Earle
Winchester Fishing Co.
Jim Winchester
Wind Dancer Guide Service
Larry L. Wright
Wind River Ranch - Arthur Davenport
Wind River Wilderness Tours
Wind Rush Farms
Quint & Cicely Drennan
Windsinger Lodge
Sandra, Pahl & Bill Gottschalk
Windsock Lodge/Hastings Bros.
Outfitters Tim & Donna Hastings
Windy Way Charters -Allen Girens, Jr.
Wine Lake Camp
Herb Pugmire & Ann Sherman
Wings Robert Gretzke
Wings of Adventure - Jeff Conners
Winnetou Resort
Hank & Betty Thierauf
Winston D. Coleman
Winter's Guide Service - Jon P. Winter
Winterhawk Outfitter, Inc.
Larry L. Amos
Winterhawk Outfitters
Wisconsin Charter Association, Inc.
Wisconsin John Guides Again
Wistaria Guiding - Gary Blackwell
Wit's End Guest Ranch & Resort
Jim & Lynn Custer
Witch Bay Canadian Outposts
Randy & Cindy Thomas
Witer King Charters - Ralph E. Lohse
Wits End Corinne Heidemann
Witte Ranch - Patrick J. Witte
WMS, Inc.
Wogenstahl's Canadian Resort
The Wogenstahls
Wolf Adventure Tours
Wolf Country Fishing
Scott & Roberta Ravenscroft
Wolf Creek Guide Service
Steve Butts
Wolf Creek Outfitters
Jeffrey D. Berkenmeier
Wolf Creek Outfitters, LLC
Jason Ward
Wolf Lake Wilderness Camp
Wolfe's Guide Service
Wolfe Bros. Guide Service
Dennis R. Wolfe
Wollaston Lake Lodge Ltd.
Brian & Sharon Elder
Wolseley Lodge Jules Morin
Wolverine Creek Wilderness Cabins
Thomas H. Rench
Wolverine Guide Service
Richard A. Labert
Wolverine Lodge
Renee & Fred Bettschen
Wolverman Wilderness Outfitters
Walchuk & Degenhardt & Slager
Wolverton Outfitters-Keith Wolverton
Woman River Camp
Dary & Diane Wilkinson
Woman River Fly-In Outposts
Les & Sandy Schultz
Women's Flyfishing - Celilia Kleinbauf
Women Sail Alaska
Theresa Tavel & Karen Walter
Wood's Alaska Sport Fishing
Jack Wood
Wood River Lodge - John D. Ortman
Woodhouse Camp
The Woodhouses
Woodland Echoes Cottage Resort
Ken & Carol Turner
Woods Bay Lodge
Doris & Uwe Liefland
Woods Sport Fishing - John Wood
Woodside Guide Service
Capt. Don Williams
Woodsman's Sport Shop & Fishing
Serv.
Woodstock Guide & Outfitting
Jack Sours
World Class Outfitting Adventures
Jason D, Larry & Carolyn Clinkenbeard
World Class Sportfishing

Mike Arthur
Worldwide Outdoor Adventures
Randy Beck
Wright Point Resort
Joe & Carrie Whitmell
WRP Fly Fishing Outfitters - Bill Page
WW Outfitters
William A. White
Wy'East Expeditions
Michael R. Gehrman
Wycon Safari, Inc. - Wynn Condict
Wyoming Rivers & Trails
Liz & Matt David
Y-Knot Charter Service
Richard D. & Betty J. George
Yaak River Outfitters
Patrick "Clint" Mills
Yakutat Bay & River Charters
Flank Deveraux
Yakutat Lodge - Ken & Jill Fanning
Yakutat Outfitters - Robert Fraker
Yampa River Outfitters
Randall W. Baird
Yamsi Ranch - Gerda Hyde
Yankee Angler - Bradford White
Yankee Charters - Capt. Bernie Burby
Ye Olde Tackle Box - Ken McIntosh
Yellow Breeches House
Yellowater Outfitters - Roy G. Olsen
Yellowhorn Outfitters/Sand Tank
Outfitters Peter A. Cimellaro
Yellowstone Catch & Release
Outfitter - Gary David Clount
Yellowstone Fly Fisher
Mike Sprague
Yellowstone International Fly
Yellowstone Llamas - William Gavin
Yellowstone Outfitters Hunting &
Fishing - Lynn Madsen
Yellowstone Raft Co.
Chris Lyness, Julia Page
Yellowstone Troutfitters - Steve Perry
Yentna Station Roadhouse
Dan Gabryszak
Yes Bay/Mink Bay Lodges
Kevin M. Hack
Yeshna Guided Tours
Stanen & Caeen Hay
Yoda Guide Service James W. Dawson
& Gary J. Young
Yohetta Wilderness Adventures, Ltd.
Goetz Schuerholz
Young's Fishing Service, Inc.
Jack LaFond & Bill Young
Young's Outfitting - Stanley Young
Young's Wilderness Camp
Perry & Carol Anniuk
Young Lake Lodge
Steve & Debbie Vincent
Younger Brothers Guiding &
Outfitting - Glen Younger
Youth Future Barry Lywak
Yukon Don's, Inc.
Yukon Don & Kristan Tanner
Yukon Fish Guiding Service
Gregory Landeis
Yukon Hunting & Guiding Ltd.
Rod Hardie
Yukon River Tours
Paul & Mary E. Starr
Yvon & Son's Bear Hunt
Yvon & Gilles Goudreau
Z & S Outfitters, Inc.
Carl R. Zapfee
7 Bar J Outfitters - Mark Story
Zachar Bay Lodge
Martin & Linda Eaton
Zelazek Guide Service
Dave Zelazek

Peel off your address label and place here

PLEASE NOTE: The Business or Professional you
are invited to rate is printed above your name
after "referred by..."

Picked-By-You Questionnaire
Top Guided Flyfishing

Name of your Field Guide:_____
(Person that guided you in the field)

Date of Trip_____Location_____ Day trip ☐   Overnight trip ☐

Was this a Family Trip where your children were actively involved in the activities?   Yes ☐   No ☐

Technique used: _____

Species caught or observed: _____

Catch ☐   Catch and Release ☐

Outstanding   Excellent   Good   Acceptable   Poor/Inferior   Unacceptable

1. How helpful was the Outfitter (Guide, Captain or Lodge) with travel
    arrangements, fishing regulations, permits etc.?.. ☐ ☐ ☐ ☐ ☐ ☐

2. How well did the Outfitter (Guide, Captain or Lodge) provide important
    details that better prepared you for your fishing trip (clothing, equipment,
    information on the fish and the water, list of "take along", etc.)?................. ☐ ☐ ☐ ☐ ☐ ☐

3. How would you rate the Outfitter's (Guide, Captain or Lodge) office skills
    in handling deposits, charges, reservations, returning calls before and
    after your trip?.. ☐ ☐ ☐ ☐ ☐ ☐

4. How would you rate the accommodations (tent, cabin, lodge, etc.)?............ ☐ ☐ ☐ ☐ ☐ ☐

5. How would you rate the equipment provided by the Outfitter (Guide,
    Captain or Lodge) during your trip (boats, tackle, rods, airplanes, etc.)?...... ☐ ☐ ☐ ☐ ☐ ☐

6. How would you rate the cooking (quantity, quality and cleanliness of the
    service)?.. ☐ ☐ ☐ ☐ ☐ ☐

7. How would you rate your Guide's Attitude — Politeness — Disposition?..... ☐ ☐ ☐ ☐ ☐ ☐

8. How would you rate your Guide's knowledge of the area?............................ ☐ ☐ ☐ ☐ ☐ ☐

9. How would you rate your Guide's knowledge of the fish (feeding cycle,
    habits, type of flies to be used, etc.)?... ☐ ☐ ☐ ☐ ☐ ☐

10. How were your fish prepared for trophy mounting and/or for the trip home?
    (For Catch and Release write N/A)... ☐ ☐ ☐ ☐ ☐ ☐

	Outstanding	Excellent	Good	Acceptable	Poor/Inferior	Unacceptable

11. How would you rate the skills and the attitude of the Staff overall?............ ☐ ☐ ☐ ☐ ☐ ☐

12. How would you rate the quality of the waters?... ☐ ☐ ☐ ☐ ☐ ☐

13. How would you rate the quality of the fish?.. ☐ ☐ ☐ ☐ ☐ ☐

14. How would you rate the flexibility of your Guide or Captain to meet your goal(s) ?.. ☐ ☐ ☐ ☐ ☐ ☐

15. How would you rate the overall quality of your fishing experience?............ ☐ ☐ ☐ ☐ ☐ ☐

	Good	Fair	Poor

16. How would you describe the weather conditions?...................................... ☐ ☐ ☐

17. Did the Outfitter (Guide, Captain or Lodge) accurately represent the overall quality of your experience (quality of waters, fish, accommodations, etc.)?... ☐ Yes   ☐ No

18. Did you provide the Outfitter (Guide, Captain or Lodge) with truthful statements regarding your personal needs, your skills and your expectations?.. ☐ Yes   ☐ No

19. Would you use this Outdoor Professional/Business again?........................ ☐ Yes   ☐ No

20. Would you recommend this Outdoor Professional/Business to others?..... ☐ Yes   ☐ No

Comments: _____
_____
_____
_____
_____
_____
_____
_____
_____
_____
_____
_____
_____
_____
_____
_____
_____
_____

Will you permit Picked-By-You to use your name and comments in our book(s)? ☐ Yes   ☐ No

Signature_____

Outfitters, Guides & Lodges by Fish Species

Artic Grayling

Alaska Fish & Trail Unlimited
George Ortman Adventure Guiding
The Complete Fly Fisher
Tracy Vrem's Blue Mountain Lodge

Artic Char

Alaska Fish & Trail Unlimited
George Ortman Adventure Guiding
George River Lodge
Tracy Vrem's Blue Mountain Lodge

Bass

Largemouth Bass

G & W Guide Service
Tim Bermingham Drift Boat Guide
   Service
The Hungry Trout

Smallmouth Bass

M & M's Whooper Hollow Lodge
Tim Bermingham Drift Boat Guide
   Service
The Hungry Trout
West Branch Angler & Sportsman's
   Resort

Striped Bass

Chesapeake Bay Charter
The John B. Gulley Flyfishing Guide
Service
Tim Bermingham's Drift Boat Guide
   Service

Barracuda

Fly Fishing Paradise

Bonefish

Fly Fishing Paradise

Dolly Varden

Esper's Under Wild Skies
George Ortman Adventure Guiding
Solitude River Trip
Tracy Vrem's Blue Mountain Lodge

Drum(s)

Capt. Doug Hanks
Chesapeake Bay Charter
Look-N-Hook Charters

Mackerel(s)

Chesapeake Bay Charter

Northern Pike

Alaska Fish & Trail Unlimited
George Ortman Adventure Guiding
George River Lodge
Les Enterprises du Lac Perdu
Mike Wilson's High Mtn. Drifters
The Hungry Trout
The Reel Life
Tracy Vrem's Blue Mountain Lodge

Permit

Fly Fishing Paradise

Outfitters, Guides & Lodges by Fish Species

Trouts

Brook Trout

Alpine Anglers
Broken Arrow Lodge
Dragonfly Anglers
East Slope Anglers
Esper's Under Wild Skies
Gander River Outfitters
George River Lodge
John Henry Lee Outfitters
Kelly Creek Fly Fishers
Les Enterprises du Lac Perdu
Libby Sporting Camps
Mike Wilson's High Mtn. Drifters
Rocky Fork Guide Service
The Battenkill Angler
The Complete Fly Fisher
The Hungry Trout
Tim Bermingham's Drift Boat
  Guide Service
Tite Line Fishing

Brown Trout

Alpine Anglers
Broken Arrow Lodge
Dragonfly Anglers
Eagle Nest Lodge
East Slope Anglers
Grossenbacher Guides
Hatch Finders
Heise Expeditions
John Henry Lee Outfitters
Kelly Creek Fly Fishers
M & M's Whooper Hollow Lodge
Mike Wilson's High Mtn. Drifters
Rocky Fork Guide Service
Serene Fly-Fishing Adventures
The Battenkill Angler
The Complete Fly Fisher
The Hungry Trout
The John B. Gulley Flyfishing
  Guide Service
The Reel Life
The Reflective Angler
The Troutfitter
Tim Bermingham's Drift Boat
  Guide Service
Tite Line Fishing
West Branch Angler & Sportsman's
  Resort

Cutthroat Trout

Alpine Anglers
Broken Arrow Lodge
Classic Alaska Charters
Dragonfly Anglers
Eagle Nest Lodge
East Slope Anglers
Esper's Under Wild Skies
Fishing on the Fly
George Ortman Adventure Guiding
Heise Expeditions
John Henry Lee Outfitters
Mike Wilson's High Mtn. Drifters
Rocky Fork Guide Service
Solitude River Trip
The Complete Fly Fisher
The John B. Gulley Flyfishing
  Guide Service

Lake Trout

Alaska Fish & Trail Unlimited
East Slope Anglers
George Ortman Adventure Guiding
George River Lodge
John Henry Lee Outfitters
Les Enterprises du Lac Perdu
M & M's Whooper Hollow Lodge
Mike Wilson's High Mtn. Drifters

Rainbow Trout

Alaska Fish & Trail Unlimited
Alpine Anglers
Broken Arrow Lodge
Bruce Slightom
Dragonfly Anglers
Eagle Nest Lodge
East Slope Anglers
Esper's Under Wild Skies
Fishing on the Fly
George Ortman Adventure Guiding
Grossenbacher Guides
Hatch Finders
Heise Expeditions
John Henry Lee Outfitters
Love Bros. & Lee
M & M's Whooper Hollow Lodge
Mike Wilson's High Mtn. Drifters

Outfitters, Guides & Lodges by Fish Species

Rocky Fork Guide Service
Serene Fly-Fishing Adventures
Solitude River Trip
Sweet Old Boys
The Battenkill Angler
The Complete Fly Fisher
The Hungry Trout
The John B. Gulley Flyfishing Guide
  Service
The Reel Life
The Reflective Angler
The Troutfitter
Tim Bermingham's Drift Boat Guide
  Service
Tite Line Fishing
Tracy Vrem's Blue Mountain Lodge
West Branch Angler & Sportsman's
  Resort

 Steelhead Trout

Bruce Slightom
Fishing on the Fly
Serene Fly-Fishing Adventures
Sweet Old Boys
Tim Bermingham's Drift Boat
Guide Service

 Spotted Sea Trout

Chesapeake Bay Charter
Gander River Outfitters
Look-N-Hook Charters

 Snook

Capt. Doug Hanks
Look-N-Hook Charters

Salmons

 Atlantic Salmon

Gander River Outfitters
George River Lodge
Libby Sporting Camps
M & M's Whooper Hollow Lodge

 Chinook (King) Salmon

Alaska Fish & Trail Unlimited
Bruce Slightom
Classic Alaska Charters
George Ortman Adventure Guiding
Serene Fly-Fishing Adventures
Sweet Old Boys
Tim Bermingham's Drift Boat
Guide Service
Tracy Vrem's Blue Mountain Lodge

 Chum (Dog) Salmon

Classic Alaska Charters
George Ortman Adventure Guiding
Tracy Vrem's Blue Mountain Lodge

 Coho (Silver) Salmon

Alaska Fish & Trail Unlimited
Classic Alaska Charters
George Ortman Adventure Guiding
Sweet Old Boys
Tracy Vrem's Blue Mountain Lodge

 Pink(Humpback) Salmon

Classic Alaska Charters
George Ortman Adventure Guiding
Tracy Vrem Blue Mountain Lodge

 Sockeye (Red) Salmon

Alaska Fish & Trail Unlimited
Classic Alaska Charters
George Ortman Adventure Guiding
Tracy Vrem's Blue Mountain Lodge

Outfitters, Guides & Lodges by Fish Species

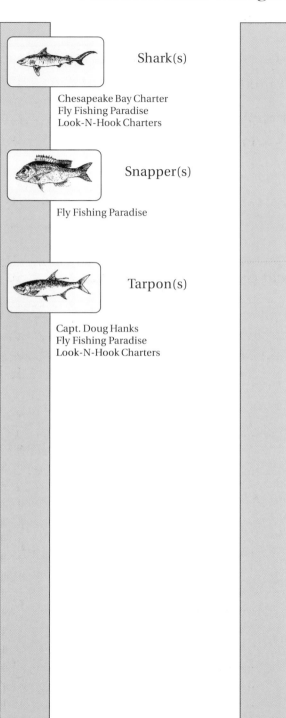

Shark(s)

Chesapeake Bay Charter
Fly Fishing Paradise
Look-N-Hook Charters

Snapper(s)

Fly Fishing Paradise

Tarpon(s)

Capt. Doug Hanks
Fly Fishing Paradise
Look-N-Hook Charters

Index of Outfitters, Guides & Lodges
by State/Province

Index of Outfitters, Guides & Lodges
by State/Province

Index of Outfitters, Guides & Lodges
by State/Province

Alphabetical Index by Company Name